Contents

A History of
St Matthew's, Highfield
1867–1993

written and compiled by
GORDON A. COOKE

to mark the Centenary
of the building of the
Memorial Church, 1894

To Mildred Mary and Marjorie Anne

A History of St Matthew's, Highfield, 1867–1993
written and compiled by Gordon A. Cooke

Published by St Matthew's Fellowship, Highfield, November 1993

Text copyright © Gordon Cooke, 1993

ISBN 0-9522386-0-8

Typeset in old style Monotype Ehrhardt by Carnegie Publishing, 18 Maynard St., Preston
Printed and bound in the UK by Cambridge University Press

Foreword

by the Vicar of St Matthew's, Highfield
Revd W. H. Harrington, AKC

I am the only building in Billinge Road that stands for time and eternity. I proclaim that which the whole world needs, that which is beyond value and which no words can adequately describe—God, and the assurance of His Eternal Presence and Love. I am a kind of witness in stone to the power of God in our demented and distracted world.

This is what St Matthew's Church says to me, and, I trust, to many who see its spire from miles around. These words give some indication of the inestimable worth that our parish church has been, and still is, to the people of Highfield, Pemberton and Winstanley. This book, which has been researched with meticulous diligence, dedication and love by Mr Gordon Cooke, is, I believe, a history you will treasure. We are indebted to Gordon for his years of researching and compiling and I am deeply grateful to him. I warmly commend it to you; it will give you clear insights of the innumerable people who in the past 130 years, inspired by the love of God and neighbours, have made St Matthew's parish what it is today. As the present incumbent of this parish I place on record my deep appreciation of all who in the past, both clergy and laity, have helped build and maintain the rich heritage which is ours.

I am sure this story about St Matthew's, with its illuminating photographs, will captivate you, as it has me, and may it inspire you as it does me to see that, as far as I am able under God, the next one hundred years may provide local historians with a story of service to God and community, growth, opportunity and challenges well met.

Bill Harrington
August 1993

Acknowledgements

I am very grateful to the following people who have all helped in the compilation of this book:

Mr Donald Anderson, Parbold.

The Late Mr James Anderson.

Mr Roger Arden, Registrar, Liverpool Diocesan Registry.

Mr John Aspinall.

The Late Mr John Berry.

The Librarian, Hatfield Hall, Durham University.

Brigadier D. H. B-H-Blundell, Wichenford, Worcester.

Mr Harry Brighouse, Up Holland.

Mr G. H. Buchan, Christ Church, Barnton.

Revd Canon W. H. Bullough, Churchtown, Southport.

Mr & Mrs R. O. Butts, Up Holland.

Revd W. Bynon, St Peter's, Newton-le-Willows.

Dr J. A. Cooke, Edinburgh.

Mrs M. J. Cooke, Edinburgh.

Mr W. P. Cooke, Dinnington.

The Staff of the Carmarthenshire Record Office.

The Carmarthen Antiquary, Vol. XXIII, 1987, for the article on Cilycwm.

The Staff of Clitheroe Reference Library.

Revd Rodney Dakin, Rector of Littleton, Staines, Middlesex.

Mrs E. Dale-Jones, Carmarthen.

Revd Walter Drain, Christ Church, Chatburn.

The Late Mr E. G. Elliott.

Mr Trevor Evans, Llandovery.

Mr Fred Foster, Highfield.

Mr & Mrs H. F. Gaskell, Highfield.

Miss Sally Gaskell, Highfield.

The Guardian newspaper for permission to reproduce the extract on page 47.

Mrs Ethel Hall, Highfield.

Revd W. H. Harrington, St Matthew's, Highfield.

Mr Fred Holcroft, Winstanley.

The Late Mr T. Hughes.

Mr Graham Jarvis, Headmaster, Highfield C. E. School.

Mr Gerald Johnson, Duffield, Derbyshire.

Revd Alan Kettle, former Vicar of Cilycwm.

Mr Brian Lancaster, Highfield.

The Diocese of London Record Office.

Mr Jack Lowe, Highfield.

The Staff of Liverpool Family History Library.

Mr Bernard Miller, West Derby, Liverpool.

The Staff of the National Union of Teachers.

The Staff of the Archives de la Ville de Nice, France.

Mrs A. Perrin, Weston Super Mare.

Mr Alan Powell, Holy Trinity, Bickerstaffe.

Registry of Births, Marriages and Deaths, Clitheroe.

Mrs H. Saint, Winstanley.

Mrs Helen Sayer.

Miss Diane Smith, Crank, Rainford

Revd John Southern, St John the Divine, Pemberton.

Miss A. Stockley, Highfield.

Mr & Mrs D. Tomos, Penyfedwfawr, Cilycwm.

The Master and Fellows of Trinity College, Cambridge, for permission to reproduce the picture and extracts from Munby's Diary on page 5.

Mr Chris Tyne, Liverpool Diocesan Registry.

Miss E. Twigg, Highfield.

Dr. P. A. N. Wainwright, Winstanley.

The Staff of the National Library of Wales.

The Staff of Wigan History Shop.

The Editor and Staff of the Wigan Observer for permission to reproduce articles from that newspaper.

The Staff of Wigan Record Office.

Mr & Mrs Ken Williams, Cilycwm.

Mr Hedley Woods, Wigan.

Many thanks too, to all those who it would be impossible to list, who have supplied photographs, programmes and articles.

Preface

A S A SCHOOLBOY I hated history, but later discovered the joys of the Bible, which is the world's greatest history book. An interest in family history really started me off on the search and the discovery of what history is all about. My interest in the history of Highfield started on my first visits to this beautiful church in 1946, and was encouraged many years ago when the late Mr Thomas Hughes lent me the 1923 Bazaar Handbook containing the first short history of the parish, and other papers and documents about the church and parish. Since then I have steadily collected any relevant material as it came to hand and when the plans were first discussed to celebrate the Centenary of the present building in 1994, I offered to write an illustrated brochure.

An appeal for photographs and documents produced much more information. So many people in the parish have been so helpful as were so many people outside the parish to whom I wrote for information. The list of acknowledgements on the previous page shows how wide the search has been, and how many people have helped to make this history possible.

I have been privileged to serve with the last four Vicars and work with them as Reader and Church Treasurer and for some time as Organist, and have been very much involved in the life of the parish over these years. I am very grateful to the Vicar, Revd W. H. Harrington and to the Parochial Church Council and the Committee of St Matthew's Fellowship for all their encouragement over the past months and years. What started out as an idea for a brochure soon grew bigger and bigger and I knew that the brochure was rapidly becoming too big, but everyone encouraged me to go on and so finally here it is.

From the list of people who have helped in so many ways I must pick out four for special mention: Mr Donald Anderson of Parbold for information, pictures and advice, Mrs Edna Dale-Jones of Carmarthen for help with research on Revd Thomas Evans, Mr Chris Tyne of Liverpool Diocesan Registry for help with Diocesan Records and research and Mr Nicholas Webb of Wigan Record Office for his help with parish records and other local sources.

Gordon A. Cooke
Winstanley
July 1993

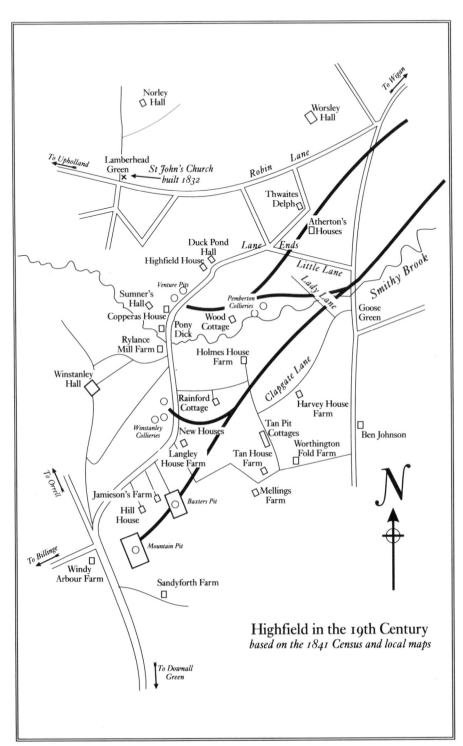

Highfield in the 19th Century
based on the 1841 Census and local maps

Beginnings

THE PARISH of St Matthew Highfield contains the districts of Highfield and Winstanley, which today are suburbs on the south of the Metropolitan Borough of Wigan. Two hundred years ago they were not even large enough to be described as villages. 1867 saw the building of the first church in the district and in 1994 the parish will celebrate the centenary of the building of the present Memorial Church, but it will not be until 2010 when St Matthew's will celebrate its centenary as a parish.

There was a church in Wigan before the year 1200 which was then in the Diocese of Lichfield, founded in 664. Upholland Church, which was within the old parish of Wigan, had been a Priory Church, which was a daughter house to the Benedictine Priory of St John at Pontefract, with a prior and twelve monks, founded in 1319 by Robert, 1st Baron Holland. Billinge Church, also within the old Wigan parish, was founded in about 1540 just before the Diocese of Chester was founded in 1541. The present church at Billinge was built in 1718.

The area of Highfield and Winstanley is almost equidistant from these three churches and it involved a walk of three or four miles to the nearest church for worship, baptisms, weddings and funerals. People have always found a way to overcome problems, and in the 19th century, confirmation candidates were taken in swept-out coal trucks down the colliery line from Winstanley to Seven Stars or Wigan Pier and from there walked to Wigan Parish Church.

In 1832 St John's Church, Pemberton was built. It was what was known as a 'Waterloo' Church. The Battle of Waterloo had been won in 1815, and in 1819 the government gave one million pounds as a thanksgiving for victory to build new churches. This was added to by another half million pounds in 1825. St John's was built with some of this money and was consecrated on 26 September 26 1832, as a chapel of ease to Wigan Parish Church. A district was assigned to St John's, by an order in Council dated 1 February 1838; this consisted of the township of Pemberton, which included Highfield, and part of the township of Orrell.

A Curate-in-charge was appointed to Highfield by the Vicar of St John's when the Iron Church School was built in 1867. The present Memorial Church was built in 1894, extended and consecrated in 1910 when the district became a parish in its own right.

Up to 1966, when the parish boundaries were redrawn to take account of the M6 cutting through the area, most of the houses on the A571 (Pemberton Rd) from Pony Dick to Windy Arbour were in Billinge Parish; and up to 1974, at the reorganisation of Local Government, were in Billinge and Winstanley Urban District. The Parish boundary now extends as far as the M6 motorway, and the Wigan Metropolitan Borough boundary extends as far as Billinge Church.

Winstanley is an old place-name, first appearing in Pipe-rolls in 1206 as Unstanesle, and in 1212 in the Book of Fees as Winstanesle. It means 'Wynstan's Leah'; Leah is an old English word meaning 'an open place in a wood, a part in a wood with the trees scattered so that grass can grow'—a glade. (*Concise Oxford Dictionary of Place-names*). Highfield is a comparatively young name, meaning what it says, and comes from the name Highfield House which stood on the site of St Matthew's Close.

The 1841 Census

In 1841 there was a census throughout the whole of Britain. The census returns for Winstanley and Highfield give a very good picture of the parish as it was in those days.

In the area covered by the present parish of St Matthew's there were only 80 separate addresses or houses. If you walked through the parish from North-east to South-west starting from Little Billinge Road near the garage, there was a farm there and a quarry called Thwaite's Delph. Moving up Billinge Road, there was a group of houses called Atherton's Houses on the Left hand side. There was a farm at the corner of Little Lane or Lane Ends as it was called. There were more buildings near Queen St but nothing else until you came to Highfield. No railway or station, no Enfield Street, but there were several coal pits on the left hand side of the road, nearer to the Wood through which ran the brook, including the Engine Pit and the Bye Pit opened about 1815.

There was a farm called Duck Foot Hall or Duck Pond Hall near to Highfield House. There was no school or school house, no Iona, church or vicarage, just open fields until you came to Copperas House which stood opposite the entrance to Summersales. (Sumner's House) which stood in the fields behind. The Venture Pit was opened near here in 1842. At Pony Dick there was the Inn and a corn Mill (Rylance Mill) from which the bridge over the Smithy Brook gets its name, also Rylance Mill Farm. Billinge Road was originally called Rylance Mill Lane.

A little further up the hill on the right was Wigan Lodge, still standing today, one of the entrances to Winstanley Hall which estate occupied the right hand side of the road up to Windy Arbour. There were no other buildings until the top of the hill on the right where the Bankes Winstanley Collieries were busy. The cottages for the workers were on the left hand side of the road, called the new houses, still standing today, though one complete row was demolished to make way for the bungalows. Between here and Windy Arbour, there were three farms and Croppers House which was inside the Park.

On the left-hand side of the road there were several farms where now there is the Winstanley Housing Estate. Here we used to have our Rogation Walk but that's another story in itself. There was also a row of cottages in Clapgate Lane. Spread across the area were many colliery railways carrying coal from the pits at Winstanley and Highfield to the canal at Crooke, Seven Stars or Wigan Pier.

Of the 80 separate addresses 20 were farms at which lived 118 persons. 132 persons lived in the New Houses at the top of the hill, 65 lived in Rylands Mill Lane (Billinge Rd) and 45 lived in Clapgate Lane. The population was about 465 persons. 179 were employed men, young men and young women. 104 were wives, widows or unemployed young ladies. 182 were children under 15. The main occupations were: Farmers & Farmworkers, 47; Weavers, 34; Nailmakers, 23; Coalminers, 17; Servants, 16; Black-smiths, 9. The rest of the occupations—beerseller, miller, bricklayer, grocer, pig butcher, laundress, toll collector, etc. only had one or two persons each.

This census, along with the 1845 map of the area, gives a picture of a largely rural area, but showing the beginnings of the industry that was to come and completely change the area in the next fifty years. The second half of the 19th century was a period of tremendous growth in the parish due to the rapid growth of the collieries, the mills and the railways. One family in particular had the greatest effect on our parish than any other. They were the Blundell family.

The Blundell family

Jonathan Blundell, the founder of the Coal Business, was the fourth son of Alderman Bryan Blundell, merchant and master mariner, one of the founders and chief benefactor of the Blue Coat Hospital in Liverpool. He was a Protestant descendant of the Roman Catholic Blundells of Ince Blundell. Jonathan and his brothers were owners of several

The late COLONEL BLUNDELL, C.B.   MAJOR CUTHBERT BLUNDELL, O.B.E.

Colonel Henry Blundell-Hollinshead-Blundell CB and his nephew Major Cuthbert Leigh Blundell-Hollinshead-Blundell, the two principal benefactors of St Matthew's Church, School and Parish. Portraits taken from the 1923 Bazaar Handbook.

ships during the eighteenth century which traded in gold dust, ivory and slaves as well as coal. Jonathan himself had been involved in collieries in the Orrell coalfield.

When Jonathan died in 1800, his son Henry took over the business and bought land in Pemberton on which Pemberton Collieries were subsequently built. In 1815 He sank the Engine Pit and the Bye Pit, and between 1815 and 1827 eleven shafts were sunk at Pemberton, and a railway was built to the canal at Seven Stars. Henry died in 1832 and his son Richard took over the business and bought Highfield including Highfield House from Bedford Kenyon. In 1842 The Tanhouse Colliery at the Tanpits and the Venture

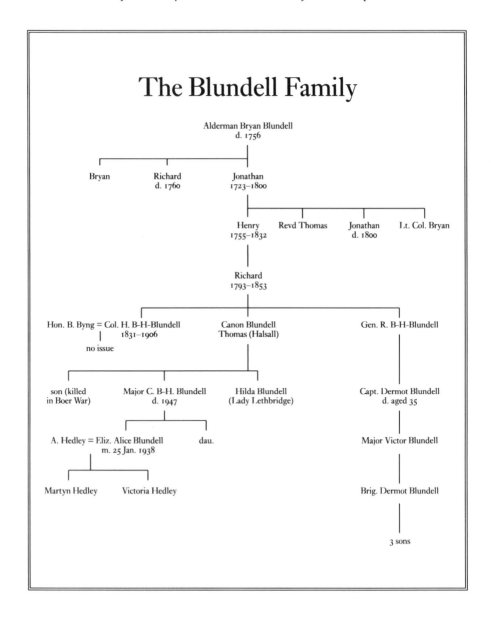

The Blundell Family

Alderman Bryan Blundell
d. 1756

Bryan   Richard d. 1760   Jonathan 1723–1800

Henry 1755–1832   Revd Thomas   Jonathan d. 1800   Lt. Col. Bryan

Richard 1793–1853

Hon. B. Byng = Col. H. B–H–Blundell 1831–1906 | no issue   Canon Blundell Thomas (Halsall)   Gen. R. B–H–Blundell

son (killed in Boer War)   Major C. B–H. Blundell d. 1947   Hilda Blundell (Lady Lethbridge)   Capt. Dermot Blundell d. aged 35

A. Hedley = Eliz. Alice Blundell m. 25 Jan. 1938   dau.   Major Victor Blundell

Martyn Hedley   Victoria Hedley   Brig. Dermot Blundell

3 sons

Colliery near Summersales were opened by Richard Blundell. In 1848 the Liverpool and Bury railway was opened through Pemberton Station, providing easy access from the collieries to all parts of Lancashire and further afield.

In 1853 Richard died and his son Henry took over the business. This was the Henry who was to build the Iron Church, our present Church and our Church Schools. He must have been a very impressive person. He was educated at Eton and Christ Church, Oxford, where he obtained a BA. He passed through Officer training at Sandhurst and served in the Crimea after the fall of Sebastopol, and was involved in the Nile Expedition, 1884–5. He was MP for Ince from 1885 to 1892 and from 1895 to 1915. He married the Hon. Beatrice Byng, daughter of Admiral Byng. She was a maid of honour to Queen Victoria, and in her memory he built our church. The School Managers' minutes of meetings indicate that he was a very regular attender at the meetings, and the newspaper reports of events show that he was very often in attendance at many of the functions in the Parish.

He was helped in the business by a very good team of management. He was still at Sandhurst, aged 22, when he inherited the business in 1853 and he appointed William Armstrong as his general manager. Armstrong appointed William Greener of Durham as manager of Pemberton Colliery and by 1863 after only ten years, output had reached 200,000 tons per year.

This account of the Blundells and their collieries gives an idea of what was happening in the parish during the first half of the nineteenth century.

A. J. Munby's visit

An eye-witness account by A. J. Munby, the famous diarist, describes a journey he made through the district in March 1865 as follows:

17th March 1865

Friday is Wigan market day; and just as I saw farmers' daughters yesterday driving in their milk-carts, so today I saw them driving market-carts: notably one rosy and strapping maiden, who had a woollen kerchief tied over her bonnet, and mittens—but not gloves—on her rough broad hands, and who was loading her cart at a shop door.

There were many women in the crowd in Standish Gate; more women than men: and among them, servant maids, not giddy and flaunting, but homely and quiet. One, a nice looking buxom girl in working frock and coarse apron, and with bare thick red arms, was showing her hands to a friend as I passed. They were coarse to begin with and all roughened by the frost; and she was evidently saying 'How coarse my hands are!'

The sun shone full on Wigan market place as I left it; the booths were busy with gay colours—scarlet flannel, purple woollen kerchiefs; and crowds of country women, in warm plaid shawls, and round oldfashioned bonnets, and blue or brown kirtles, moved about with baskets on their arms: and there was little or no crinoline. The booths were flanked and topped by the old town hall and the old gabled houses; and in the centre, above all, rose the fine Tudor tower of the parish church. There are few more picturesque townscapes in England than this.

I left Wigan on foot at 11.45, to walk to St Helens and see the pits en route. The high road passes no pits for the first two miles, though one or two are visible not far off on the right, near the town. But near Goose Green I turned off to the right, and the footway led me by Blundell's collieries, two in number, lying near together on the slope of the range which bounds the Wigan valley to the southwest. The first of the three pits had large workings and gear, but few people: only three women. One of these I found on the top of coal wagon under the shoot, arranging the lumps of coal. She was a strapping young woman of 27, in waistcoat, pink shirt and flannel trousers; with an honest rustic face, sensible and good looking; with bare stout arms, which like her face were amber-brown, darkened more or less with coal dust. Her name, she said, was Mary Green; she was unmarried; has worked at pit brow some years, but was brought up as a farm labourer: worked a long time on Fairtlough's farm at Winstanley, (Sandiforth farm) partly as a day-labourer, hoeing and shearing and harrowing and driving horses at plough. She never actually drove the plough itself, but her sister, who was in the same service, did, many a time. Fairtlough employed a great many women labourers, and at one time she was Fairtlough's servant, and acted as groom: groomed her master's gighorse, cleaned his gig, cleaned out the stable. That is how Mary Green was brought up. And she is not only robust, but civil, handy, thoroughly respectable in manners and appearance.

In the cabin I found two elderly male colliers and a lass of eighteen getting their dinner: meat and potatoes. The lass was called Mary Liptrot: she wore a blue coat; was healthful though not very big; has worked in factory, but prefers pit.'Aw can tak' me maat better at this work,' she said. The third girl I did not speak to, for she was busy tilting waggons, high up on the shoot: but I could see she was lusty and strong, and a steady worker.

Following the coal railway uphill, I soon reached the other pit called Venture Pit; not, I suppose, because of its belching bellying smoke; for it was the blackest pit and one of the largest, I ever saw. The shoots, galleries and stages at the brow were very lofty and large; crowds of railway trucks, empty or full, filled the spaces below; and wenches in trousers and strange coats were to be seen everywhere, some running to and fro; some mounting the ladders, some showing their black faces over the truck sides; some crawling under to grease the wheels or uncouple the waggons; some 'putting their backs into it', and by main force moving the great trucks, as railway porters do. With their legs well clad and free from petticoats, the lasses kept clambering lightly up, or dropping briskly down, or darting nimbly hither and thither among the trains of waggons with their oilcans and grease boxes; all as dexterous as lads and as strong too. In all there are 15 women at this pit. and only 5 men, overlooker included, and 2 lads: so one of the men told me. All the women were quite young, except one and she not much over 30 apparently. There was much diversity of garments: some girls wore velveteen or fustian coats, some coarse flannel smocks, some waistcoats only: some had trousers of black cloth; one had on a pair of grey tweed trousers with stripe down the side, once perhaps worn by some gay youth, now soiled and patched with all kinds of stuff.

They have no regular mealtimes at this pit; each girl gets her breakfast and dinner as she can, while someone else takes her place at work. But it was now near 1 p.m. and some of the gangs were dining. One group sat under an archway of the coke-ovens, before the furnace door, with their dinner between their knees; bowls of steaming stew, and meat pies.

There was Mary Moss, a great big wench of twenty, 5 feet 8 in height clad in a brown velveteen coat and fustian trousers, and, with her broad, homely face, looking exactly like a man; she sat with her legs crossed and her hands in her pockets, for she had done feeding and her great ironshod clogs were a sight to see: and there were two other lasses, bare armed, eating busily and unmindful of the clouds of coaldust that filled the air and blackened my paper as I sketched them.

And above this black trio of brawny maidens stood a young man, clean, pale and slim, leaning on crutches. He was lame; and he had, it appeared, brought the colliery girls' dinner, just as a navvy's wife brings her husband's, and was standing by while they ate it. This curious inversion, and the contrast between the slim white youth and his coaly and muscular sisters, was a triumph for the 'weaker' sex. Oh my sentimental friend! Fitter for work is a girl like Mary Moss than a lame and sickly youth.

After this, 8 of the wenches repaired to the coal shoots; and there, while the corves rested a space, I talked with them, and Robin the Gaffer looked on from above and added his word. All were unmarried, all had worked in factories: five liked pit much better, 2 preferred mill because it's cleaner, and 1

One of the illustrations from Munby's diary, sketched by Munby himself at the Venture Pit when he visited the collieries there in 1865.

was neutral. They were very black, these girls; black, robust and healthy; civil and quiet enough but not so grave as most, for when they were all there together, there was laughing and chaffing; but it was not at all gross or indecent. They had heard that women were to be stopped at brow; thought it hard; and some said they would work on here. They asked me for nothing; no one did, all today.

Leaving these Blundell Collieries, which lie between Pemberton and Winstanley—I crossed a little rural dell, and ascended again by the side of Winstanley Park, beyond which on the hill and close to the road I came to another pit Banks's Pit which was not agate. But one of the folk told me they have 9 women working there. I turned off the road here to the left, I followed a coalrailway which in about half a mile led me past a small disused colliery to a pit that lies alone in the heart of a narrow green valley, with woods and fields and farms all around. The shaft and gear were new, and the pit was either Bankes's New Pit or 'Baxter's', I forget which. I found there 4 men, elderly, sedate and very respectable, thrutching the corves from the pitmouth; and six women who were all employed in filling the railway trucks with coal, except one girl, who was digging coke with a spade below, and wheeling it in a large wheelbarrow. Five of the women were young—eighteen or twenty: and one a middle-aged person. All were drest in coats or smocks, and trousers: all were stout, rosy and healthy, and not very black as there was fresh air all round them; and all too were grave and earnest, girls though they were: they worked lustily when a corf load was emptied into the truck and wanted arranging with shovel and hands; and between whiles they sat silent and with folded arms, on the side of the waggon. The wheelbarrow girl, indeed whistled at her work; but the others were as staid as matrons, and hardly spoke a word to anyone: and they certainly had not altered their behaviour on my account. They took little notice of me, but girls and men were both very civil: when I dropped my map, one lass shouted to me 'Hi! ye've lost a paaper.'

There were some large collieries visible over the woods eastward, and a mile off or more, so I had not time to go to them. Mercer's pits they were called. I turned to the west, and left the valley by a field-road, passing through the farmyard of an old grey homestead, which proved to be Fairtlough's farm, where Mary Green once worked. Beyond this I again struck the main coal-railway, which runs from pit to pit all the way from Wigan, and is here a steep incline worked by a stationary engine; and I followed it up to Mountain Pit, where it ends. At this pit there are three women, and I saw them all at work. One was about forty years old, but had not worked below. She was tall and gaunt; wore a blue great coat; and her bare neck was somewhat goitrous: the only case—except occasional smallpox—in which I ever saw disease in a pitwoman.

When a colliergirl has had the smallpox, and I know two or three such, her face becomes grotesquely hideous; the pockmarks remaining white, while the rest of the skin is black with coaldust. So too this woman's throat was smooth and white, though her face was all begrimed. She was unloading a truck full of planks. The other two were girls of eighteen; they were on the stage above, thrutching the corves. Both wore their topcoats, for it was now very cold; and one was lusty and big, and both were healthy. Neither had worked in factory. All the three were somewhat dull and heavy in manner and appearance: not nimble and alert like most pitgirls.

This Mountain pit stands on the top of the range of irregular high land that forms the watershed between St Helens and Wigan. Hitherto as I looked back I had always seen the wider valley of the Douglas, with the town of Wigan in the centre, and mills and collieries scattered all round, and the heights of Shevington and Aspull Moor (on the) far horizon. Henceforth I saw all this no more: for before me, looking from Mountain Pit, lay another kind of country; small basin-like hollows, between interlacing uplands, extending as far as one could see: a long line of pit chimneys on the nearest ridge, but all rural in between.

I was now about six miles from St Helens, and it was 2.30 p.m.—A respectable old man at the coal office on the brow advised me not to go by Billinge, which lay out of sight to the right: there are pits that way, said he, but more if you go the longer route by Brackleyhurst: such as those yonder of Sammy Stock's. So I took his advice. There is a coal office on all pitbrows except the most remote: and the sentimental soul may shudder to see a smart dapper young clerk issue thereout in a lordly manner, while all around him are girls in rough coats and breeches, girls begrimed and laborious, and sweating among the coals. So also one may mourn to see a young gentleman reclining in his chair, while a servantmaid hands him coffee, after having perchance even cleaned his boots. After a blank mile along the highroad, and after passing a small colliery-village, I crossed the fields to the nearest pit, on the ...

James Anderson's Story

Donald Anderson's father, James Anderson who worked at the colliery as Head Joiner and later as foreman, tells of life in the parish during the second half of the nineteenth century:

> During the second half of the 19th century the extensive mining developments at Blundell's Pemberton Collieries transformed the quiet district known as Highfield into a sort of gigantic sub-terranean beehive which insinuated itself into the lives of almost every member of the community.
>
> Conditions in the pits were difficult and often dangerous, the work arduous and the hours long. Many of the older people were illiterate and very few of the younger ones could do little more than writing and reading and a bit of figuring. The social order of the day was accepted rather than tolerated by the local people to whom it seemed to last until doomsday.
>
> It was a commonplace sight in those days, for the grand equipages of the local magnates to be seen driving through Highfield and Goose Green where illfed and undernourished urchins clad in ragged clothes played in the streets. Yet the incongruity of the situation was far removed from the minds of the common folk, indeed on the contrary many of the colliery work people took pride in the fact that their employer's wife the Honourable Beatrice B. H. Blundell had been a maid of honour to Queen Victoria and also that Colonel Blundell himself was a Colonel in the Grenadier Guards and his brother a Major General who commanded the Poona District of India.
>
> The Social hierarchy of the period was clear and well-defined. After the Blundells who occupied the apex in the pyramid of social strata came the people who actually managed the colliery—the Greeners and the Pickerings. There was also 'Tawny Taylor' of Highfield House, the colliery solicitor and Joseph Roper who had built May Mill adjoining the colliery in the early 1860s.

James Anderson was born at Highfield in 1882 and attended Highfield Day and Sunday Schools and the old Iron Church. He worked for 50 years at Pemberton Colliery, for 40 years of which he was foreman in charge of the carpenter's shop and waggon shop. He was responsible for all alterations and repair work at the Highfield Schools as they were at that time the property of the Blundell family, the owners of the Colliery. His mother who also was born at Highfield attended Miss Greener's Sunday School which was held in the Colliery Offices in the 1860s.

Early days in the life of the church

William Greener was born in 1823 at Longbenton, Northumberland. His wife, Janet was born in 1824. Their eldest son, William John, was born in Exhall, Warwickshire, in 1853, the same year that his father William was appointed Manager of Pemberton Collieries. There were two more sons, born at Pemberton: Thomas in 1856 and Martin in 1858. Tragically their mother died in 1858 on the 30th April, and father William's sister Isabel, born in Houghton-le-Springs, Durham, in 1829, came to live with them to care for William and her three young nephews. It was this lady, Miss Isabel Greener, (who never married), who started the first Sunday school in Highfield in 1863. The short history of Highfield in the 1923 *Bazaar Handbook* says 'Miss Greener started a Sunday school in a small building used by the colliery workmen as a reading room. There were only a few people residing in the district at that time.' James Anderson says in his notes that Colonel Blundell built the Little Lane Mission Hall which was used as a reading room during the week. This building is still standing (1992). It is now occupied by Newman Roofing, 83 Little Lane.

Wood Cottage. The residence of the managers of Pemberton collieries. On the lawns in front of this house the Sunday School scholars were provided with refreshments, and sang hymns and choruses on early Walking Days and Field Treats.

After only twelve years at Pemberton, William Greener was involved in an accident on Friday 30th June 1865, at Moss House Colliery, Rainford where he was consulting engineer and manager. He was involved in a roof fall which broke his left thigh. He was taken home and appeared to be making satisfactory progress until Tuesday 4th July, when he became seriously ill, deteriorated, and the following Sunday noon, July 9th he died. He was buried at Pemberton Parish Church on Thursday 13th July. His obituary spoke of 'a kindly and generous disposition, with a large circle of friends.' While the funeral party moved from Wood Cottage to Pemberton Church, the inhabitants of the district drew their blinds as a mark of respect and esteem.

Sadly, the death of William Greener was to mark the end of his sister's work with the Sunday school, but fortunately, it was not the end of the story but the beginning.

William J. Watkin from Penshaw House, Durham, who had trained at Pease and Partners' collieries in Durham was appointed the next manager of Pemberton Collieries. He married a Miss Douglas, a sister of Mr Douglas of West Lodge, Crook who was general manager of Crook collieries. They had no children themselves, but were both to take a keen interest in the education of the children of the area, in both day and Sunday schools for the next twelve years.

Mrs Watkin took over the Sunday school from Miss Greener and the numbers attending grew so that Mr Watkin decided to hold a Men's Bible Class in the colliery offices, and their good work continued so that Captain (as he was then) Henry Blundell, the owner of the collieries, was moved to provide better accommodation for the spiritual and secular education of the inhabitants of the area.

Joshua Paley, Vicar of St John's, Pemberton had, with help from the National Society, built schools in the new parish of St John, at Marsh Green, Orrell, Goose Green and Kitt Green before he died in 1849. Highfield had grown in population as the Pemberton Collieries had grown. Plans were afoot to sink the King and Queen pits which began in 1867. In those days this enterprise was a huge commitment, but at the same time plans were being made by Henry Blundell for the new Iron School Church which was to be opened in the same year, the first of his many generous benefactions to what was to become the Parish of St Matthew, Highfield.

Revd Samuel Lancaster Laidman

First Curate In Charge

1867–1871

I N MANY WAYS, the building of the Iron School Church and the beginning of the Church in Highfield reflected what was happening throughout the country at this time. The movement of population from the countryside to the towns created problems for the churches in the towns and cities. Between 1836 and 1896 the number of parish clergy increased from 8,147 to 13,720, and the number of curates rose from 1,006 to 6,514. There were many new buildings erected, and many new districts and parishes formed. The Incorporated Church Building Society reported that between 1818 and 1896, it had helped to build 2238 new churches and extend or improve 6039 existing churches. Between 1837 when Queen Victoria was crowned and 1897, over sixty million pounds were spent on church building and restoration.

The Home Mission of the Church during this period was towards the poor, who were not keen to go to church at all because of their poor clothing, or the distance they had to travel and the time involved, or because of the ties of young families, and so to overcome these difficulties mission buildings were provided to supplement the parish churches. Over five thousand of these missions existed and this was one of the ways in which the Church of England tried to bring the poorest of the people to Christ.

Many mission buildings, which in many cases were dual purpose buildings—a church on Sundays and a school during the week—were built in the Wigan area. St Luke's, Stubshaw Cross is one example which is still in use today after over one hundred years.

By May 1867, Henry Blundell had built in Highfield, at his own expense, the Pemberton Colliery Iron Church School, the house for the Curate and the house for the Schoolmaster. This Iron building was to serve this area for the next twenty seven years as a church and school, and for nearly forty years afterwards as a parish hall.

The Revd Samuel Lancaster Laidman was appointed as the first Curate-in-Charge of the new church by the Revd Arthur Coates, Vicar of St John, Pemberton.

The Revd Laidman was the son of David Laidman and Eleanor Ann Hannah Laidman of Kirkdale. He was born in 1836 and baptised at St Mary's, Bootle on 15 October 1836. His father David is shown in Gore's Liverpool Directory as a Shipowner of Stanley Crescent, with premises at North John Street and later at Rumford Street. There is no reference to the Laidman family in the 1841 Census in Stanley Crescent which suggests that the family moved from there before 1841. Samuel Laidman obtained a L.Th. at Durham University in 1859, and was ordained Deacon in that year by the Bishop of Ripon, and began his first Curacy at St Mark's, Longwood, Hudders-field, which was then in the Diocese of Ripon. He was ordained Priest in 1861 and left Longwood in 1862 to become Curate at Holy Trinity, Bickerstaffe, where in 1865 he married Alice Ellison, the daughter of Edward Ellison, a gamekeeper. He left Bicker-staffe later that year and was for the next two years curate at Mede-Brace, Shrewsbury. He moved to Stretton, Cheshire for a very short time in 1867 before coming to Highfield, in what seems to have been a bit of a hurry, in May of that year for the opening of the new Church on Sunday 12 May. The opening was reported in the *Wigan Observer* as follows:

The Iron School Church

The school church erected near the Pemberton Collieries, through the magnificent liberality of Capt. Blundell, was opened for divine service on Sunday last. The prayers were read in the morning by the Revd S. L. Laidman, to whose pastoral care the district in which the school church is situated has been entrusted. The congregation, which was a numerous and attentive one, was addressed by the Revd Arthur Coates, incumbent of Pemberton, who enlarged upon the advantages of education, and the means of grace; and pointed out the causes to which may be ascribed the too general disregard of spiritual privileges in this locality. The Revd preacher at the same time heartily acknowledged the generosity of the gentleman who had erected that building for divine worship, and supplied all that was requisite to conduct a school for the education of the children of the district. The evening service was even more numerously attended than the morning one, and owing to the indisposition of the Revd Mr Laidman, the sermon was delivered by the Revd J. T. Wilson, curate of St John's Church. The musical portion of the services was under the direction of Mr Fannthorpe, the newly-appointed master of the school. The building, which was of iron, lined with wood, is fitted up with a chancel, vestry and book closet. When the room is being used for the ordinary purposes of a school the church is shut off by means of folding doors. Gas has been introduced, a harmonium provided, and the school furnished with the Windsor desks which answer the threefold purpose of desk, table and seat with back, as circumstances may require. The church is calculated to accommodate about 250 persons, and has been duly licensed for the performance of divine worship and the administration of the sacrament of the Lord's supper.

An indication of the speed with which the Revd Laidman was appointed is given in the dates of the documents pertaining to his appointment. The Testimonial was dated 21 June 1867 and says:

> To the Right Reverend William, Lord Bishop of Chester.
>
> We, whose names are here under-written, testify and make known that Samuel Lancaster Laidman, Clerk, Licentiate in Theology, of Bishop Hatfield's Hall, in the University of Durham, nominated to the charge of a district in the parish of Pemberton, and county of Lancaster, hath been personally known to us for the space of three years last past; that we have had opportunities of observing his conduct; that during the whole of that time we verily believe that he lived piously, soberly and honestly, nor have we at any time heard anything to the contrary thereof; nor hath he at any time, as far as we know or believe, held, written, or taught, anything contrary to the Doctrine or Discipline of the United Church of England and Ireland; and moreover we believe him in our consciences to be, as to his moral conduct, a person worthy to be Licensed to the said Curacy.
>
> In witness whereof we have hereunto set our names, this 21st. day of June, in the year of our Lord, one thousand, eight hundred and sixty seven.
>
> Oswald Penrhyn. M. A. Incumbent of Bickerstaffe.
>
> Joseph L. Bush. M. A. Vicar of Ormskirk.
>
> Robert Henry Gray. M. A. perpetual Curate of Kirkby.

The Nomination to Curacy by the Vicar of Pemberton is a very interesting document, dated 27 June 1867. It reads:

> TO THE RIGHT REVEREND FATHER IN GOD, WILLIAM, by Divine Permission LORD BISHOP OF CHESTER.
>
> I The Reverend Arthur Coates, Clerk, MA, Incumbent of Pemberton, in the County of Lancaster, and your Lordship's Diocese of Chester, do hereby nominate THE REVEREND Samuel Lancaster Laidman, Clerk, L. Th. to perform the Office of Curate in my Church of Pemberton aforesaid, and do promise to allow him the yearly stipend of one hundred and forty pounds, (and the use of a small unfurnished house, free from all rent, rates and taxes.) to be paid to him by equal quarterly payments. AND I do hereby state to your Lordship, that the said Samuel Lancaster Laidman intends to reside in the parish aforesaid, in a house situate at Highfield, distant from my Church about one mile: that the said Samuel Lancaster Laidman does not serve any other Parish as Incumbent or Curate, and that he has not any Cathedral Preferment or Benefice, and does not officiate in any other Church or Chapel.
>
> Witness my hand this twenty seventh day of June One thousand eight hundred and sixty seven. (signed.) Arthur Coates MA

The Bishop's Commission for Licensing the Revd S. L. Laidman as Curate was issued on 6 July 1867, and sworn on 24 July by the Revd Arthur Coates, Commissary for the Bishop.

Since 1830, when St John's, Pemberton was built, the baptisms, marriages and burials of people from the Highfield area had all been performed at St John's, and even after the opening of the Iron Church, they were still performed there. On 13 November 1867, Revd S. L. Laidman conducted his first Burial at Pemberton. (There was no graveyard at Highfield until 1923.) His first Marriage at St John's was not until 17

March 1868, and his first Baptism, also at St John's, was on 6 May 1869. There were no Baptisms at the Iron Church until 1873.

Annual Field Treat, 1869

The Annual Field Treat, which continued at Highfield until the 1950s originated in a Day and Sunday school festival which was held at Lamberhead Green, (St John's) in the early years of the parish of St John's, in which all the Day and Sunday school scholars from every school in the parish took part. The procession including about 1600 children, must have been a very impressive one indeed. Together with parents and friends who joined the children on the field after the procession, there must have been over 3000 people present. The 1868 and the 1869 annual SCHOOL FESTIVALS were recorded in the *Wigan Observer*. The 1869 report reads as follows:

> On Monday last the annual festival of the Sunday and Day schools of St John's Parish, took place. The order of the procession was as follows: Pemberton Amateur Brass Band; the children attending the Lamberhead Green Schools, numbering about 400, headed by the Revd A. Coates, M. A., Vicar; the Orrell scholars, numbering about 200, headed by the Revd J. T. Wilson, Vicar of Wrightington, former Curate of this parish; the Kitt Green schools, including about 300 children, headed by Mr R. Gaskell; Marsh Green scholars, numbering about 200, headed by the Revd T. Evans, curate; children attending the Pemberton Colliery schools, numbering 250, headed by the Revd S. L. Laidman; and the Goose Green scholars, numbering about 250, headed by the Revd J. Wilson, curate. There was a fair sprinkling of banners, and the procession attracted considerable attention from the numerous parents and friends of the children, as it wended its way through the village to a field at Orrell Mount, kindly lent by Mr W. White. While preparations were being made for the distribution of buns and milk, a shower of rain fell, and caused the scholars to seek shelter under a cluster of trees; but after a little patient waiting, the rain passed over. The scholars soon found their places, and the teachers were busy distributing refreshments to the recipients. Passing showers tended to spoil the pleasure; the bands however poured forth their enlivening strains of music and all present seemed determined to enjoy themselves as much as possible. Dancing as usual was a favourite pastime with the elder portion of the visitors, while the youngsters had races and scrambles for nuts. The wet caused many to go home early, and doubtless kept many friends away altogether. (There follows a list of the clergy and visitors attending.) As usual, a refreshment tent was provided for the sale of tea, sandwiches, etc. for visitors, and nuts and sweets for the children. On Tuesday evening the teachers and friends had tea in the schoolroom, and a very pleasant evening was spent.

The 1869 Wigan Directory records Revd S. L. Laidman as curate in charge of Pemberton Colliery Iron Church.

On 4 August 1870, a son was born to the Revd Samuel and Alice Laidman at Highfield Parsonage. He was baptised at St John's Church, Pemberton by his father. Even the Curate's son had to go to Pemberton to be baptised!

When the 1871 Census was taken on the night of 2/3 April 1871, the family were recorded together at the Parsonage House. It included: Samuel Lancaster Laidman,

Curate of Pemberton, aged 34, born at Walton, Lancs., Alice Laidman, his wife, aged 33, born at Ribchester, Herbert L. Laidman, their son, aged 7 months, born at Pemberton, and Agnes Pearce, Domestic Servant from Yorkshire.

The Church and School

There are, sadly, no records of services in the Iron Church until 1882, so we are unable to say what the pattern of worship was in these early days with any certainty. The services on the opening day of Morning and Evening Prayers probably continued, with the Holy Communion on occasions. It is probably fair to assume that the services which existed in 1882 reflect fairly accurately the pattern of worship in these early days. There is still in existence the first book of Common Prayer inscribed in the front cover ' Pemberton Colliery School Church. May 1867.' We know too that Mr and Mrs Watkin continued their work with the Bible Class and the Sunday School.

The Day School was all-age in these early days, that is Boys, Girls and Infants in the same building, with Mr Fannthorpe, the Headmaster and one or two assistants or pupil teachers.

The Revd Samuel Lancaster Laidman's last recorded service was a Baptism at Pemberton on Tuesday 24 October 1871. There is no record of exactly when or why

The Iron School Church on the corner of Foundry Lane and Billinge Road, with the old Parsonage House—at one time called Ivy Cottage—now Iona, and St Matthew's Church. Note the 'cobbled' road.

he left Highfield, but before the end of the year he was serving another Curacy at Garston where he served from 1871 to 1873. After this he served at Weaverham, Cheshire for two years and at Tickhill near Pontefract for two years before finally obtaining a living as Vicar of Barnton, near Northwich, Cheshire in 1877 where he served for twenty years until 1897.

During his ministry at Barnton he was active in the formation of Barnton Cricket Club as the following extracts from the Centenary Brochure of the Club show:

> The existing Barnton Cricket Club derives its origins from the Church, having been formed in 1880 by the Revd Samuel Lancaster Laidman, the incumbent Vicar of the Christ Church, Barnton. His venture received active support and encouragement from A. H. Smith-Barry Esq. the owner of Marbury Hall.
>
> The Revd S. L. Laidman had taken up his appointment as the parish Vicar in 1877, and by all accounts, was a very keen cricket enthusiast.
>
> The 1889 Fixture Card shows Revd S. L. Laidman, President, and son H. L. Laidman, Secretary.
>
> The club suffered its most serious blow of all with the sudden death of its mentor, the President, S. L. Laidman, in 1897.

In 1896, his son Herbert was a sidesman at Barnton Church (aged 26.) An inscription on the Laidman grave in Weaverham Church yard reads:

> In loving memory of the Revd Samuel Lancaster Laidman, 20 years Vicar of Barnton, and formerly curate of this parish who entered into rest April 12th 1897.

The Central Light in the East Window of Barnton Church is a Memorial to the Revd Samuel Lancaster Laidman. The inscription reads as follows: 'To the glory of God and in Memory of the Revd Samuel Lancaster Laidman, for twenty years Vicar of this Parish, 1877–1897.' On 27 April 1912 Herbert Lancaster Laidman, his son, died aged 41, and was buried with his father at Weaverham. Alice Laidman died on 7 June 1927, aged 82 years, and was also buried at Weaverham.

Revd Thomas Evans

Second Curate In Charge

1871–1881

THOMAS EVANS was born in Cilycwm, near Llandovery, South Wales on 10 January 1845, and was baptised at Soar Tynewydd Chapel on 29 January 1845 by William Prytherch, Minister. He was the fifth child of seven children born to Evan and Sarah Evans of Penfedwfawr, Cilycwm, who were married at Cilycwm Parish Church on 8 June 1832. Evan Evans was a farmer and a member of the Methodist Chapel Soar Tynewydd where he was a Deacon in 1856. He was also the Registrar of Births, Marriages and Deaths for the Parish of Cilycwm. Thomas's three brothers and one of his sisters all followed their father into farming. The village was an early centre of Welsh Methodism.

The Revd Henry Morgan, born in Cilycwm in 1855, described the village in his reminiscences published in the Carmarthenshire Antiquary Volume XXIII as follows:

> The village of Cilycwm is situated about the central part of the valley in its length and in its width. It lies four miles to the north of the market town of Llandovery. The highway road runs through the village. At the lower end of the village is built the school building and the house of the master with ample playground for scholars and garden for family. (This is where Thomas attended as a student and where he worked as a Pupil Teacher. The Revd Henry Morgan could have been one of his pupils.) The little brook, the Croewddwr, winds its silvery waters in its course from the inland farms past the school and gives great delight to the School children. The brooklet rises in the hill creek of the name and empties into the Gwenlais river a few fields below the School building.
>
> Cilycwm village consists of one main street which runs its whole length and another short street branches from it to the east over the river Gwenlais. This short street bears the name Ship Street. The inhabitants of the village have their drinking water from

springs that rise a short distance away. One spring in the meadow of Gwaen Croewddwr, with the pathway for the villagers along several fields and over several stiles; and the other on the bank of the river Gwenlais some short distance from the village by the Penystackon field. These springs were never dry in the driest weather. The village now is supplied with water carried in a pipe from the Gwaen Croewddwr spring, and the water tap is in the village. The dwelling houses of the village are now well built and houses suitable for their occupiers. The old houses, some roofed with straw and ferns, and some with the Nantyrside stone slates have disappeared and the cottages of the bylanes cleared away.

The 1851 Census for Cilycwm shows that living at Penfedwfawr were: Evan Evans, Head of Household aged 46, Farmer of 93 acres, born at Llandingat (near Llandovery) and his wife Sarah, aged 40, born at Cilycwm, together with their children, David, aged 17, Morgan, aged 14, Catherine, aged 11, Anne, aged 8, Thomas, aged 6, William, aged 4, Mary, aged 1 and Catherine Jones, aged 19, House servant.

The 1861 Census for Penfedwfawr shows: Evan Evans, Head of Household aged 55, Farmer of 94 acres, born at Llandingat and his wife Sarah, aged 49, together with their children as in 1851 except for David who had moved to a neighbouring farm known as Penlan, and Mary who seems to have died in infancy. Thomas is aged 16 and described as a Pupil Teacher, almost certainly at the village school. He had obviously been encouraged in this by either the Vicar or the Schoolmaster at the time. In the next three or four years he was influenced to enter the ministry and in about 1865 went to Queen's College, Birmingham to begin his training.

In 1868 Thomas was ordained Deacon by the Bishop of Chester, and was appointed Curate at St John's Church, Pemberton, by the Vicar, Revd Arthur Coates, M. A. and for three years helped in the ministry of a growing parish at St John's, being ordained priest by the Bishop of Chester in 1869.

The 1871 Census for Orrell shows that living at Orrell Mount Cottage, the house used by the Curates of St John's, were: Revd Thomas Evans, Unmarried, Head of Household, aged 26, Born Cilycwm, Carmarthenshire. and Revd John Thomas Wilson, Vicar of Wrightington, (who had until recently been a Curate at St John's with Thomas), John Halsall, 37, Coachman and Domestic Servant, and his wife, Elizabeth, and sons, John, aged 6 and William James, aged 1.

When Revd Samuel Lancaster Laidman left Highfield at the end of October 1871, Thomas Evans took over as Curate-in-charge at Highfield. There are still no Registers of Services, but the first Baptism at St Matthew's, conducted by Thomas Evans, was of Thomas Green, son of James, a collier, and Ellen Green of Goose Green, on 12 January 1873. This first register of Baptisms is still in existence.

As well as the normal Sunday services, the work of the Sunday School and the Bible Class seems to have continued. Mr Fannthorpe, the first Master of the School and Organist at the Church only stayed for two years and he was followed by Mr R. Dawson who was Master and Organist for the next twenty years. Mr & Mrs Watkin were also still very much involved in the work of the Day and Sunday Schools and the Church as the following report in the *Wigan Examiner* of 24 April 1874, of the Annual Congregational Tea Party shows:

BAPTISMS solemnized in the Parish of *Pemberton at Pemberton Colliery Iron Church*
in the County of *Lancaster*
in the Year One Thousand Eight Hundred and *seventy three*

When Baptized.	Child's Christian Name.	Parents' Name. Christian.	Surname.	Abode.	Quality, Trade, or Profession.	By whom the Ceremony was Performed.
1873 January 12th No. 1	Thomas	James + Ellen	Green	Goose Green Pemberton	Collier	Thomas Evans
1873 January 12th No. 2	John Thomas	Elizabeth	Catterall	Goose Green Pemberton	—	Thomas Evans
1873 January 26th No. 3	Samuel	Joseph + Alice	Starkey	Pony Dick Inn Pemberton	Publican	Thomas Evans
1873 February 1st No. 4	Sarah Alice	James + Ellen	Taylor	Smithy Brook Pemberton	Labourer at Colliery	Thomas Evans
1873 April 20th No. 5	Ellen	William and Mary Ann	Wilkinson	Highfield Pemberton	Coachman	Thomas Evans
1873 April 20th No. 6	Emily	William and Mary Ann	Wilkinson	Highfield Pemberton	Coachman	Thomas Evans
1873 April 20th No. 7	Lillie	William and Mary Ann	Wilkinson	Highfield Pemberton	Coachman	Thomas Evans
1873 April 20 No. 8	Mary Elizabeth	William and Jane Maria	Melling	Highfield Pemberton	Printsewer	Thomas Evans

The first page of the first Baptism register, the oldest surviving register of the Church.

Annual Tea Party, 1874

The annual congregational tea party in connection with the Pemberton Colliery Iron Church was held on Tuesday evening last, and was very largely attended, upwards of 400 persons partaking of tea. The subsequent proceedings were presided over by the Revd T. Evans (curate in charge), and among the clergy and gentlemen present were the Revs. Chadwick, W. T. Sparrow, T. Higham (St Catharine's, Wigan), J. Cronshaw (St Thomas's, Wigan), T. F. Fergie (Ince), J. T. Wilson, (Wrightington) W. Howe; Messrs W. J. L. Watkin, T. Shortrede, G. Henderson, S. Brown, J. Brown, &c. The choir of the church gave an excellent selection of glees and part-songs, Mr Dawson accompanying on the pianoforte; songs were also given by Mr Hall (Wigan) and Mr Darlington (Billinge), and recitations by several of the schoolchildren.

The chairman said it was customary on occasions of this kind to say a little as to how they had gone on during the past year since their last congregational gathering. He would like to see more unity amongst them and to see each doing his best, for each could do something, however little it might be. The help and assistance for which he was now asking was not of a pecuniary character, but he wished them to strive to get people into the church and the Sunday school. He was glad to say the Sunday school was in a very flourishing condition. They had on the books 290 scholars, 275 of whom were present last Sunday afternoon. They had some very good teachers, and he was greatly indebted to Mr and Mrs Watkin for the attention they paid to the Sunday school. (Applause) His thanks were also due to others for the interest they manifested. It would give him pleasure to see more volunteers in this department. Many present would be able to teach, but if they could not do that they certainly might bring some of the people in Victoria Street up to the school. There were some in the street named whom it seemed impossible to bring to the school. As he heard it said by a clergyman the other day, they stood in the street like chimney ornaments instead of attending school and church.

As his hearers were aware, there was a clothing club in connection with the school, and last year the subscriptions to the club amounted to £337. (Hear, hear.) The interest on that amount, when divided among the contributors, was very small; but there was this advantage, that, whereas children previously spent their pennies needlessly, they now saved them by means of the club, and where three or four members of a family contributed to the club a considerable sum was saved during the course of the year.

Since he had come amongst them there had been Christenings in the church, and during the last year this rite was performed on 49 children. There seemed to be some misunderstanding in the matter, and he would, therefore, tell them there was no charge whatever for Christening nor for churching, but in the latter case women could contribute whatever they thought proper.

In the day school there was a good number on the books, but he wished they could improve the attendance. He had heard of a clergyman somewhere in Lancashire who took for his text the words 'All men are liars,' and commenced his sermon by saying, These words were spoken by David. He must have said them in haste, but if he had been in this parish he might have said them at leisure. He (the chairman) did not say they were all liars, but he said some of the parents amongst them were very negligent. Those having charge of the school had done their best to get the children to attend regularly, and he wished the parents would see that they were regularly sent, because, if not, it was a great disadvantage to all concerned. The children could not progress, and there was a loss to the school. What was paid in school pence went a very little way towards paying the teacher, and unless a child attended a certain number of times in the year the Government inspector refused to examine him. Several were not examined last year from this cause, and their parents were offended; but their non-examination was also a loss to the school. The last time they were visited by the inspector 53 should have been examined, but only 39 appeared. He admitted that it was very cold on the morning of the examination, but he thought an effort should have been made by the parents to get the children to school, because the absence of the remainder of those who should have been examined meant a loss of about £7 to the school.

The day school had every encouragement. Colonel and the Hon. Mrs Blundell did their utmost towards the education of the children of that part; they had given prizes for sewing, good attendance, and many other things, and Mr Watkin and Mr Pickering had also kindly assisted them. There were, therefore, advantages and privileges there which could not be obtained at any other school, and he hoped the people would show by sending their children regularly that they valued those advantages and privileges. The night school for boys had been very well attended, but that for girls had been a failure. Some were under the impression that they had to pay half a crown to attend the night school. That was to some extent a mistake. Half a crown had to be paid, but if the youth attended 40 times out of 60 the money was returned to him. This plan was adopted to prevent the classes dwindling from a large number to a very few as the season progressed. This year there had been five failures with regard to the attendance. The half crowns of those who failed were given as prizes to the others (Hear, hear).

Since their last tea meeting a band had been started, which had cost altogether £13. 18s. Mr Watkin kindly advanced the money for the flutes, and the children who had bought them were allowed to pay for them as they were able, and he was glad to say they were almost all paid for and they would soon be clear of Mr Watkin. (Hear, hear and laughter.)

Before he (the Chairman) came to Pemberton they had no monthly offertory at that church, and on the first Sunday of its adoption they realised 18s. He was glad to say it was now a little better, but there was still room for improvement. By its means they generally get about 28s. or 30s. but seldom above the latter sum, and he asked them to put their shoulders to the wheel and try to get a little more money. Mr Watkin wished him to say they were in debt. It was quite true. (Laughter) According to a paper in the porch they were about £6 8s. in debt, and unless the amount of the offertory increased they must have collections oftener. Colonel Blundell was so good to them that they could not expect everything from him, and they ought to do something for themselves (Hear, hear).

He again invited them to have a little more unity amongst themselves and to do their best for the good of the church and of the district. They had a good congregation, but they desired a still larger one, as there were so many who went nowhere. He was sorry to say he was getting quite tired of asking people to come to church. They were good promisers but poor at fulfilment. He hoped these would mend, and that they would soon have the place filled from corner to corner. (Applause).

The Revd J. Cronshaw delivered an address, in which he referred to the necessity for lay co-operation in order that the church might be prosperous, and impressed upon his hearers the great desirableness of the laity reading such works as would thoroughly inform them what were the principles and teachings, and doctrines, and the form of government of the Church of England.

The Revd T. Higham, in the course of some excellent remarks, said he took objection to one statement made by the chairman. He was perfectly willing to give an education for nothing to those who could not afford to pay for it, but not to those who could. The chairman had done a thing in that parish which he hoped no other clergyman would do, and that was after a scholar has paid his fee he had given it back to him. If there were any young men or boys present who had received their halfcrowns again he would tell them if he had his health and strength he would not sleep in his bed until he had brought the money back again (hear, hear).

Social Conditions

We heard in the first chapter of the social conditions of the area, but the following letter to the editor of the *Wigan Observer*, reported on 12 December 1874, gives a very vivid picture of the conditions under which the poor of the area lived:

Dear Sir,

At this present time when the sanitary conditions of our towns and villages is exciting considerable attention, I may perhaps be excused for calling attention to one or two facts which merit the attention of the members of the Pemberton Local Board. It is a well-known fact that the Messrs Blundell and Son are extending their works at a very rapid rate in this township, and to meet the requirements of their numerous workmen a large number of houses have recently been erected, and it is to the sanitary conditions of these that I now call attention. The traveller to Liverpool has often, I dare say, noticed the pretty row of houses facing the Pemberton Railway Station which bears the aristocratic name of Alexandra Terrace, and I have heard many complimentary remarks on their neat appearance, but there are very few who observe two dirty rows of cottages in the hollow immediately behind, bearing the loyal name of Victoria Street.

Last Monday I was tempted by what I had heard to make an examination of their sanitary condition, and from what I saw I cannot but be surprised that the giant diseases in the shape of cholera and epidemic fevers visit this neighbourhood, and attach such an evil reputation to it as would put Darwen and Skelmersdale in the shade. Not one of the houses have any backyards, a cartroad runs between the ashpits and the back doors, and which it is no exaggeration to say more resembled a marsh in the fen country than anything I have ever seen. True the women have been wise enough to connect their back doors with the ashpits by planks, but how awkward it must be for anyone returning home on a dark night. The water was so deep at one persons back door that he had utilised it in a very strange manner. A large drake was making himself quite at home as I passed.

It is only within the last month, I am informed, that any drains have been laid to these houses, and even now the ashpits and gardens are totally without any sewers, so that the stench is at times unbearable. Messrs Blundell's manager is the chairman of our local Board, and is pushing a very costly sewage scheme on the ratepayers. Would it be too much to ask him to provide at once proper sanitary arrangements at home.

Hoping Sir that you will insert this in your next issue,

I am your obedient servant, PEMBERTON.

For Thomas Evans, work amongst such dreadful conditions must have been very difficult. Fortunately there is beautiful countryside next door to this industrial background, and there were happy times for Thomas, and he was not to be alone in his work for any longer, for on the 14 March 1876, he married Alice Taylor of Orrell at St John's

Church, Pemberton. Alice was the daughter of Israel Taylor, who had died in 1874 and had been a Linen Manufacturer. They were married by the Revd David Edwards, who sounds like a friend of Thomas, not by the Vicar of Pemberton, Revd John Leach. Alice soon became involved in the work of the parish.

Sunday School Treat, 1876

In July of the same year the Annual Sunday Scholars' Treat was held, this year the procession taking a slightly different route. It was reported in the *Wigan Observer* on 21 July 1876 as follows:

> On Saturday last the children attending the Day and Sunday schools in connection with the Iron Church, Pemberton, had their Annual Field Day. The children assembled about two o'clock in the afternoon and soon started in procession preceded by the 'Pemberton Red Jacket Band' and the Revd T. Evans, and the Teachers walked with their respective classes.
>
> By special invitation, the procession proceeded as far as Mr George Holland's, Winstanley, (Copperas House) where the children, amounting in number to 463 were supplied, through the liberality of Mr Holland, with nuts, gooseberries, biscuits, milk and etc. . There was also a large table tastefully set out and heavily laden with good things suitable for the occasion for the accommodation of the teachers. The band was also provided for.
>
> After a most enjoyable half hour, the procession returned through Winstanley Park, by kind permission of Mr Shortrede, (Squire Bankes's Agent) and proceeded to Wood Cottage, where they were welcomed by Mr and Mrs Watkin and friends. Assembled in front of the House the children sang Hymn Number 364 Ancient and Modern.
>
> Again the procession was resumed and proceeded in front of Alexandra Terrace and then returned to the field. Here they were supplied with tea and buns, and their readiness to partake thereof after their long procession was manifested by the quantity consumed and the ample justice done to both.
>
> Among the ladies and gentlemen present on the field were Revd J. Leach, Revd T. Evans and Mrs Evans, Mr and Mrs Watkin, Mrs Douglas (Chesterfield), Mr and Mrs Pickering, the Misses Pickering, Mr and Mrs Henderson, Mr and Mrs Humble, Mrs Booth, Dr and Mrs Fisher, Mr and Mrs Shortrede, Mr G. Holland, Mr and Miss Johnson (Wigan), Mr Jones (New Brighton).
>
> The children were well attended to, and every effort was and had been made to contribute towards their enjoyment. A large quantity of nuts were distributed among them, and through the kindness of Mr Watkin, a number of swings had been erected, with sundry other things which added much to the children's amusement. About nine o'clock in the evening the doings of the day came to a close. The children were assembled and arranged to have the remnant of the provisions distributed amongst them, and after singing the National Anthem, all left the field for their respective homes highly pleased with their day's entertainment.

New Boys' School

In the nine years since the opening of the Iron School Church, the population of the area had grown with the development of the colliery and the mills. The school had been all age in one building, and now that more room was needed, a building across the road which had probably been a barn connected with Duck Foot Hall, was converted to provide new accommodation for the boys, and the girls and infants were left in the old building. Again the scheme was most generously financed by Colonel Blundell. It was probably brought into use as a school from the beginning of the Autumn term, but was not officially opened until October 1876, as the following account in the *Wigan Observer* of the 27th of that month shows:

> On Monday an entertainment was given in celebration of the opening of the new schools built by Colonel Blundell. Mr W. J. L. Watkin was voted to the chair, and in a short speech stated that this was an entertainment where the performers were almost entirely children attending the schools. The programme was a lengthy one and consisted of glees, catches and recitations by the children and several musical selections by the Misses Rose and Ashurst, the Misses Moorfield, Mr Dawson, and Master Johnson. The singing of the children was extremely good throughout and did credit to their teachers, who must have taken very great pains with their training.

> After the programme had been gone through Mr Pickering was called upon by the Chairman to address the meeting. On rising he expressed his complete satisfaction with the manner in which the children had acquited themselves and said they showed they had been carefully and conscientiously trained. No-one but teachers knew what uphill work it was to train children in this manner, and he, therefore, asked the thanks of the meeting for Mr Dawson, the Master, his assistant, and the two lady teachers. He advised parents never to keep their children from school for any trivial reason, but to give them a fair chance of availing themselves of the opportunities placed in their reach.

> Mr Dawson, the Master, in acknowledging the compliment payed him and his assistants, said he was proud to preside over such a school, the building of which was an example of the well-known generosity of Colonel Blundell to his work-people, and he hoped the parents of children would not fail to avail themselves of it.

> The Revd T. Evans, in addressing the meeting, said he had often been asked when he intended to open the school, but he was now happy to be able to say the children had opened it themselves. Alluding to a large quantity of clothing which was suspended across the end of the school he said these articles had been made by the children, and had passed before the scrutinising eyes of the Inspectors who expressed themselves pleased with the work. The articles were for sale, and the proceeds would be devoted to a general fund. The materials of which the goods were made had been presented by Mrs Watkin, and he proposed calling it 'Mrs Watkin's Charity'. This was not the only entertainment to take place in the school; he intended to commence a series of Saturday evening readings, and etc., the price of admission to be a penny or more as was found best. The money thus acquired would be devoted to prizes for the children of the day school. Not only would prizes be given to successful competitors at examinations, but they would also be given for attendance, so as to act as an inducement for regular

attendance. The average cost for every child at school amounted to 1 shilling or 1 shilling and 3 pence per week, while the school pence was only three pence weekly, so that parents ought to send the children regularly.

Upon the proposition of Mr Evans a vote of thanks was passed to Mr Simpkin for the loan of the piano and to Mr Watkin for the able manner in which he had performed his duties as Chairman.

Mr Watkin, in reply to the vote, said it afforded him great pleasure to preside over such an assembly, and on such an occasion. Though he had no children himself, he took a great interest in the children of others. He found the birth rate of that township was three times the death rate, and soon the school accommodation would need to be increased; if necessary they were prepared to double it. he wished while he was speaking to say a few words about the garden and cottage prizes offered by Colonel Blundell. Two thirds of the whole tenants viz. 196 were found to be entitled to prizes which were in sums of 5 shillings to 10 shillings each, amounting in all to £69 9s. 6d. One man named William Massey, though he had been an invalid for many months, had kept his cottage and garden in a very nice condition indeed, and would receive a prize of £1.

The schools are fine, roomy and lofty buildings, well ventilated and furnished by the North of England School Furnishing Company of Darlington, in the latest and the most approved manner. The proceeds of the entertainment were £6 3s. od.

It can be seen from the above report how involved Mr and Mrs Watkin were in the life of the Church at Highfield, and the young Church owed them a great deal for all their work and generosity. But the life of a colliery village was never without its tragedies, and in 1877 one of the worst explosions in the Wigan coalfield took the life of Mr Watkin and thirty four others. The King and Queen pits were connected for ventilation purposes and when the explosion occurred a cloud of dust and smoke appeared from one of the shafts indicating that an explosion had taken place below ground. Mr Watkin, Mr Cook and Mr Laverick and several others went down as an exploring party. Six

J. W. L. WATKIN   R. F. COOK   R. LAVERICK
(Manager of the Pit)   (Certificated Manager)   (Underlooker)

THE COLLIERY ACCIDENT AT PEMBERTON—THE FIRST RESCUING PARTY, ALL OF WHOM WERE KILLED

Mr J. W. L. Watkin, Manager, and his colleagues who were killed while leading the rescue at the tragic mining accident at Pemberton Colliery in 1877.

hundred men were evacuated from the workings and Mr Watkin, Mr Cook and Mr Laverick decided to push forward to try to save any more men. After a while, and no word from the three, the others decided to go to see what had happened. They were found to have been gassed, having tried to make their way back. Word of the terrible tragedy soon spread round the whole Wigan area and mine officials came from many other collieries to see if they could help, but the news of the deaths cast a dreadful gloom over the whole area. The Revd Thomas Evans and the Revd John Wood, then a Curate at Pemberton, were both at the colliery, and to Thomas Evans was given the awesome task of telling Mrs Watkin of her husband's death. The young Church must have been devastated and Thomas Evans and his wife must have had a very difficult time for the next months comforting the widows and their children.

William John Greener, the son of William Greener, the first manager of Pemberton Collieries, who had trained under Watkin, and had held posts in Durham and Yorkshire, became the next manager of the collieries, at the age of twenty-three, and he too, like his predecessor, was to become very involved with the life of the Church and the School over the next twenty years.

Some time around the middle of 1879 Thomas's wife Alice began to be ill, and having suffered for some months her doctors advised a change to a milder climate. Thomas took her that Autumn to southern Europe. From letters written to friends she appeared to be making favourable progress, but a telegram from Rome sent at the end of February 1880, announced her death on 24th February. Her obituary in the *Wigan Observer* said that 'The members of the Church and the families will greatly miss the kind and charitable visits of their pastor's late wife.' She was forty-four and was buried in Rome.

In her will Alice left personal estate under £8,000, most of the estate going to Thomas.

The 1881 Census for Pemberton on 3 April records Thomas Evans, widower, aged thirty-six, Curate of Highfield, born Carmarthen, living at Ivy House (The Parsonage) with Anne Arrowsmith, 41, Servant, born Winstanley.

Sunday School Treat, 1881

Thomas must have involved himself in the work of the parish during these sad years. In July 1881 we find him again leading the activities at the Sunday Scholars' Annual Treat, reported in the *Wigan Observer* on the 9th of July:

On Saturday last, the treat provided annually for the Sunday scholars in connection with the Iron Church, was held in the field of the Highfield Cricket and Football Clubs. The weather, upon which depends almost entirely both the quality and the quantity of the enjoyment to be derived from all outdoor amusements, was as beautifully fine as the hearts of the most anxious could wish; the sun—it deserved its share of praise—shone splendidly, and hotly, too, if the rapid manner in which bottled refreshments disappeared is any criterion. The band, without which all outdoor proceedings seem incomplete nowadays, was the Pemberton Temperance, which kindly gave its services for the occasion, and the style of whose performance needs no comment; the judges in the many contests in which they have so successfully competed have decided that long ago.

The scholars, to the number of 530, assembled at the church at two p.m. ; where they were arranged in processional order by the superintendents and teachers, and then, with band playing and colours flying, joyfully wended their way along the route to Little Lane and Spring-bank. From the girls, the majority of whom were dressed in white (which colour, and with good reason, appears to be the general favourite for these occasions), to the band with their yellow-faced scarlet jackets and brown helmets, with waving red plumes, the procession made an exceedingly favourable impression of their appearance upon the minds of the numerous spectators who mustered strongly along the whole line of route, and was the object of much criticism. But a subject for much more congratulation, and which must be exceedingly much more gratifying to the esteemed pastor of these schools (the Revd T. Evans) and to all concerned in their welfare will be found in the fact that (as regularity of attendance at Sunday school, as in all other cases, is the first great step towards the success of that school, and which may therefore be taken as a criterion of its prosperous condition), the attendance of the scholars is of such a high standard, for out of the 530 who took part in the proceedings a good percentage have never been absent during the year; the rest at the worst have not missed four times a quarter, as all who have were excluded from the day's treat. The processionists on their return were marched into the field, and there regaled with buns and tea (the walk, it was found, had not in the least impaired their appetites).

After the conclusion of the repast the public were admitted into the field at a nominal charge, and the recreation portion of the day's amusements commenced. Races for the scholars, both male and female, with handsome prizes for the successful, were conducted under the management of the Revd T. Evans and Messrs Dawson and Ritson at the starting point, and Messrs Taylor and Crossley at the winning post. Flat and hurdle races, open to all on the field, were also run for money prizes. There were tugs of war for those who wished to distinguish themselves by the exhibition of their strength ; there were kissing rings for those people of an over affectionate disposition ; there was dancing for those accomplished in that accomplished art (whenever the band chose to play dance tunes, which might have been oftener). There were several other games, the names of which are probably not yet determined on, nor probably ever will be.

But the greatest feature in the day's programme, and the one that caused the greatest amount of amusement to the spectators, was the obstacle race arranged by Mr Crossley, who ran himself as an inducement to others. The first prize for this race was 12s., second 6s., third 4s., and fourth 4s. The new Vicar of Pemberton, the Revd Harry Mitchell, MA, who had scarcely arrived on the field before he was installed a general favourite, officiated as starter in this peculiar race, whilst Mr T. R. Taylor acted in the capacity as judge. The course, about 300 yards long, contained some half dozen obstructions placed at intervals. First came a water jump of 15ft.; then two flights of hurdles; next came a sort of skeleton scaffolding, consisting of upright poles 10ft. high, with horizontal bars fixed firmly to the top, and about 16ft. long, the idea being to climb the uprights, swing along the horizontal bar, and then drop off at the end; further on a huge baulk of timber was secured 10 inches above ground, under which the competitors had to crawl; and lastly, barrels of 17 inches diameter were placed for them to wriggle through. In the first heat Robertson alone cleared the water jump, the rest not succeeding in doing so, to the intense satisfaction of the spectators, who were densely packed at this point, expecting and obtaining considerable amusement from the repeated failures of the competitors. Robertson, however had to give first place to Winstanley, who passed him in the climbing performance. In the second heat both T. Taberner and W. Dixon succeeded at the water, and after mastering the other obstructions came in first and second respectively. In the final all the men took a bath for a start, amid roars of laughter from the delighted spectators; the remainder of the impediments were got over more successfully, and eventually Taberner won with his hands down; Winstanley 2nd, Robertson 3rd, and Dixon 4th, Taberner owing the ease of his victory to his superior activity in the rigging.

The best thanks of the teachers and scholars are due to the manager of the Pemberton Collieries, Mr W. J. Greener, who kindly erected the swings and made all the necessary preparations for the obstacle race, which, as have been seen, were very considerable; and it is a source of deep regret that he was prevented by illness from being present on the occasion. This, the most successful of the many treats given at Highfield was brought to a close by the band playing the National Anthem.

Thomas's work at Highfield was coming to a close. His last recorded Baptism at Highfield was of Sarah Jane Fouracre of Mill House, on Sunday 21 August 1881.

Teachers and Choir Outing

On the previous day, Saturday 20 August, the Sunday School Teachers and the Choir had their Annual Outing, this year to Knowsley Park, the home of Lord Derby. The Curate did not accompany them on this occasion, for on the same day, in the evening, a testimonial presentation was to be held. The *Wigan Observer* reported the outing as follows:

The weather of the month of August has held out to excursionists, picnic parties and ruralists hopes of enjoyment. To appoint particular days for rural sports and pleasures is exceedingly critical and seems only to portend certain disappointment. Saturday last was the day chosen for the annual picnic of the Sunday School Teachers and Choir of the Iron Church, Pemberton. The steady downpour of rain last Friday made the committee despond, but Saturday morning dawned favourably, and by noon the weather was all that could be desired. Assembling in front of the iron structure, about sixty Sunday School Teachers and Choristers were comfortably seated in two large vans specially retained for their conveyance which sped away with their burden, joyous and exhilarated. After a delightful progress through the parishes of Billinge and Rainford, by the kind permission of Mr Hale, Lord Derby's agent, the park was entered at Knowsley and then came the most enjoyable part of the day. For three miles and a half, the vehicles drove slowly, stopped at intervals, giving the inmates opportunities of enjoying the magnificence of the undulating and well-wooded park, inhabited by herds of deer and cattle romping on the grass, rollicking in the pure fresh air. Emerging from the park at Prescot, the horses were refreshed and the party drove home, their appetites sharpened by the long and splendid drive. On arriving at the schools at 7.30 p.m. the ruralists sat down to a well-catered tea varied with the creature comforts of this life, and judging from the silence which immediately prevailed, ample justice was done to it. When the members of the party had attended the presentation to the Revd T. Evans, they again adjourned to the boys' schoolroom, where they finished the evening with dancing and games of an innocent kind, at the conclusion of which they dispersed, having spent a most delightful day.

Presentation to Revd T. Evans

The report of the presentation made to Thomas Evans on behalf of the members of the Church and his last service and sermon at Highfield were also reported in the *Wigan Observer*:

> It was known definitely three weeks ago, that the ministry of the Revd T. Evans, curate of the Iron Church and chaplain of Col. Blundell's employees, would terminate. Although the time was short a committee was at once formed for the purpose of raising a testimonial as a tribute of respect and esteem in which he is held by all who know him. The solicitations of the committee met with a hearty response which far exceeded their most sanguine expectations. The result was the purchase of a most handsome present consisting of a silver tea-urn and a case of four silver salt-cellars with accompanying spoons.
>
> The members of the congregation, teachers and choir assembled on Saturday evening at 8.30 p.m. for the purpose of seeing the above presented. Mr W. J. Greener kindly presided, and after a few introductory and appropriate remarks, made the presentation, reading the following address: 'To the Revd Thomas Evans, Reverend and Dear Sir, Your friends in the neighbourhood of Highfield have learned with much regret that you are on the eve of leaving them, thus bringing to a close, a ministry among them extending over nine years. They feel they cannot allow you to go away without some token of the regard in which they hold you and therefore desire your acceptance of the accompanying. While bidding you farewell they trust that you may long be spared to fulfil the duties of your calling in the same kindly and conscientious spirit which has marked you in the past. They beg to subscribe themselves, Reverend and Dear Sir, Yours faithfully, etc. etc.'
>
> The Revd T. Evans responded, dwelling upon the events of his past ministry, some of which had been of a calamitous nature, while others had been cheering. He referred to the rapid growth and efficiency of the Day and Sunday Schools, and hoped that they would continue in prosperity. In conclusion, he thanked many kind friends for the readiness and voluntary manner in which they had assisted him, and expressed his regret at leaving them and his deep sense of gratitude for the final token of respect. Mr Dawson, on behalf of the committee moved a cordial vote of thanks to the chairman for the interest he had taken in promoting the testimonial and also to Mr Crossley, who at the sacrifice of much time and trouble had undertaken to illuminate the above address.

Mr Evans' Farewell Sermon

The Revd T. Evans, who leaves Highfield for Littleton Rectory, Staines, preached his final sermon in the Iron Church last Sunday. Accommodation had been made in anticipation of a large congregation and every seat was occupied soon after six. By means of additional chairs the church was densely packed. Every available space was occupied and scores of people were unable to gain admission. The musical portion of the service consisted of Burnett's Unison Services in F. The psalm was sung to the three following single chants consecutively, Rimbout in Eb, Ousley in F minor, and Woodward in Bb. and the hymns were 342, 260, and 279 in Hymns Ancient and Modern.

The Reverend gentleman preached from I Chronicles 28: part of the 9th verse 'If thou seek him, he will be fond of thee, but if thou forsake him, he will cast thee off for ever.' and alluding to the occasion on which the above words were used, he said the text was most becoming to parents, teaching them what should be their chief desire on behalf of their children. These words were also very appropriate for a minister to his congregation. The present occasion was one of peculiar solemnity and interest to himself, inasmuch as they were aware that he was, in all probability delivering to them his last words of counsel and monition as their minister from that pulpit. He urged them to seek after God with their whole hearts. They should rest, not in a formal routine of duties or in a partial conformity to His revealed will but should see that their hearts are right with Him, and they should never rest until they had the testimony of their own conscience, that in simplicity and Godly sincerity they had their conversation in the world. Such a state of mind was most desirable for every one of them, and it was the best preparation, no less for the duties of this life, than for the enjoyment of the life to come. The words of his text contained a promise and a warning, and from these it was evident that God would deal with them according as they behaved themselves towards Him. Their happiness both in time and in eternity depended upon their present diligence and faithfulness. Let them therefore beg help from God that they might so devote themselves to him now as to be approved by Him in the day of Judgement.

Continuing, he said, Though I may be far away in years to come, if spared, I shall ever feel a keen interest in your welfare, spiritual and temporal, and though miles and miles may intervene between us, my thoughts will often revert to you, and my prayers be offered that His blessing may be with you. It is now nearly ten years since I entered upon my duties amongst you. As I look back through these years during which I have gone in and out among you, I am reminded of many changes which have taken place. I have seen afflictions, sore and grievous invading your families. I have known houses by death, sudden and awful, desolated. Sickness in manifested forms have entailed suffering and distress. More than once, bad trade has cast the gloom of anxiety over our district. I trust it may please God to give you better times and that He will soon, of His mercy, spare you from those awful accidents which work such desolation, and of which we all have so vivid a remembrance.

I miss tonight many a face that was once familiar. Many a voice, that once mingled with ours at these services, has been hushed by death, though hushed as to the services on earth, yet audible I trust in the worship of Heaven. In ten years what changes happen, the boy developes into manhood, the girl into womanhood, and often, while time is moving, buds, once promising, untimely fade. Those who gave hopes for heaven, under the corroding influence of the world fall away, forget their Saviour and serve the world, the devil and the flesh. In ten years to come, some who are now earnest, regular and diligent in their religious duties perhaps will be found walking in the ways of the world and utterly careless of their souls. Something may have offended them. Some honour or notice which they looked for has not been given, or some new formed attachment has perhaps, like a rank and noxious weed choked and stifled the plant religious life within them. They are not only treading the broad road themselves, but by their example, perchance their counsel, leading others away from God. I trust, my friends, that in ten years from now it may be found not to have been thus with any of you. Remember the apostles practice.I press towards the mark for the prize of the high calling of Christ Jesus. He keepeth the mark and the prize was before him. Even so, my brethren, do ye in like manner persevere. Remember to seek God. Seek him in the service of His sanctuary. Seek Him by holiness of living. Seek Him in dutiful obedience. Seek Him in prayer and watchfulness, for 'If thou seek Him, He will be fond of thee, but if thou forsake Him', and brethren, awful is the warning, He will cast thee off for ever. May the Holy Spirit so guide and aid you by His divine influence that you may be saved from the awful doom of a backslider, and be amongst those, who, when Christ comes with glory, shall receive those blessed words of commendation: 'Well done, thou good and faithful servant. Enter thou into the joy of thy Lord.'

I feel I cannot conclude my discussion without testifying the regret which it is impossible for me not to feel in the prospect of the approaching severance of the ties which now for years have bound us to each other. I remember with gratitude the kindnesses more than I can number, which I have received from you. Kindnesses which by their spontaneity and lack of ostentation have impressed me the more deeply, and especially are my thanks due to the teachers, both in the Sunday and the Day schools, as also to the choir, church officials and many others, who, with much steadfastness and diligence have assisted me in the conduct of our schools and services. In many other ways help has been rendered with a readiness that has deeply impressed me, but it would be utterly impossible for me, in the time at my disposal now, to adequately advert to each instance, and to thank in detail every friend. Be assured, your friendly aid will not be forgotten by me. I pray that you may have reward of God and trust you will ever strengthen the hand of my successor as you have strengthened mine, and that God will prosper His work among you, and, if spared, that we shall have the opportunity of meeting from time to time. We have had joys and sorrows. Events have occurred that will never be forgotten, and that will cause a feeling between us wherever and whenever we meet. Finally, my brethren, I humbly and earnestly commend you all to the care of Almighty God. May His Fatherly hand be ever over you. May His Holy Spirit be ever with you, and so lead you in the knowledge and obedience of His word, that in the end you may attain everlasting life.

Thomas preached this farewell sermon on Sunday 21 August 1881, and must have left Highfield very quickly, for on the following Thursday, 25 August 1881, he married again, this time to Eline Alice Robin at the Parish Church of St Giles in the Fields, Bloomsbury and Westminster. He moved to St Mary Magdalene's Church, Littleton, near Staines for a short time. Records there show that he performed one Baptism, one Marriage and one Funeral in October and November 1881, but his stay there is not recorded in any edition of Crockford's Clerical Directory or in the London Diocesan records.

Thomas and Eline seem to have moved back to Thomas's birthplace at Peny-fedwfawr, Cilycwm for on 19 September 1882, a son, Emile Thomas was born there. Father Thomas's occupation given on the Birth Certificate was Clergyman (No cure of Souls), and the Registrar was Wm. Evans. This was Thomas's brother, who became Registrar for the village after his father.

Three years later a daughter, Sophia was born at Carmen Villa, Walton Rd, Swansea, where the family lived until 1888 when they moved to Henllys near Llandovery. From time to time during these years Thomas officiated at funerals and weddings at the Parish Church, Cilycwm. On 20 March 1887, Thomas returned to Highfield and preached at both morning and Evening Prayers. This is recorded in the Iron Church Service Book started in 1882.

Henllys is described in *Historic Carmarthenshire Homes and their families*, by Francis Jones as follows:

> Near the banks of the Tywi, 1½ miles north of Llandovery. Sometimes known also as Henllys Fawr. It was a double pile house of two storeys (and an attic storey) each with five windows. The grounds at one time included lands on both sides of the river, which was crossed by a footbridge raised upon two projecting rocks. Henllys was for 7 generations home of the Lewis family. In the middle of the 18th Century the last generation of the main line died. From 1788–1815 it was the seat of Colonel David Williams. The house is still in use today.

An article in the *Western Mail*, 23 September 1977 headlined: 'Squatter bids £45,000 for Georgian House' describes the nine-bedroomed Henllys Court as a Georgian Mansion and 123 acres of land near Llandovery, and in a footnote says:

> The squatters may be sitting on more of an asset than they realise. It is believed by some that the estate holds a buried chest of gold coins and gems brought from India in the 18th century by its first owner Colonel David Williams, who is buried in nearby Llandingat Church.

The 1891 Census for Cilycwm records that at Henllys Fawr, Llandovery. lived Thomas Evans, aged 46, Head, Clerk or Clergyman in Holy Orders, born Cilycwm. speaking Welsh and English, an employer, and his second wife, Alice Olive aged 34, from Jersey, speaking only English, together with his son, Emile Thomas Evans, aged 8, born in Cilycwm, speaking Welsh and English, and daughter Sophia S.A., aged 5, born in Swansea, Glam., speaking Welsh and English. In the same house lived David Thomas, aged 46, Farm Bailiff, Anne Davies, aged 26, Cook, Domestic, and Anne Richards, Housemaid.

In the same Census for Cilycwm. William Evans, farmer, Thomas's brother, aged 43, and Catherine Evans, his sister, aged 48, and Anne Walters , a servant, are still living at the family home Penyfedwfawr. In 1895 William also appears in a trade directory for Cilycwm as a farmer.

In 1894, another daughter, Eline, named after her mother, was born at Henllys. Thomas was very involved in local affairs during these years. He was the representative of Cilycwm Parish on the Carmarthenshire County Council, and was a Justice of the Peace. He was a most generous benefactor to the parish. In 1901 the family moved to 10 Market Square, Llandovery, and in the same year erected a granite water fountain in the square at Llandovery as a memorial to the late Dr F. W. Lewis who was their family doctor and the Medical Officer of Health for the borough.

Thomas left Llandovery in 1903 and during the next five years he lived at Aberayron and Aberystwyth. Because of failing health Thomas had resigned his seat on the County Council and eventually moved to Geneva in Switzerland for two years and then to Nice in the South of France in 1910 where he spent his declining years. The move must have been good for him for he lived there for another ten years.

In the 1911 Census for Nice Thomas is living in the Villa Lisette, 79, Avenue de California, Nice, with his wife, Alice, and daughter Eline, an English lodger and a French Cook.

In 1918 the family moved to Villa Vitoria, Avenue Cyrille-Besset where Thomas died on 17 February 1920. The Funeral Service was held at the Holy Trinity Anglican Church on 19 February.

Obituaries appeared in the Carmarthen Journal as follows:

February 27th 1920. *District News*, Llandovery.

On Thursday last news reached Llandovery of the demise of the Revd Thomas Evans formerly of Henllys, near this town, who passed away on the preceding Tuesday at Nice, where he had gone to reside. The departed gent was about 80 years of age, and during the years he was at Henllys he was the representative of Cilycwm parish on the Carmarthenshire County Council, a seat which he resigned owing to ill health. Prior to his departure from the neighbourhood the Revd and Mrs Evans erected at their own expense a costly granite water fountain as a memorial to the late reverent Dr F. W. Lewis who was their medical attendant and medical officer of health for the borough. This they subsequently handed to the Llandovery Corporation in January 1901 during the May-oralty of Mr Thomas Phillips of Picton Court. Deceased leaves widow, one daughter and one son (Mr E. Evans.) A nephew of the departed is Mr Evan Williams of Brynawel surveyor and inspector of nuisances under the Llandovery Corporation and Llandovery District Council.

March 5th 1920. District News, Cilycwm.

Last weeks papers announced the death in France of the Revd Thomas Evans, a native of this parish, and at one time its most generous benefactor and its representative on the County Council. Latterly on account of failing health he spent his days at Nice in France, where he was buried last week. On Sunday morning a memorial service was held in the parish church. The congregation including Mr Emile Evans of Aberystwyth (son), many local relations, and general sympathisers, amongst others being Mr & Mrs C. P. Lewis and Mrs Lewis, Llandovery. Taking his text Paul 39 v. 4, the Vicar, Revd E. Jenkin produced an eloquent sermon in Welsh, extolling the virtues of a man who had per-formed his part and by his generosity and sympathy had endeared himself in the hearts of all. Appropriate hymn tunes, a powerful sermon and a fine rendering of the Dead March made the service an impressive one.

The 1921 Census for Nice shows Mrs Evans still living in the Villa Vitoria with a companion, an English Housekeeper, and David Jones, an accountant from Aberyst-wyth. Mrs Evans Died on 29 September 1928 in Nice.

Revd
John Wood

Third Curate
In Charge

1881–1908

JOHN WOOD was born at Bolton in 1828. He was the son of James and Alice Wood. Nothing else is known of his childhood or early years. In 1852, on 26 April, he became Schoolmaster at Chatburn, Lancashire, at the age of twenty-four. He was to stay here for the next twenty-three years. In 1857 he married Elizabeth Ann Ardern and between 1858 and 1873 eight children were born to them, William Henry in 1858, Edward James in 1860, John Thomas in 1863, Annie Harriet in 1865, Samuel in 1867, Susan Catherine in 1868, Robert Lucius in 1870 and Lucy Mary in 1873. One child, Samuel, died aged one day, but the rest survived. The families are recorded in the 1861 and 1871 Censuses for Chatburn. John Wood was the enumerator for both these censuses for Chatburn and the neighbouring villages.

In the 1871 Census Lucius King, Curate of Chatburn was living as a lodger with the family. He was obviously well thought of by John and Alice for the last two children were named after him, and it was perhaps through his influence that John decided to enter the ministry. In the school log book is the following entry for 27 April 1870.

> Mr Wood with the consent of managers became matriculated at Oxford as an unattached member and commenced residence for his first term. He is expected to find a substitute during his absence.

John's son William Henry began five years pupil teaching at Chatburn in April 1872, and his younger brother, Edward, followed in his footsteps a year or two later.

In 1874 John obtained his BA at Worcester College, Oxford, and in 1875 on 24 June he left Chatburn and was ordained Deacon by the Bishop of Chester. He served his first Curacy at St Catherine, Wigan from 1875 to 1877. In 1876 he was awarded his MA, and in the same year was ordained priest by the Bishop of Chester.

On 29 March 1877 John's son Edward James Wood left Chatburn to continue his pupil teaching at St Thomas's Schools, Wigan, obviously to be nearer the rest of the family, and the following month, on the 12th April father John was appointed to his second curacy at St John's, Pemberton and so began his long association with Highfield. In the Nomination to Curacy, the Revd John Leach, Vicar of Pemberton, promised to pay John Wood the yearly stipend of £170 in equal quarterly payments. He was to live in the parish in a house situated less than a quarter of a mile from the Church. In the 1881 Census for Orrell, taken 3/4 April, John and his family were living in Ash Leigh, Ormskirk Rd. At this time Thomas Evans was still in charge at Highfield. Soon after John arrived at Pemberton he was involved in the tragedies of the mining industry, for in October 1877 he was at the Pemberton Colliery disaster with Thomas Evans when W. J. L. Watkin, the Manager, and thirty four men were killed. (See Chapter 3)

John Wood became curate in charge at Highfield after Thomas Evans had left at the end of August 1881. His first recorded baptism at the Iron Church was on 2 October 1881.

In January 1892, John Wood began a new Preachers Book. This is the first extant register of services. The only earlier register in existence is the Register of Baptisms which was started by Thomas Evans in 1873. The book is dated 1 Jan 1882, and at the foot of the page inside the front cover is inscribed 'This Iron Church was opened on May 12th, 1867, and the first sermon preached by the Revd Arthur Coates, Vicar of Pemberton, The Revd S. L. Laidman being first Curate in charge was succeeded by the Revd Thomas Evans who had charge till 1881.'

Among the earliest entries are the following:

Jan. 1, 1882, 10.30.   Jno. Wood   1 Peter 1-12 Christmas with the angels.

Jan. 1, 1882, 6.30.   Jno. Wood   Psalm 128. 8 Good luck in the name of the Lord.

Sep. 17, 1882, 7.30   T. B. H. Blundell   Matt. 9. 9 The call and obedience of St Matthew.

(T. B. H. Blundell was Rector of Halsall and brother of Colonel H. B. H. Blundell.)

The *Wigan Observer* reported one of John Woods earliest Walking Days at Highfield in July 1883 as follows:

Field Day, St Matthew's, Highfield

Saturday week was an eventful day for the children of Highfield, being as it is very often called 'The Walking Day'. The procession, headed by the Goose Green Band, left the Schools shortly after 2 o'clock, the girls as usual walking first, followed by the infants, the children of Little Lane and the boys of Highfield bringing up the rear; making a total of about 700 children. The Revd J. Wood, together with Messrs Moorfield, T. Barton, and Rigby, (Sidesmen), led the procession down Tunstall Lane, up Enfield Street, and down the Colliery Lane, to Wood Cottage, the residence of the Manager, Mr Greener, who received the children at the gates and arranged the children in groups upon the different lawns. The sight was a very pretty one to see, so many children of all sorts, and of all sizes, their white dresses, clean collars, etc., enjoying themselves to their hearts content. The children after singing 'Brightly Gleams our Banner', were served with tea and buns by Mr Greener, Mr T. Greener, Mr Pickering, and the teachers. After tea they filed out through the gates, where each one on passing through received a large handful of nuts. The rest of the evening was spent on the cricket field, where the children enjoyed themselves with a variety of amusements till about nine o'clock.

Parish Magazine

A parish magazine was first published in January 1884, and has been published continuously ever since. Sadly there are very few copies of magazines before 1914 in the Church archives, and from then onwards the bound copies are not continuous, but what there are give a good picture of life in the parish at the time of their publication.

The earliest surviving extract from a parish magazine was reprinted in the May 1937 magazine as follows: 'FIFTY THREE YEARS AGO', Extracts from the First Magazine, Pemberton Colliery Iron Church.'There will be Evening Prayers and special sermons in the Pemberton Colliery Iron Church each Thursday evening during the season of Lent. The number sold of this magazine in February was 234, and we should be glad if our many friends would help us by introducing the Magazine into the families of their friends and neighbours.'

This seems to have been from the March 1884 magazine, not the first which was published in January.

The April 1937 magazine printed the following extract: ' "FIFTY YEARS AGO", Extract from the Highfield Magazine, April 1887.' It will be encouraging to the Reverend Edward Francis Forrest to have a hearty welcome given to him next Saturday 2nd April, at the parish Church. It is hoped the congregations of the various district Churches will attend in large numbers and join in prayer and worship for a blessing upon their Pastor and upon the work he is called upon to promote in this large and important Parish of Pemberton.'

The next, most important surviving extract from the early days of the parish was a description of the laying of the foundation stone of the Memorial Church in 1892 which is reproduced later in this chapter.

The earliest surviving complete magazine is dated Vol. XI. Dec., 1894.

Congregational Tea Party, 1885

The Congregational Tea Party had by now become an annual event, and one of the highlights of the year. It was often reported in the local press and presented a picture of what was going on in the district. In 1885, the Mayor of Wigan presided and his speech indicated a good understanding of the life of the church in the area. *The Wigan Observer* printed the following report:

On Monday evening, the annual tea party and entertainment, in connection with St Matthew's Highfield, took place, when a good number sat down to tea. After tea, the Mayor of Wigan (Mr Alderman Park.) presided, and amongst those present were the Revs. J. Wood, curate in charge, J. H. Ireland, Mr W. J. Greener & etc. The Mayor said it gave him great pleasure to be there to support their worthy clergyman, who he knew was doing a great and good work in that part of the Parish of Pemberton. He had known Mr Wood for a considerable number of years, and he had always found him to be an industrious, hard worker, earnest, and very desirous of promoting the interests of the people under his charge. It was always a pleasure to see a room well filled, and it must be very gratifying to their worthy clergyman to find himself surrounded by so many parishioners and so many smiling countenances. he knew that a great and good work was being done in the township of Pemberton, which was now getting to vast dimensions. The population, which had become very large, was composed mostly of the working class and the Church had been doing a noble work providing for the spiritual wants of that population. The church in Pemberton, with the able support of its labourers and friends, had succeeded in raising no less than five schools and additions, since their esteemed Vicar (Mr Mitchell) came late to the township of Pemberton. (Cheers) He thought that was an evidence of the progress that the church was making in that parish and when they knew that, they must pardon him for saying that the church was entitled to their consideration, their sympathy and support. Some of them who could not give money might say a few words to their neighbours, and thus pave the way for the ministers; others might assist him by coming and acting as teachers in the Sunday school, others might, by attending the church, set a good example, and those who were able might assist with their purse. Fortunately for them the Church of England had not politics. She was the church of the people and was entitled to the support of the parish. Several admirable schools had been provided in that great township of Pemberton, schools for the education of the working classes of that great community, - and he was sure that not only the people had done well, but that the great employers had also done their share, for they had come forward most admirably to support those schools, which he believed had been done entirely by voluntary contributions.

The Revd J. Wood said that only a few days ago, after a long waiting, they received the report of the government as to their schools, and he was very happy to be able to say that they were reported most satisfactory. They had received excellent in every department, which was very gratifying to the teachers and to the parents. The children and the teachers had worked hard to bring about that good result. They had established a cookery class which he thought would be most useful to the scholars in after life. They ought to think a great deal more about when and what they should eat. They had gone backwards in the matter during the last thirty years. They took too much tea, and if they had to fight the Russians, they would have to have different diet and return to the old fashioned way of living. (Laughter.) The object of the cookery lessons was to help the girls to provide good and nutritious dinners cheaply and he had no doubt it would succeed very well.

During the evening an entertainment was given, the scholars in particular distinguishing themselves. The 'Shadow Pantomime', under the direction of Mr M. Mercier, was a great feature in the entertainment. Mr P. Fearnley, as the Clown, and Mr G. Makinson as the Pantaloon, acquitting themselves very well. Mr Dawson (Headmaster), presided at the pianoforte.

17 January 1886 must have been a very proud day for the Revd and Mrs John Wood, for on this day their son Edward James, who had been ordained Deacon the previous year by the Bishop of Exeter, preached for the first time in the Iron Church at the Evening Service. This was the first of many times that Edward was to help his father at Highfield during the following years.

In April of this year, the Vestry meeting of the parish was held in the vestry of the Parish Church, St John's, Pemberton. The Register of Services records the election of sidesmen for Highfield and Little Lane Mission as follows: Messrs J. W. Greener, G. Ashurst, T. Barton, John Nicholson, William Rigby and James Tyrer were elected for Highfield and Messrs J. Bell, and Robert Ashton, for Little Lane.

Eisteddfod for Choirs, 1886

In November of the same year (1886) Mr J. A. Pickering, Commercial Manager of Blundell's Collieries and Churchwarden at St John's started what was hoped might be an annual event—an Eisteddfod for the church choirs of the Parish. The *Wigan Observer* reported the event in great detail:

A movement has been started in Pemberton for the improvement of the choral music in the various churches in the parish, and at the present moment there is every promise that not only will the present object be fully attained, but that in addition an increased interest will be awakened in matters musical in the populous township. Mr Pickering, one of the active churchwardens of Pemberton Parish Church, has been the principle mover in the matter, and he holds the dual offices of treasurer and hon-secretary in connection with the movement. This gentleman, desirous to affect the improvement referred to, cast about him for a feasible plan, and he determined to take a leaf out of the Welsh people's book and have an Eisteddfod or musical contest for the Church choirs in the parish. A better plan could scarcely have been adopted. Such gatherings have been extremely useful to the Welsh people, and have been the means of maintaining a spirit of patriotism and an interest in Welsh poetry and song. The Eisteddfod at Pemberton is sure to bear similar results. When competing for a prize a conductor will give very careful attention to the matter of training his choir, and the singers will enter into the work with enthusiasm, and in this way the members become more intelligent musicians, the benefit of which the churches will gain in a more enlightened rendering of the music during the service. But this is not all. The friends of each choir will take more interest in it on account of the contest, and a taste for music will thus be instilled in the minds of the public. All this we predict will take place in Pemberton if the Eisteddfod is to be an annual event, and Mr Pickering will have the credit of not only effecting an improvement in the rendering of the music used in the worship of God, which in itself will be a most praiseworthy achievement, but of giving a stimulus to the study of the most charming of all arts—music—in the district. Mr Pickering himself made all the arrangements for the contest. He offered two prizes—the first £10, and the second £5; the third £3 3s., came from the entrance moneys paid by each choir, and Colonel Blundell gave a consolation prize of £2 2s. The following choirs entered the competition: St John's choir, Lamberhead Green, conductor Mr Jno. Smith, accompanist Mr C. D. Mortimer, of Hindley; St Luke's, Far Moor, conductor Mr Gilbody, accompanist Miss Berridge; St

Matthew's, Highfield, conductor Mr Dawson, accompanist Mr R. Moss, Wigan; and St Mark's, Newtown, conductor Mr Minton, accompanist Mr Kerfoot. The event came off on Tuesday night, in the Boys' National Schoolroom, Lamberhead Green, Pemberton. The keenest interest was manifested in the proceedings, the room being crowded. Colonel Blundell, MP, occupied the chair, and amongst those present we noticed the Revs. H. Mitchell, J. Wood, W. Walker, J. H. Ireland, J. H. Newberry, F. D. Cremer (Vicar of Upholland), W. Berridge, Messrs J. Pickering, W. H. Harbottle, I. Knowles (Ince), R. Daglish, F. Robinson, J. M. Ashurst, T. H. Harbottle and W. Taberner. The plan of the contest was as follows: A book of anthems and glees was fixed upon by the organiser, and the competing choirs were told that the pieces they would have to sing would be selected from that book. This compelled the competition to practice the whole of the music, as, of course, they were not informed which particular piece of music they would have to render. It was decided by ballot in what order the choirs had to sing and what piece they had to render, and as the conductor was told what the piece was just a few minutes before ascending the platform, it will be seen that each choir was tested in the best possible manner. The judges were Mr Alexander, organist of the Wigan Parish Church, and Mr James Dawber, Mus. Bac., who were located in an apartment adjacent to the platform, where they could hear but not see the competitors. The contest was divided into three stages. In the first stage St Matthew's choir was drawn to sing the anthem 'My God, my God, why hast Thou forsaken me?' (Reynolds), and St Luke's came next, the anthem 'Out of the deep have I called thee' (Mozart) being allotted to them. St Mark's had the third anthem which was 'Turn thy face from my sins' (Attwood). and St John's had the fourth, namely 'I will lift up mine eyes unto the hills' (Clarke Whitfield). The first stage was closed by the combined chorus singing the anthem 'Christ, being raised from the dead, dieth no more.'. An interval of fifteen minutes here took place, during which Mr H. McEleney, late bandmaster of the Carbineers, played a couple of solos on the clarionet, Mr Mortimer being the accompanist. In the second stage each choir rendered the glee by Bishop 'Who is Sylvia? What is she?' being drawn to sing in the following order: 1st St Matthew's, 2nd St John's, 3rd St Mark's, 4th St Luke's. In the third stage the choirs were drawn in the following order: 1st. St John's, glee 'Stay, prithee, stay' (Bishop); 2nd St Matthew's, chorus, Spirits advance (Bishop); 3rd St Luke's, glee spotted snakes. (Stevens); and 4th St Mark's, glee, When winds breathe soft. (Webbe). As will be seen below St Luke's carried off the first prize, and we may here add that with regard to the conductor, Mr Gilbody, that the members were so satisfied with the training he had given them that on Saturday night they presented him with an ebony baton, with silver mountings, bearing a suitable inscription. The Eisteddfod was in every way a great success, and this should furnish grounds for the promoters to repeat the entertainment yearly.

Colonel BLUNDELL, who was received with applause, said that while the judges were deciding upon their award, he thought it was his duty to thank the audience for their quiet attention and for the fair manner in which they had heard the competing choirs, and he thought he might say on the part of all of them who had had the pleasure of listening to the music that had been rendered in their hearing that night, that whatever might be the merits of the four competing choirs, each one of them had given them a great deal of pleasure. (Applause) It would have been impossible for the choirs to have sung as they had done without having given a great deal of attention to the work. He was sure he was speaking the opinion of a great many present when he said that the attention that had been given by the instructors and the manner in which the choirs were led was very pleasing indeed. (Applause.) he said he thought he might say they were very much indebted to Mr Pickering. (Applause.) who had with his usual ability and energy got up that charming entertainment, which he hoped, and he believed they all hoped, would be frequently repeated. (Applause.) He would not trouble them with any more words, as they would soon hear the award of the judges. He would just say, however, that he was glad to be able to announce that there was a consolation prize of two guineas for the unsuccessful choir. (Loud applause.)

The Revd F. D. CREMER said he was sure he was giving expression to their feelings as well as his own when he said how delighted he was with the treat they had had that night. He never thought that Pemberton could have produced, on so short a notice, such a really grand musical display as they had had that night from the different choirs. (Applause.) They all knew what a name Leeds had gained for its musical festivals and how people went there from miles around. Perhaps Pemberton in the future would be so distinguished, and people would come from miles around to the Pemberton Eisteddfod. He was sure they all owed a deal of gratitude to Mr Pickering for organising the entertainment, and they might warmly congratulate him on the success of the event. (Applause.)

Mr Pickering then ascended the platform and read the judge's award. He said the first prize was taken by St Luke's choir. (Loud applause.) The second prize was awarded to St Matthew's choir—(applause)—and the third to St John's. (Applause, mingled with hooting).

Colonel Blundell then handed the prizes to the successful competitors, and the consolation prize to St Mark's choir.

The Revd H. MITCHELL said he had a very pleasant duty to perform, and that was to propose a vote of thanks to a gentleman whom they were always delighted to have amongst them, and that was to Colonel Blundell, for presiding over the gathering that night. (Applause.) No words of his were necessary to commend the vote of thanks to them. They had all known Colonel Blundell so long that any words of praise from him would be quite out of place. (Applause.) The motion was carried with applause.

Col. BLUNDELL, in reply, begged to return them his hearty acknowledgements for the way in which they had received the vote of thanks, and also to their worthy Vicar, Mr Mitchell, for the kind manner in which he had proposed it. He could only say that his thanks were due to those gentlemen who gave him the opportunity of listening to that beautiful music, and he was sure he only hoped that everybody in the room had enjoyed it as much as he had. (Applause.) The National Anthem was then sung, and the proceedings ended.

(There follows a tabulated statement of the points gained by each choir.)

The 1891 Census for Highfield, taken on 5 April, records that Mrs Wood was not at home at the time. Revd John Wood was recorded, aged 63, Clerk in Holy Orders, Curate in charge, and of the children still living at home, John Thomas was aged 28, and described as a student, undergraduate of Oxford. Anne Harriet was aged 25, with no occupation recorded, and Robert Lucius was aged 20, and is described as a medical student. Susan (23) and Lucy (18) are missing. It is quite possible that Mrs Wood may have been ill at the time, possible being nursed at the home of a relative, possibly in hospital, for five months later on 3 September, sadly, aged 54, she died, and was buried at St John's Churchyard, Pemberton.

The Memorial Church

During 1891, and probably earlier, plans must have been afoot for the building of the Memorial Church by Colonel Henry Blundell in memory of his wife who had died in 1884. No doubt the Revd John Wood, as Curate-in-charge would have been involved in the preparations, along with the Vicar of the parish, Revd E. F. Forrest, although

Architect's impression of the Church showing originally proposed wall and lych-gate.

the parish and particularly the district of Highfield were indeed fortunate in that they did not have to raise one penny towards the cost of the new Church or the new Schools, which were built by Colonel Blundell at the same time entirely at his own expense.

Architect's drawing of the church by Paley Austin and Paley.

Colonel Blundell was very wise in his choice of architects for the Memorial Church. Professor Nikolaus Pevsner in his work 'The Buildings of England. South Lancashire.' says of the architects, 'Paley and Austin, whose office was at Lancaster, were local architects, are of the highest European standard of their years,' and he describes St Matthew's as, 'one of their first flight.'

There must have been a great deal of excitement in the district, knowing that they were to have a new Church of their own. The Iron Church had served them well for nearly twenty five years, used as Church, School and Parish Hall. The district was growing rapidly and the numbers merited a separate building, but they must have been overwhelmed by the generosity of their benefactor.

In September, 1891, George Fouchard, a colliery workman, who had carved a portrait of Colonel Blundell in cannel from one of the Colonel's own pits, and who, in 1894 at the time of the dedication of the new Church, was to exhibit a beautiful model of the new Church in the old Iron Church, obviously a man of considerable talents, wrote the following poem as an expression of gratitude to Colonel Blundell:

St Matthew's Colliery Iron Church
Highfield, Pemberton

These lines, by a working man, are most respectfully dedicated to Col. Blundell, CB, MP, donor and patron; in commemoration of his further munificent gift of a new stone church to replace the above.

In the long years gone past, oh Lord, Thou hast blest
Thy house at the corner, our little Iron Church;
At its altar Thy children, from youth to old age,
Have rejoiced hand in hand in their offerings of praise.

Whilst here upon earth to all mortals Thou said,
He that Me honours, him I'll honour give;
For this work to Thy name-sake dear Lord God of love,
Thou hast built him a mansion more glorious above.

May the hearts of Thy people be touched to respond
To the blessings received through Thy servant their friend;
May the seed he has sown spring forth into bloom,
Till Thy courts are enriched with its fragrant perfume.

Oh! help us to bring in the wanderer, the poor,
To point the right way and feast them from Thy store;
Guard us and Thy church from all dangers unseen,
Thy blessing we crave for our country and Queen.

Written by George Fouchard
September, 1891. Highfield

Foundation Stone Ceremony

There must have been a good deal of activity on and around the site of the new Church during the next months, digging and laying the foundations, and laying the first stones of the walls, but eventually the day for the laying of the Foundation or Corner stone arrived, St George's Day, 23 April 1892. The Parish Magazine for May 1892 records the events of the day as follows:

> The foundation or corner stone was laid by Colonel Blundell, CB, MP, on the 23rd April, 1892, at 3 o'clock in the afternoon, in the presence of a very large assembly of people, clergy, ladies, gentlemen, parents, and children of the schools.
>
> Saturday last was a day which will be long remembered by all interested in Ecclesiastical Work at Highfield, being associated as it was with the laying of the Foundation Stone of the New Memorial Church, Highfield, with St Matthew as its Patron Saint. Though the Ceremony was somewhat marred and curtailed by the prevailing atmospheric conditions a great amount of interest was manifested in the ceremony by the display of streamers from the windows of the houses in the neighbourhood, and the gathering of large crowds on the route of the procession, and in the enclosure of the Church Building.
>
> At 2-30 the proceedings commenced, when the Clergy, sidesmen, gentlemen, scholars, teachers, and colliery officials assembled on the Highfield Cricket Ground, and accompanied by the Pemberton Band, sang the National Anthem. At three o'clock promptly the procession was formed, and marched in the following order to the scene of the ceremony:—Infants, with hands joined, four deep, led the way, then Little Lane, girls, Highfield; boys, Highfield; Men's Bible Class, parents and friends, men of the Choir, colliery officials, sidesmen, and gentlemen; the clergy. On arriving within the enclosure the various sectioned marshalled themselves in the spaces allotted to them, and independent observers secured all available positions which commanded a view of the proceedings. The Clergy present were the Revs. Canon Blundell (rector of Halsall), Canon Bridgeman (Rector of Wigan), E. F. Forrest, J. H. Newberry, H. Mitchell (Prescot), J. Leach (Kirkby), H. F. Lloyd, E. A. Dury. E. J. Wood, J. Wood (curate-in-charge, Highfield), W. Walker, & J. Llewellyn; the laymen included, in addition to Colonel Blundell MP, Mr J. W. Greener, Dr Hartley, Mr Tom Brown, Mr J. Pickering, Mr P. Partington, Mr G. Ashurst, sen., and Messrs Paley and Baines (Messrs Paley and Austin, architects, Lancaster.) The ceremony was commenced a little after the time announced, and the prescribed form was gone through.
>
> Mr GEORGE ASHURST, senr., then said he had a most pleasant duty to perform, which was that of presenting to Colonel Blundell a silver trowel, the gift of the congregation, which was inscribed to the following effect:—'Presented to Colonel Blundell, by the congregation, on the occasion of laying the foundation stone of St Matthew's Church, Highfield.' In handing the trowel to Colonel Blundell, he begged his kind acceptance of it.
>
> The Revd J. Wood, before placing the customary receptacle beneath the stone, read the contents of the document affecting the structure, which was as follows:—'Memorial Church, St Matthew's, Highfield. The foundation stone was laid by Colonel Blundell,

CB, MP, on Saturday, the 23rd day of April, 1892. Revd E. F. Forest MA, Vicar of Pemberton: Revd J. Wood MA, Curate-in-charge of Highfield,' followed by the names of the Wardens for this year, and the sidesmen for that part of the parish.

Colonel Blundell, in responding, said he received the trowel with much gratitude from the congregation, presented to him by his old friend, Mr Geo. Ashurst, and with which he would shortly have to lay the foundation stone of the Church which was to be erected there. He had for many years—or at least for six or seven years—desired to build a Church there, but had not been able to do it till then in the way which he had desired to do. It was a memorial church to the memory of his dear wife, who died in 1884, and who, from the day of her marriage in 1863, to her death, took a deep interest in the welfare of the schools adjoining. Though living at a distance she never failed to examine the registers, and always took care that the religious instruction should always accompany secular instruction. She also always took a deep interest in improving the needlework and the cooking many years before they became part of the school course. She had not the honour of commencing the school there, for he thought the germ of the present school was in the Sunday school commenced by the late Miss Greener, but from the time she married she took the utmost interest in those schools, and it was her wish that a church should be built there. She desired that it should be of a pure style of architecture and excellent material, but with nothing tawdry or fantastic, and he was endeavouring, in the structure about to be raised, to carry out these ideas to the best of his ability. (Hear, hear, and applause.) He hoped that the church would not only be a memorial to her, but would be useful in that increasing district, and would be an object of interest to the many children who had been brought up in the school, and the many bright young faces he saw around him, showed that they took an interest in what was now being done. He again begged to thank the ladies and gentlemen of the congregation for the beautiful trowel with which he had been presented, and also thank his old friend Mr George Ashurst who had presented it to him. (Applause.)

The ceremony of laying the stone was then performed, the usual Scriptural declaration being duly pronounced.

Canon Bridgeman then pronounced the benediction, and an adjournment was made to the schoolroom, where tea was served to the clergy, sidesmen, colliery officials, teachers and members of the choir. In the boys' and infants' schools and the iron building tea was served to the scholars.

The Church, on the plan, consists of a nave 20 ft. wide and 60 ft. long, a chancel same width and 47 ft. long, the choir being placed under the central tower, north and south transepts, the south transept being arranged for the organ; north and south aisles to nave externally form transepts. 34 feet westwards, each opening out into the nave by two arches. The porch, outer and inner, is on the north side of the nave, and the vestries on the south side of the chancel. The tower is 26 feet square at the base, 70 feet high to the top of parapet and is surmounted by a spire 70 feet high. The roofs which are open timbered are to be covered with green Westmorland slates, and the aisle roofs with lead. The architectural style of the Church is Early English. It is to be built of stone; the facing of walls inside and outside, also the dressings being of 'flecked' Runcorn. All the woodwork of roofs, seats and fittings throughout will be of oak. The heating will be by hot water pipes enclosed in channels under the floors, to which a supply of fresh air will be conducted from the outside and let into the church warmed. The contractors for the whole works are Messrs J. Hatch and Sons, of Lancaster. The architects are Messrs Paley, Austin and Paley, of Lancaster.

In 1893, John Wood's son Edward James, after having served several curacies including two years at Prescot, was appointed Vicar of Whiston. It must have been a proud day for his father. Sadly his mother was not alive to share the event with them.

After two years work on the new Church, the building was ready for use, but first there were the last services in the Iron Church. In a way, these were probably sad occasions for many who had been involved in the worship and services there. The first service book, started in 1881, records the preachers and texts for the day. At the morning service, John Wood preached on the text Rev. 15: verses 4 & 5. 'Who shall not fear thee, O Lord, and glorify thy name? for thou only art holy: for all nations shall come and worship before thee; for thy judgements are manifest.

And after that I looked, and behold, the temple of the tabernacle of the testimony in heaven was opened:'

At the last service, Evensong at 6.30 p.m., the Vicar of Pemberton, Revd E. F. Forrest preached on the text 1 John. 2: verse 18.'Little children, it is the last time: and as ye have heard that anti-christ shall come, even now are there many anti-christs; whereby we know that it is the last time.'

Dedication of Memorial Church, 1894

Wednesday 4 July 1894, was the great day for the district, the dedication and licensing of the new Church by the Lord Bishop of Liverpool, John Charles Ryle. The *Wigan Observer* describes the event as follows:

> The usually somewhat quiet township of Highfield wore an animated appearance on Wednesday afternoon, and from the display of bunting from the housetops and the large number of people in holiday attire, it was evident that an occurrence of an uncommon character was to take place that day. The reason of it all was to be found in the fact that the consecration service, by the Bishop of Liverpool, Dr Ryle, of the Memorial Church was to take place. The Church, we might state, has been erected by Col. Blundell, CB to the memory of his wife, and the site of it is on the left-hand side of the road proceeding to Winstanley, and is a little further west than the Iron Church, which has been the centre of church work in the village for a considerable time. Preparatory to the commencement of the consecration service the Sunday School scholars, men's Bible Class, and congregation assembled in the Iron Church, and from thence walked into the New Church, a short distance away. Amongst those present at the ceremony were the Bishop of Liverpool, Dr Ryle, Colonel Blundell, C. B. Canon Blundell, Canon Bridgeman, Wigan, Canon Fergis, Ince, Canon Mitchell, Prescot; Revs. E. J. Wood, Whiston; J. Leach, Kirkby; E. J. Forrest, Pemberton; G. F. Grundy, Aspull; Howard St George, Billinge; R. G. Matthew, Wigan; E. A. Dury, Wigan; F. B. A. Miller, Hindley Green; T. Taylor, Ince; T. Gleave, Newtown; C. J. Buckmaster, Hindley; H. F. Lloyd, Wigan; H. W. M. Gunning, Wigan; E. Kingsbury, Wigan; A. D. Schreiber, Rainford; H. Martin; T. H. Leeson, Charnock Richard; W. Berridge, Lowton; J. Wood (curate in charge of Highfield); Messrs J. Pickering, W. J. Greener, G. Ashurst, P. Partington, G. Dickson, Dr Hartley, and Austin (Messrs Paley, Austin and Paley, architects of the Church.) On assembling in the Church the Revd Canon Bridgeman read the lesson, after which the

Interior of the 1894 Church before the 1910 enlargement. Note the Pulpit on the south side. The Dossal frame behind the altar was given to St Luke's, Orrell, in 1926.

Bishop of Liverpool delivered a discourse based on the following text—' For I know that my Redeemer liveth, and that He shall stand at the latter day upon the earth; and though after my skin worms destroy this body, yet in my flesh shall I see God:' Job. 19th Chapter, 25th and 26th verses. He said—Having heard that text on that solemn occasion they would very likely ask what was the reason he had selected it. He had chosen it because he believed that it contained the two greatest truths it was possible to put before a Christian congregation—truths which he hoped would be heard from that pulpit as long as that Church stood, and as long as the Church of England has one minister to defend her. These two great truths were the redemption of man from sin and the resurrection of man's body, and were the things he put before them as the first things preached within the walls of that place.

He expounded these themes and concluded by praying that God might bless that house for ages yet to come, after he and most of them were lying in their graves. He prayed that work might be done there when prime ministers, generals, and admirals were lying in their graves and their work forgotten, and that the work done within the walls of that church would stand for evermore.

In the evening a special service was held in the church, when the Revd Canon Bridgeman preached.

We may add that previous to the afternoon ceremony Mr Fauchard of Highfield, exhibited in the Iron Church, a beautiful model of the New Church, which attracted considerable attention.

(Incidentally, this was not the Consecration Service, the Consecration of the Church did not take place until 1910.)

The first three Baptisms in the new Church were performed on 15 July 1894, and were of Ellen Berry of Alexandra Terrace, Beatrice Alice Shepherd of Billinge Rd, and Thomas Taylor of 577 Ormskirk Rd.

BAPTISMS solemnized in the Parish of *Pemberton St Matthews Memorial Church* in the County of *Lancaster* in the Year 18*94*.

When Baptised.	Child's Christian Name.	Parent's Name.		Abode.	Quality, Trade, or Profession.	By whom the Ceremony was performed.
		Christian.	Surname.			
1894 July 15 No. 249	Ellen	John + Jane	Berry	Alexandra Terrace Highfield	Fireman & Colliery	Jno Wood
1894 July 15 No. 250	Beatrice Alice	Gabriel + Mary Ann	Shephard	Billinge Road Highfield	Engine driver	Jno Wood
1894 July 15 No. 251	Thomas	John + Jemima	Taylor	577 Ormskirk Rd	Collier	Jno Wood
July 8 1894 July 22 No. 252	Peter	John + Catherine	Ashurst	Goose Green Pemberton	Labourer	Jno Wood
7 July 1894 July 22 No. 253	Christina	William + Mary Jane	Anderson	No. 12 Maybile Highfield	Contractor in Coal mine	Jno Wood
June 19 1894 July 29 No. 254	James	William + Catherine	Simmy	Junotall Lane, Pemberton	Collier	Jno Wood
June 20 1894 July 29 No. 255	John	George + Margaret	Finney	Little Lane Pemberton	Collier	Jno Wood
June 17 1894 Aug: 5 No. 256	Thomas	James + Jane	Edleston	Goose Green Pemberton	Engine driver	Jno Wood

First Baptisms in the new Church, July 1894. There were no marriages until the Church became a Parish Church in 1910, and no Burials until the graveyard was opened in 1923.

Actual payments	Memorial Church	Schools
Building Contract	£8,872: 1: 0	£4,046.19.9
Heating apparatus	160: 0: 0	117: 0. 0
Draining & Sundries	94.10:10	31. 6. 1
Architect's fees	589:11: 0	211. 6. 10
Marble pavement	175: 0: 0	
Bell & fittings	149: 7: 0	
Pulpit	134:16: 0	
Oossal	18: 8: 0	
Fence	36, 10: 9	
Total	£10,230: 4: 7	£4,406. 11. 11
Value of site	£250. 0. 0	£500: 0: 0
Insured in the Manchester Fire Office	£3,300. —	£1,800

25 July 1895

Details of costs of building Church and Schools, sent in a latter to Revd John Wood from Mr J. A. Pickering, Colonel Blundell's agent in July 1895.

Dedication of Organ

There had been an organ in the Iron Church which was sold to Mount Zion Methodist Church when that Church was opened, also in 1894, and a new organ was erected in the new Church and dedicated on St Matthew's Day, Friday 21 September. The *Wigan Observer* records the event as follows:

On Friday evening (St Matthew's Day), services were commenced in St Matthew's Church, Highfield, on the occasion of the dedication of the new organ and the harvest thanksgiving services. The preacher on Friday evening was the Revd. S. A. K. Sylvester, MA, Vicar of Roby, and the organ recital, particulars of which will be found below, was given by Mr Lawrence, ACO, of Leeds. On Sunday morning the Revd E. F. Forrest, vicar of Pemberton, was the preacher, the Revd J. Frances MA, vicar of St Stephen's, Liverpool, preaching at night. The collections amounted to about £10, in aid of the organ fund. Mr J. W. Duddle gave the recital at the conclusion of the evening service. The church was beautifully decorated, the chancel especially having had a deal of beautiful floral work done to it. The following are the particulars of the new organ and programmes of both recitals. The organ has been erected by Wilkinson and Sons, of Kendal, and has two complete manuals CC to G, 56 notes each, and pedal organ CCC to F, 30 notes:

Great Organ

1. Open Diapason	8 feet tone	
2. Claribel	8	”
3. Dulciana	8	”
4. Principal	4	”
5. Suabe Flote	4	”
6. Fifteenth	2	”
7. Clarinet	8	”

Swell Organ

8. Bourdon	16 feet tone	
9. Violin Diapason	8	”
10. Gedacht	8	”
11. Salicional	8	”
12. Voix Celeste	8	”
13. Gemshorn	4	”
14. Horn	8	”
15. Tremulant		

Pedal Organ

16. Sub-bass	16 feet tone	
17. Violoncello	8	”

Couplers

18. Swell Super-Octave to Great
19. Swell to Great
20. Swell to Pedals
21. Great to Pedals

Accessories

Two double-acting composition pedals to Great
Two double-acting composition pedals to Swell
One Swell Pedal
30 concave and slightly radiating pedals.

The whole is enclosed in a beautiful oak case, designed by Messrs Paley and Austin, and made by Messrs Hatch and Sons, of Lancaster. The front pipes of the organ are all of spotted metal.

Friday evening's recital, which was given by Mr H. M. Lawrence, ACO, organist of All Soul's Hook Memorial Church, Leeds, was a treat, listened to by a crowded audience, the following being the programme:

Opening Voluntary, Theme in A	Hurd
Grand Fantasia in F minor	Mozart
Andantino in D Flat	Chauvet
Concertstruck in A minor	Spark
Canzone in A minor	Gulimant
Rond's di Campanoli	Morandi
Selection from 5th Symphony	Widor
(a) Allegro	
(b) Allegretto	
(c) Toccato(finale)	

Mr J. W. Duddle's recital on Sunday evening was also of an enjoyable character, and was composed of:

Grand Offertoire in F	Weby
Andantino Tranquillo	Calkin
Moderato in Bb	Calkin
Sanctus-Benediction	Mozart

An Educational Dispute

A very distressing dispute arose in the schools between the Revd John Wood and the three Head Teachers of the schools during the Autumn Term 1895. Sadly, the dispute was not confined to the district, and a report appeared in The Schoolmaster (The Official Magazine of the National Union of Teachers) for 7 December 1895, and a full copy of the report was printed in the *Wigan Observer* of the same date as follows:

The Educational Dispute at Pemberton
Dismissal of Teachers
An Appeal to Col. Blundell, MP

We have received an advance copy of a report which will appear in The Schoolmaster for December 7th, and which deals with the above-named dispute. The report is headed: 'The tenure problem in 1895. Three head teachers dismissed.' and it opens as follows: 'During the past two months the Law Committee of the Executive of the National Union of Teachers has had under its consideration the case of the head teachers of the Pemberton Colliery Schools. The time has now arrived when the committee consider it advisable to make public the details of this case, as all attempts at an amicable and just settlement of the difficulty have failed. The particulars we give below are based upon documentary evidence in the possession of the committee and the results of a personal inquiry made by Mr Organ.

The teachers, Miss Ashurst, Miss Rowlinson, and Mr Duddle are the respective head teachers of the three departments of the Pemberton Colliery School. Miss Ashurst has been connected with the school as a scholar, pupil teacher, assistant and headteacher; Miss Rowlinson was appointed in April, 1888; and Mr Duddle in February, 1889. Against none of these teachers has a complaint been lodged, either as to personal character or professional work during all these years, and yet each of them has received notice of dismissal.

THE TEACHERS' PROFESSIONAL RECORDS—At the time of writing we have before us the full copies of the reports of Her Majesty's inspector and also of the Diocesan inspector for the whole period during which these teachers have had charge of the Pemberton Colliery Schools. Space will not permit us to quote them fully, but we are able to state with confidence that no school managers in the country are able to produce a better series of reports. Where fault is found it is laid to the doors of the managers, who until recently have not supplied sufficient accommodation, and even now the reports show that the head teachers have succeeded in spite of many difficulties arising from the fact that the managers have not supplied sufficient teacher help.

Then follow the last two reports in each department, and the 'Managers' opinion of Mr Duddle, who so late as June of this year, obtained a testimonial from the Revd J. Wood, acting manager of these schools, and the man who is largely responsible for the dismissals.

THE CHURCH CONCERT—When appointed, Mr Duddle agreed to be organist and choirmaster, and also to teach in the Sunday school. He has faithfully carried out this engagement, although the duties in connection with these offices have steadily increased. It appears to have become the annual custom for the three head teachers to take upon themselves the responsibility of organising a concert, the children of the school being performers. This year the head teachers found that they could not undertake the work in connection with the organisation of a concert without expending energy which was needed in their schools, and they accordingly took no steps to prepare for the concert. During the last week in August the Revd J. Wood (curate-in-charge and corresponding manager) went to Mr Duddle, and said 'I want you to begin thinking about the congregational tea party concert which will be held sometime in October.' Mr Duddle informed the Revd J. Wood that he felt that he could not undertake the work. It appears that the Revd J. Wood then went to each of the head mistresses. To Miss Rowlinson he said, 'What are the girls doing for the concert?' Miss Rowlinson's reply was.'Do you not think someone else might take a turn at the work this year, Mr Wood?' This aroused Mr Wood's wrath and he dashed out of the room with the words, 'I see which way the wind blows.' A similar performance occurred in the school of Miss Ashurst.

Mr WOOD OPENS FIRE—Two days after the refusal, Miss Ashurst and Miss Rowlinson each received a letter, of which the following is a copy: 'Dear Miss——. The managers of the Pemberton Colliery Schools are of the opinion that it is part of the duty of head teachers to prepare the children attending the schools in certain exercises and work as illustrations of the efficiency of the scholars and for the pleasure and satisfaction of the parents. This being so you are asked to furnish the managers with an immediate explanation of your refusal; to say you have no time is unsatisfactory. Yours truly (signed) Jno. Wood.' We will continue the train of the narrative with reference to the two ladies, and then deal with Mr Duddle's case. On September 12th Mr Wood again wrote to Miss Ashurst: 'I have waited a considerable time in the hope of receiving a full and satisfactory explanation of your refusal to comply with the reasonable request of the managers, and which, as a public servant, they hold the opinion that it was your duty cordially to fall in with for the benefit of the children and the satisfaction of the parents. In the absence of such explanation I am compelled, with very much regret, to tell you that the managers have decided to revise at once your agreement with them, and to reconsider the terms of the said agreement. In pursuance of which I am directed to serve you with the following notice of determination of your engagement as infants mistress of the Pember-ton Colliery Infant School.

To Miss MARY ANN ASHURST—Notice is hereby given to Miss Mary Ann Ashurst, head mistress of the Pemberton Colliery Infant School, that, after the expiration of three calendar months from this 12th day of September, 1895, the engagement between the said Miss Mary Ann Ashurst and the managers at the Pemberton Colliery Schools will come to an end. Dated this 12th day of September, 1895. Signed on behalf of the managers, JOHN WOOD, acting manager and correspondent. P.S. The revised agreement will be preferentially offered for your signature and acceptance, if you shall within fourteen days state in writing that it is your wish to continue as head mistress of the infants' department, Highfield.

REPLY OF MISS ASHURST TO THE ABOVE—14th September, 1895. Revd Sir, I am in receipt of yours of the 12th, and I may say that I gave you my answer when you brought your note of 31 August. Further than that I did not consider it was necessary for me to go. I had the pleasure of being the headmistress of the Infants' School before you came, and I may inform you that there never was any agreement between the managers and myself as regards anything, and that concert work, and in fact all extrane-ous work, was always considered as voluntary work of love, and was given as such. As it is such an important communication I shall have to consult my friends before I can give you my further reply. Yours respectfully, M. A. ASHURST.'

There is intermediate correspondence, in which the Revd John Wood for the first time speaks of referring the matter to Col. Blundell, MP, who is the proprietor of the schools and one of the managers. It will be noted that in the preceding letters of Mr Wood he assumes to write 'on behalf of the managers.' We have, however, ample evidence that the managers were not consulted. The three managers of the school are Col. Blundell, MP, the Revd F. Forrest, vicar of the parish, and the Revd J. Wood, curate-in-charge and corresponding manager. We have reason to believe that the Revd F. Forrest does not agree with the action of his brother managers.

THE MANAGERS' OFFER—On 1 October Miss Ashurst received the following: 'Dear Miss Ashurst, The managers of Highfield Schools would be glad to have answers from you to the following questions as soon as convenient; but the answers should be, if possible, in my hands not later than Friday, 4th October, 1895: Fixed annual salary as head mistress of the infants' school. Fixed annual salary for the preparation of some of the school children for the annual tea party entertainments, if you consider such preparation of them as outside your duties as infants' mistress at the Highfield Schools. Fixed annual salary for any other work (if any) which you consider as outside your duty as infants' mistress at Highfield. Please state its nature, and let all your answers be as definite as possible.—JNO. WOOD, acting manager, Highfield Schools.'

MISS ASHURST'S REPLY—4th October, 1895. To the managers of Pemberton Colliery Schools. Sirs, - I beg to state that I have given the questions submitted to me by the managers—per the Revd J. Wood—my most careful attention, and appended I ask you to find answers to the same: 1. Fixed annual salary as schoolmistress of the infants' school. The same salary as at present receiving. 2 and 3. I would like to state in answer to these questions that I consider they have nothing to do with the duties of the schoolmistress, and that the performance of them will be looked upon as purely voluntary on the workers' part, and ought in my opinion to be undertaken in that spirit of voluntaryism which will make it pleasanter for all parties concerned. Sincerely hoping that these answers will meet with your approval and materially assist in repairing the breach which has so unfortunately been made. I am, yours respectfully, M. A. ASHURST.

THE MANAGERS' MEETING—It appears that after this there was a meeting of the managers. As a result Miss Ashurst received the following memorandum: 'The managers of the above school will be happy to renew your engagement as infants' mistress as from January 1, 1896. Salary £80 *per annum* (fixed). Bonus of £2, or £4, or £6, payable January 1 each year on report of acting manager—fair, good, or excellent in respect of punctual and diligent work, giving religious and secular instruction both to pupil teachers and school children in strict accordance with the approved timetables. JOHN WOOD, acting manager.' Miss Ashurst accepted this.

THE HEAD MISTRESSES WIN—It will be noted that in the enclosed offer there is no condition as to the performance of extraneous tasks, and therefore there is every reason to congratulate Miss Ashurst on having maintained the position which she at first took up, viz., that she had a right to refuse to perform any duties which were not specified at the time of her engagement.

MISS ROWLINSON'S CASE—We do not propose to give the details in Miss Rowlinson's case, as generally they run on similar lines to those in the case of Miss Ashurst; but, unfortunately, it is necessary for us to deal more fully with the case of Mr Duddle, as no amicable settlement has been effected.

Mr DUDDLE'S CASE—We have stated that at his appointment Mr Duddle undertook the performance of certain extraneous tasks. His weekly work in connection with these three tasks at the time of his appointment was: (a) Choir practice, about one hour: (b) Superintendence at two meetings of the Sunday school; (c) Playing the organ at two plain services. His present weekly work is: (a) Attendance at three choir practices, about three hours; (b) The conduct of more elaborate musical services; (c) Instead of merely superintending the Sunday school, he conducts a large Bible-class consisting of eighty young men. It should be understood that Mr Duddle was both eager and willing to continue his work in connection with these young men, and that no objection had been raised by him to continuing to perform the increased duties which have been laid upon him in connection with the Church and Sunday school. He does, however, object to being compelled to undertake the organisation of a concert in addition to his other heavy extraneous tasks. It should be clearly understood that the salary for these extraneous tasks has been taken from school funds.

THE PROCEEDS OF THE CONCERTS—The proceeds of these concerts are not devoted to school purposes, but to the purposes of the church. The teachers do not know the amount which is raised by these concerts, as Mr Wood does not communicate the financial result to them. Until the last year or two the teachers used to pay all expenses, and when asked, Mr Wood raised serious objections to refunding the most trifling amount. The very children were expected to buy their own tambourines and dresses. Preparation for the concert occupied the teachers every evening for six weeks previous to the date of the performance, and the teachers assured us that the preparation for these concerts interfered very considerably with the progress of the school work. It cannot be too often stated, that because these teachers have refused to undertake work which in their opinion was detrimental to the education of the children committed to their care, they have been dismissed from posts which they have occupied with credit to themselves and to the satisfaction of all concerned.

PRIVATE WORK A CONDITION OF PUBLIC OFFICE—On September 14th, 1895, Mr Duddle received from Mr Wood a letter, the following being the last paragraph: 'I will cause a new memorandum of agreement to be drawn up for your acceptance and signature. You know, I believe, exactly what the new terms are—£140 *per annum* for the mastership of the boys' school as long as you give satisfaction to the managers in respect of its duties, and £10 additional for organ, choir, and concerts. The mastership both of school, organ, and choir must go together. At any rate, that is the present idea. On behalf of the managers I beg to thank you for all past services, and with the hope of a further amicable arrangement of work for these important schools.' It will be noted that the sum of £10 is offered as the salary for work in connection with the organ, choir, and concerts, and at the same time it is stated that £140 *per annum* is to be given to Mr Duddle as schoolmaster, and that the undertaking of the choir and organ duties is a condition of appointment as master of the schools. In other words the managers of the Pemberton schools tell Mr Duddle that they have the power to give him the headmastership of a public elementary school, the funds of which are largely provided from public sources, and that they will give to him this headmastership if he will consent to an arrangement by which they obtain the services of a man for private work at a salary which hardly deserves to be qualified as nominal.

Mr DUDDLE'S REPLY—3rd October, 1895. To the managers of the Pemberton Colliery Schools. Gentlemen, I have given the communication received from the managers of the above schools my careful consideration, and beg to submit replies to queries. 1. Fixed annual salary as schoolmaster. £150 *per annum*. 2. Fixed annual salary as organist and choirmaster. As this question does not enter within the province of my duties as schoolmaster, I feel that the matter could be more satisfactorily arranged at an interview between the minister, churchwardens and myself. 3 and 4. With reference to these two questions I may state that I am not anxious to receive payment for the performance of such duties, but prefer that all such work be taken up on the clear understanding that I should be treated in every respect as other voluntary workers would be. Trusting these replies will meet with your approbation, and that the present unfortunate circumstances may be brought to an amicable solution, I am gentlemen, yours faithfully, J. W. DUDDLE.

It will be noted that Mr Duddle in the above asks for '£150 *per annum*' as schoolmaster. In this respect the manager saw his chance and seized upon it as a pretext for refusing to appoint Mr Duddle. Here is Mr Wood's reply, and we call special attention to the sentence, 'Organ and Choir voluntary and without further remuneration.' This sentence is typical of the whole position. Mr Woods says, 'Do my private work or I will oust you from your position, although the situation is a public one'. October 15th, 1895—Dear Mr Duddle, I regret much to have to inform you that the managers of the Pemberton Colliery School decline to entertain the offer of your services as schoolmaster for £150 *per annum*. However, as they do not wish to make a change hurriedly or to put you to any unnecessary inconvenience in the matter, they will readily consent to extend the current notice till the last day of the inspection, July, 1896, on the following terms if you prefer this arrangement and will say so at once. The same rate of pay to 30th June, 1896, i. e. £90 *per annum* and one-fourth grant, 30s. per week till last day of inspection after June 30th 1896. Organ and Choir as before till last day of inspection, July, 1896, voluntary and without any further remuneration. The managers would require a written assurance and engagement that you would remain as schoolmaster up to and including the last day of inspection, July, 1896, and fulfil punctually and diligently the several duties of schoolmaster, giving the required religious and secular instruction both to the pupil teachers and the school children in strict accordance with the approved timetables. My instructions are that otherwise your duties will terminate 14th December, 1895. Yours faithfully, JNO. WOOD.'

REPLY OF Mr DUDDLE—17th October, 1895. Revd Sir, - I beg to acknowledge the receipt of your letter of the 15th. After carefully considering the contents of the same I beg to state—as it seems I have quoted a salary which the managers regret they are not able to accept—that I should be willing to undertake the duties of schoolmaster for the sum of £140 *per annum*, the sum which you proffered me. If you could let me have the managers' opinion on the matter as early as possible you would greatly oblige. Yours faithfully, J. W. DUDDLE.'

Mr WOOD'S REPLY TO ABOVE—18th Oct. 1895. Dear Mr Duddle, I am profoundly sorry for the issue, but the managers think that the matter had better be closed in one of the two ways proposed in my note of the 15th inst, and whichever you prefer. Yours truly, JNO. WOOD.'

Mr DUDDLE NOT HEARD BUT CONDEMNED. On October 22nd Mr Duddle wrote to Mr Wood. The following is a copy of his letter: '22nd October, 1895. Dear Sir, I am sorry my last offer—the offer which you yourself proposed—has not been effectual in bringing to an amicable settlement the unfortunate breach between the managers and myself. As a consequence I should deem it a favour if you could inform me as early as possible whether or not I could meet the managers as a body, in order to have an opportunity of laying my whole case before them, and of learning from them the reasons for my dismissal. Yours faithfully, J. W. DUDDLE.'

Mr Wood wrote a long letter in reply, refusing to arrange for an interview, but stating: 'Still I shall be glad to confer with you, or any of the teachers individually, as being the acting manager and responsible for the work of the schools, otherwise the matter is closed.' Further correspondence followed, but no satisfactory settlement has been effected, and the following letter of Mr Wood's sufficiently indicates the present position: 'Nov. 6th, 1895. Dear Mr Duddle, —I wish to say that your engagement here as master terminates, according to notice given, on Dec. 14th, 1895, and to inform you that I am now advertising for a new master. Yours truly, JOHN WOOD.'

THE OPINION OF THE PARENTS, &c.—The dismissals came to the knowledge of the Pemberton parents, and a petition, signed by over 500 persons, was presented to the managers in favour of Mr Duddle. The young men in the village testified their appreciation in the form of a petition, and the choir also adopted the same course.

WHAT WILL THE MISTRESSES DO?—It must be plain that the dismissals in these three cases are for the same cause. It is not, however, so necessary to the Revd J. Wood that the mistresses should take part in extraneous tasks. The managers have therefore offered them re-appointments. It is with the greatest satisfaction, however, that we state that both these ladies are prepared to stand by Mr Duddle. Miss Rowlinson has already informed the managers that if Mr Duddle goes she will go also. Miss Ashurst is prepared to adopt the same course should she be advised to do so, but we trust that there will be no necessity for such a procedure on her part. Both these ladies have acted most loyally, and we beg to offer them our thanks on behalf of the profession generally.

AN APPEAL TO COLONEL BLUNDELL, CB, MP—The key of the present position is in the hands of Col. Blundell, who is the Conservative member of Parliament for the Ince division of Lancashire. He is also the proprietor of the colliery to which these schools are attached. He is the voluntary subscriber, and he has full power to do as he will in this case. It is not too late for him to intervene in the interests of peace and goodwill. We are loth to believe that he has a full knowledge of the circumstances of the case. His character for fair play and public spirit stands high in the estimation of his workmen and constituents. We appeal to him to use his powerful influence to bring about an amicable settlement of this unhappy dispute, and we can assure him that by doing so he will earn the gratitude not only of hundreds of Lancashire folk, but also of the thousands of teachers who are the masters and mistresses of the voluntary schools in England and Wales.

Sadly we have no detailed record of the event in the Parish Archives. There are no details in the Managers Minute Books covering these events. The first entries in the first existing minute book are as follows:

A meeting of the Managers of the Pemberton Colliery Schools was held in the Pemberton Vicarage on Monday, September 30th at 3.45 p.m. Present were the Col. Blundell, Revd E. F. Forrest, Revd J. Wood. Notices given to the teachers assented to were confirmed. Revised agreement offered but not accepted. It was resolved to ask the teachers what they wanted.

A meeting of the Managers at Highfield Parsonage at 4 p.m. on Dec. 23rd 1895. Present Col. Blundell, Revd E. F. Forrest and J. Wood. Proposed by Colonel Blundell and seconded by Revd E. F. Forrest, that Mr William Williams be and is hereby appointed as Headmaster of the Pemberton Colliery Boys School and that Miss Ada E. Hitchen, be and is hereby appointed Headmistress of the Girls School. Resolved Unanimously. Signed. John Wood. Correspondent.

It seems a pity, as was pointed out in a later edition of The Schoolmaster, that in spite of the fact that John Wood had been a schoolmaster himself for twenty-three years, and should therefore have been able to understand the situation from both points of view, that he and the Head teachers were not able to resolve the situation. But this was not a purely local issue. The same problem was repeated many hundreds of times all over the country, sadly, some heads of Church schools were expected to perform tasks connected with the Church involving many hours of out of school activities, for little or no reward, and sometimes little or no appreciation, while their colleagues in state schools were often better paid and had no extraneous duties beyond their normal teaching hours. This problem was not solved nationwide for many years.

The First Vestry Meeting

The first annual Vestry was held in Highfield on 21 April 1896. The Vestry was a meeting of the incumbent or curate-in-charge and the ratepayers of the parish or district. In the past it had been responsible for many duties in the parish of church and state. At the meeting of the Vestry, which was held each year in Easter week, the Churchwardens and the sidesmen were elected, though in the case of Highfield which was not yet a parish, the elections were for sidesmen only, the Churchwardens for the parish being elected at Pemberton.

At this first meeting, Revd J. Wood was in the chair and those present included Messrs J. W. Greener, T. Barton, W. Moss, W. Williamson, Geo. Ashurst, Sen., Geo. Ashurst, Jun., W. Richardson, G. Dickson, J. Johnson and Geo. Monks. Among the business of the meeting recorded were the following items: William Williams, Headmaster of the Boys school, was to act as organist and choirmaster for twelve months at £10 *per annum*, payable quarterly. John Berry was appointed apparitor, bellringer and organ-blower at £10 *per annum*, payable quarterly. The ironwork on the church doors was to be painted, and grass cut round the church. The ventilation door over the chancel arch was to be made draughtproof. The heating apparatus was to be started on Friday to secure the satisfactory temperature of the church for Sunday. a problem that was to continue for many years! Fortunately the coke for the heating system in those days was supplied by Colonel Blundell direct from the collieries.

Death of W. J. Greener

Another serious colliery tragedy occurred on Monday 1 February 1897, when Mr W. J. Greener, the General Manager of Pemberton Collieries and a sidesman at Highfield, was killed in an underground accident reported by the *Wigan Examiner* as follows:

> During Monday forenoon a report reached Wigan that a serious accident had occurred at the Pemberton Collieries belonging to Messrs Blundell and Son, and that Mr Greener, the General Manager had been killed and Mr Daniel Toman, Underground Manager seriously injured. A representative of the *Wigan Examiner* was despatched to the Collieries, and obtained confirmation of the sad event. It appears that there had been a reported flow of water and an escape of gas in the Bye Pit, and about half past eight Mr Greener descended the mine with the intention of making an inspection of the workings. He was joined by Mr Toman, and the two proceeded along the engine plane. On their journey

they met a boy, and Mr Greener asked him how far the set, meaning the tubs, was off. The boy answered 'Quite close, Sir.' to which Mr Greener replied 'Alright !' There was room on each side of the rails but by some means or other both Mr Greener and Mr Toman seem to have failed to realise the dangerous position in which they were placed, as apparently they were travelling between the rails, and before they could step aside were caught by the tubs which, it is said, are hauled through the mine at a rapid rate. Mr Greener was evidently first struck on the head as he was in a stooping attitude owing to the lowness of the mine, and he sustained frightful injuries—a large wound on the forehead, spine lacerated, two broken ribs on the left side, both thighs dislocated, and a knee dislocated. Mr Toman appears to have been thrown on one side by the tubs, this would tend to explain his miraculous escape. When picked up Mr Greener was still living, and he expressed a desire to be taken to his wife. Steps were at once taken to have him removed from the mine. In the meantime, Dr Graham of Wigan, had been summoned, and on reaching the collieries he descended the shaft, and met the carriers at the pit eye. An examination then revealed the fact that Mr Greener had expired. Consequently Dr Graham proceeded to render what assistance he could to Mr Toman, who was found to be suffering from a mutilated thigh and shoulder, and the smashed limbs having been set, Mr Toman was conveyed from the pit to his home, Brook Cottage, Pemberton. The body of the deceased gentleman was removed to Mr Greener's residence, Wood Cottage, close to the collieries. Dr Hartley, of Pemberton had also been called to the mines, and he was also in a position to render medical aid. Mr Greener was about forty four years of age, and had been General Manager of the Pemberton Collieries for nineteen years. He married the daughter of Mr James Pickering, agent of the Collieries, and he leaves a widow and nine young children to mourn his loss. He was a staunch Conservative, and was prominently identified with the Church life of Highfield. It is a melancholy fact that his father, who was General Manager of the same Collieries, lost his life about the year 1853 from injuries sustained at the Rainford Colliery, and that the succeeding General Manager, Mr Watkin, was killed at the disastrous explosion of 1877. The accident has created a painful impression in the Wigan district, where the deceased gentleman was exceedingly well-known. Colonel Blundell, CB, MP, was early acquainted with the facts of the sad event and the gallant Colonel immediately travelled to Highfield. On enquiry yesterday (Tuesday), we were informed that Mr Toman's condition was satisfactory, and there were high hopes of his ultimate recovery.

The Inquest. Mr Brighouse, the County Coroner has fixed the inquest for half past ten on Wednesday morning at the Blundell Arms, Pemberton. The funeral will take place tomorrow (Thursday) afternoon when there will be a service at St John's Parish Church, Pemberton.

This was another serious loss to the church. The Greener family had been very closely involved with the church since its beginnings in the area. It was Mr Greener's aunt who had started the first Sunday school thirty-four years earlier.

The pattern of worship and activities in the church at Highfield was by now well established and was to continue with very little change for many years. From 1882 when the Preachers' Book was begun to record the services and preachers, there had been a regular 10.30 a.m. Morning Service and Evensong at 6.30 p.m., and in the early days Holy Communion was celebrated at 12 noon after Morning Prayer on the first Sunday in the month only. The number of Communicants on Easter Day 1882 was 41. The numbers attending services was recorded on 4 June 1882 as Morning 219, Evening 190,

*A class from the Boys' School in 1897, Queen Victoria's Diamond Jubilee year.
Mr William Williams, Headmaster, and scholars.*

Total for day 409. The number of Communicants on Easter Day 1896 was 69. From this year Holy Communion was celebrated after Morning prayer on the first and third Sundays each month. Sunday School was held twice on each Sunday, at 9 a.m. and in the afternoon. The Superintendents in 1900 were Boys, Mr R. A. Southworth, Girls, Mr Geo. Dickson, Infants, Miss A. Barton, and Little Lane, Miss M. Dickson. The Men's Bible Class was led by Mr William Williams, Head of the Boys' School, and the Secretary was Mr W. Richardson. There was a Sunday School Sick Society, and a Sunday School Clothing Club to help with the welfare of the district. The Field Treat was held on a Saturday early in July each year, and 'Sermons' Sunday was held annually at the end of July. The Congregational Tea Party still continued as an annual event.

The second Vestry meeting held on 26 April 1897, records the names of those present and the fact that the Accounts, properly audited were submitted, and as well as the nomination of sidesmen, a voluntary book was provided for the organist for use before services. From 1898, the meeting of the Vestry was held on Easter Tuesday.

By the turn of the century John Wood had celebrated his 72nd birthday, but he continued in harness for another eight years. He ministered at Highfield for twenty-seven years as curate-in-charge. He must have been very happy here since he never moved away to become a Vicar or a Rector in his own right. He was not only involved in Parish work. The annual report of the Liverpool Diocesan Finance Association for 1901 records that he was the Treasurer for the Rural Deanery of Wigan—responsible for the collection of Diocesan Contributions from the parishes in the Deanery.

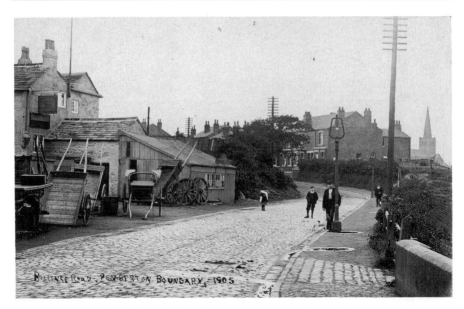

The Pony Dick Inn and Starkey's Wheelwright's workshop in 1905,
before the family built their houses on the opposite side of the road.

In 1903 special services were held in aid of the new Liverpool Cathedral Fund. In 1905 there was a proposal to have the organ cleaned and in 1906 there must have been problems with the number of children in church for sidesmen were to come to church earlier to supervise children! The question was asked. Should children be let out before the sermon? The decision was left for the future.

Death of Col. H. B-H-Blundell, 1906

The whole district of Pemberton must have been shocked to hear of the death of their benefactor, Colonel Henry Blundell in October 1906. His funeral was held quietly, at his own request, at Halsall, as the report in the *Wigan Observer* tells:

> The remains of the late Colonel Blundell, CB, were not consigned to their resting place with pomp and circumstance. The ceremony was of that plain and simple character which accorded well with the tenour of his life. Followed to the graveside by sorrowing relatives and a numerous band of friends and workers in the fields of labour and politics, he was buried under the sheltering trees and under the shadow of the ancient church of his people. The obsequies were on Tuesday afternoon, and those from this district attending the funeral left by the Southport express shortly after one o'clock, and were afterwards conveyed to Halsall by a special train from Chapel St Station. The members of this party made their way along the pleasant country lanes to St Cuthbert's Church, where the service was to take place. They found themselves preceded by many others,

who had made the journey from Pemberton by waggonettes; and people were also flocking to the church ground from all the neighbourhood around. To whatever part of the estate one might turn the same was seen—persons of all degrees making their way to pay a last respect to one who had been so great a benefactor to them and to the district. Every cottage or villa had its drawn blinds—the township was indeed in mourning.

The fine old church was quickly filled long before the appearance of the chief mourners. It is an ancient structure standing well out in its setting of level agricultural country. The interior is plain, and almost severe with its grey-stone columns and oaken roof. Exquisite windows in the chancel and continued some way down the aisles, give a sense of warmth and colour, otherwise its rugged strength and noble dignity impresses the stranger.

The organist played the opening phrases of Chopin's 'Funeral March,' and had reached the tender refrain of the trio when the tolling bell announced the coming of the cortege. Many of the visitors had waited until the arrival of the coffin and the family mourners, and they followed in the rear as the melancholy procession, headed by surpliced clergy and choir made its way along the churchyard. An affecting sight was the two lines of schoolgirls dressed in sober black, each child holding in her hand an innocent nosegay of white flowers—a touching tribute to one whose delight was in the young. The coffin of the departed Colonel was carried by men of the estate, and was covered with the most beautiful wreaths, one of pink roses offering a strong contrast to the white flowers of the others. By the time the funeral party had reached the chancel the church was crowded with mourners, the central passage of the nave being completely blocked. The opening sentences of the funeral service being concluded, the choir led the congregation in the hymn, 'Christ will gather in His own,' and the 90th Psalm, 'Lord thou hast been our refuge from one generation to another'; and the lesson from St Paul's Epistle to the Corinthians was read by the Revd J. Wood, the Vicar of St Matthew's, Highfield. Then followed the hymn, 'On the resurrection morning, ' and the organist softly played 'O rest in the Lord,' as the coffin was taken from the church into the graveyard outside. There in the presence of the assembled people the body was lowered and the last rites were observed, the choir singing with appropriate expression 'Now the labourer's task is o'er.' The funeral service was conducted by the Revd Canon Leigh (Rector of Halsall), cousin of the deceased, and the other clergy officiating were the Revd J. Wood, St Matthew's, Highfield, Pemberton; the Revd D. J. Thomas, Vicar of Lydiate; the Revd E. T. Gabriel, Curate, Pemberton Parish Church; and the Revd R. E. Whittaker, curate, Halsall.

The Chief Mourners

The chief mourners were General Blundell (brother) and Mrs Blundell, Miss Blundell (sister), Mr Cuthbert Blundell and Captain D. H. Blundell (nephews), Mrs Alston, Miss Upperton, and Mrs Keppell (nieces), Commodore Keppell, Mr A. R. Alston, Revd Canon Upperton, Colonel Leigh and Mr R. Leigh, Major and Mrs Marshall, Capt. H. Townshend, Mr G. H. Eaton, the Earl of Lathom, the Marquis de Casteja, Count Andre de Casteja, Count Emmanuel de Casteja, Sir W. E. M. Tomlinson, the Revd H. H. Hall, Dr Pendlebury, and Mr Burton.

Many institutions, varied in character, in which the deceased Colonel took a warm interest, were represented at the funeral. (Those with a local interest were listed). Among other gentlemen who were in church and at the graveside (another long list.) were Revd E. F. Forrest, E. Douglas, W. J. Greener, and J. C. Pickering. The long list of wreaths

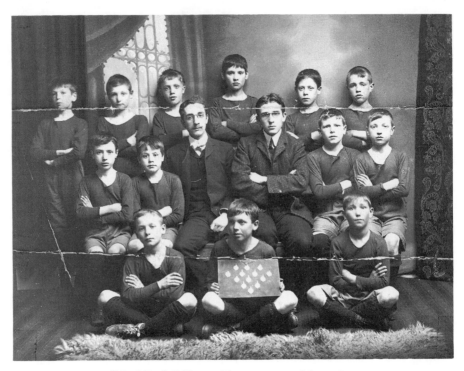

School Football Team, with runners-up medals, 1906–7.
Back row: T. Bannister; ? Ball; W. Heaton; Joe Statter; ? Bradshaw; Joe Banks.
Middle row: A. Robinson; H. Lowe; Mr Millard, Mr Anders (teachers); W. Thomas; ? Travena.
Front row: J. Parkes; J. Hudson; J. Sammons.

included St Matthew's Men's Bible Class; The Mothers, St Matthew's Memorial Church; Minister, Sidesmen, Congregation, and Sunday School Teachers and Scholars, St Matthew's, Highfield.

There followed reports of Memorial Services held at St John's Church, Pemberton, at Highfield Church, and a report of references at the Wigan Technical College.

The following obituary is preserved at Wigan Library:

In grateful and affectionate remembrance of Colonel Henry Blundell Hollinshead Blundell CB, Colliery Proprietor, Philanthropist and Politician, born 1831, died September 28th 1906, at London, and was buried at Halsall, near Ormskirk, Lancs. He served his Queen and Country in the Crimea 1855, Canada 1860 and the Sudan, Egypt in 1884–86. He was Colonel in the Grenadier Guards, Adjutant of the Home District and Deputy Lieutenant of the County of Lancaster and a Free Burgess of the City of Liverpool; MP for Ince Division 1885–92 and 1895–1906, and a real friend to the poor.

The Revd John Wood, preaching at a Memorial Service to Colonel Blundell at Highfield on the following Sunday said:

We all mourn after a great loss today. Colonel Blundell was our best friend—so good to us, he had endeared himself by his life to a large circle of friends, that it is difficult to realise he is gone, and that so suddenly. His end was peace. His has been a good and pure life. he tried to do justice to all. We all know of his great and generous liberality. His purse was open and ready for every real necessity, and for the help of every creed. Thoroughly impartial, many therefore had experience of his goodness. We here have examples of his goodness in our beautiful Church and Schools. He bore the charge of Education at Highfield more than forty years ago; starting schools before there was any government inspection or grant. Religious Instruction for the children had his great consideration, and he encouraged it in these schools, as you all know.

Have we been sufficiently thankful for all this? If not, may God forgive us. We cannot ask him now. He is beyond mortal questions, and free from a too thankless world, a world of sorrow and care. May God give us grace, like him, to take heed unto the thing that is right, for that shall bring a man peace at the last.

Revd J. Wood retires

At the 1908 Vestry, the Revd John Wood was absent sick, and Mr Southworth took the chair. From the register of services for February, 1908 onwards, the services were taken by many different ministers. By July, John Wood was taking services again but his handwriting in the register was very shaky. He was now 80 years old and had served the Church at Highfield faithfully for twenty-seven years. His last service was on 15 November 1908 at 6.30 p.m., when his son, Revd E. J. Wood, Vicar of Whiston, preached. His retirement and presentation were recorded in the *Wigan Observer* as follows:

The Revd John Wood MA gave his final address to a large congregation at the Highfield Church on Sunday evening after the sermon. He briefly stated that owing to his age and infirmities he felt it was necessary for him to resign. The parish was growing very largely and it required, he said, a younger clergyman than himself. He very heartily thanked the whole of the congregation and parishioners of Highfield for all the kindness and sympathy he had received from them. He also thanked all the sidesmen for the good work they had rendered making the members of the congregation as comfortable as possible, and he thanked the organist (Mr Williams.) and the whole of the choir for the excellent service rendered, as well as the two superintendents of the boys and girls Sunday Schools, and all the teachers who had worked so nobly in such a good cause. Mr Wood then went on to say he was not removing very far from them, not more than twenty miles, and he hoped to be remembered by them in their prayers. He trusted they would also pray very earnestly for their new clergyman and help him all they could to make everything a success with the blessing of God. He need hardly say that his very long association with them would always remind him of the people of Highfield. He then thanked the Bishop and his chaplain, and all the clergy who had been so kind to him, and rendered him such valuable help. In conclusion, he pronounced the benediction of blessing, and afterwards went to the west end of the church and shook hands with all the congregation and bid them farewell. The congregation then dispersed.

On Monday evening, a deputation, representing the congregation, sidesmen, choir, the Day and Sunday schools and gentry and clergy of the district waited upon the Revd John Wood and presented him with a purse of gold, which had been very liberally subscribed on his behalf. The Mothers and the Ladies Bible class presented their teacher Miss Wood with a valuable tea service.

Death of Revd J. Wood

Revd John Wood died at Ainsdale on 14 June 1911. A note in the Register of Services on the 17th says simply.The Revd J. Wood, MA, for twenty-seven years minister at Highfield, entered into his rest 14 June 1911. Funeral Service held at Highfield 17 June 1911. The Revd Parker Johnson, writing in the Parish Magazine in August 1937, said of Revd John Wood.He left an indelibly good impression on this parish by reason of his long service in pioneer work of building up the foundation of this parish on a high spiritual level. The *Wigan Observer* gave details of the funeral on the day of the funeral, Saturday 17 June 1911, as follows:

> It is with regret that we announce the death of the Revd John Wood, formerly Vicar of St Matthew's Church, Highfield, the sad event occurring on Wednesday morning at his residence, 63 Liverpool Rd, Ainsdale, near Southport. The deceased clergyman, who was 63 years old, had been in poor health for some time, and it was in consequence of failing health, in fact, that he retired from the vicariate of Highfield between two and three years ago when he retired to Ainsdale. The Revd John Wood was educated at Worcester College, Oxford, and he became Deacon in 1875, Priest in 1876. From 1875 to 1877 he was curate at St Catharine's, Wigan, and in 1877 he went to Pemberton, being located at Highfield. From 1881 he was the incumbent of St Matthew's, Highfield, where the late Colonel Blundell built the new church as a memorial to his deceased wife. The Reverend gentleman leaves a grown up family of four sons and three daughters, his wife having predeceased him many years ago. One son is a doctor at Huyton, and another is the Vicar of Whiston, while the two other sons have held important government positions in India and the Malay States. The funeral takes place today, Saturday, at St John's, Pemberton, the first part of the Burial Service being held at St Matthew's Highfield at half past two. The body will be conveyed by road from Ainsdale, and after the service at St Matthew's, a procession of the Choir, Sunday School scholars and members and officials of the congregation will proceed to the place of interment at Lamberhead Green. An invitation is extended to all who knew the deceased clergyman to join the procession.

A stained glass window in the south aisle of the Church was erected in his memory in 1917. It depicts the Presentation of Christ in the Temple. The inscription underneath the window reads: 'This window was erected to the glory of God and in loving memory of the Revd John Wood, MA, Curate in charge of this district, 1881 to 1908, by members of his family and parishioners. At rest June 14th, 1911.'

Revd John Woods

Fourth Curate In charge, 1909–1910

First Vicar, 1910–1936

I N THE 1881 Census for Walton, Liverpool, living at 30 Hornby Rd are John Woods, senior, aged 30, a prison warder, and his wife, Elizabeth aged 31. Their children are: Robert, aged 6, John, aged 4 and Edward H. aged 1. All the family are recorded as being born in Walton. With them is living the Revd Robert T. Saulez, Incumbent of St John the Evangelist, Walton, a new church built in 1880. The St John's parsonage was not built until 1883, and so the Woods home was being used as the parsonage house. From this it is very clear that the family were very involved in the life of the Church. This would have had a great effect upon the young John.

The 1891 Census for Walton again records the family living at 30, Hornby Rd. John Woods, senior is now aged 38, prison warder, Elizabeth his wife is 40, now recorded as born at Melling, Lancs. Son Robert is 16 and a pupil teacher, John is 14 and an Office Boy (Port). Another Robert (probably Edward) is 8 and a scholar, and Lizzie, a daughter is 1.

In about 1899, aged 22, John Woods went to Bishop Hatfield Hall, Durham, where he obtained a Licentiate in Theology (Exhibitioner) in 1902. He was ordained Deacon in 1903 by the Bishop of Durham and was appointed Curate of St James, Stockton in the same year. He was ordained Priest in 1904 again by the Bishop of Durham. He obtained his BA in 1906. He left Stockton in 1909 to move to Pemberton after six years in his first curacy. John Woods married Gertrude Dobson Pattinson, of Darlington, some time during this period.

John Woods' testimonial in his application for a licence to officiate in the Mission Church of St Matthew, Highfield, in the Parish of St John, Pemberton, was dated 11 January 1909. John Woods began his work in the district in February 1909. Major

Cuthbert Blundell immediately took steps to create a parish from the existing district, and so one of John Woods first tasks was to prepare for the beginnings of parochial life in the district. Building operations to have the Church enlarged commenced in October 1909, and all the legal preparations had to be gone through for the district to become a Parish with John Woods as Vicar. According to the Bishop's Acts Book for Highfield, St Matthew's, the Church site was conveyed to the Ecclesiastical Commissioners on 6 August 1909, and an agreement as to Patronage was made on 29 October 1909. In the midst of all these preparations a daughter Kathleen was born to Revd and Mrs Woods on 5 February 1910, and John Woods was awarded his MA in 1910.

The Consecration of the Church, 1910

The extensions to the Church were completed and the Consecration of the whole Church was carried out on 22 July 1910, by Dr Chavasse, the Bishop of Liverpool. The *Wigan Examiner* contained the following report:

> On Friday of last week the new portion of this church, which has been added to meet the increased demand for extra accommodation by the parishioners, was opened and consecrated by the Lord Bishop of Liverpool (Dr Chavasse.), when the sacred edifice was crowded to its utmost capacity. The original portion was erected as a memorial to Lady Blundell by the late Colonel Blundell CB, at a cost of over £10,000, and the alterations have been made at the expense of his nephew Mr Cuthbert B. H. Blundell, at a cost of over £2,000, and consists of an extension to the south aisle to full length of the church, and the nave carried westward. The architects were Messrs Paley and Austin (Lancaster), and Messrs R. Rathbone and son, (Atherton) were the contractors.
>
> At the opening, in addition to the Bishop, there were present the following clergy: Revs. Canon R. G. Matthew (Rector of Wigan), J. Woods MA (Vicar designate of the church), E. F. Forrest MA, W. R. Johnson, MA, C. F . Holt, F. B. A. Miller, W. A. Wickham, J. W. P. Lovatt, F. C. Bayman, J. A. Goode, and J. Hayhurst, Mr Cuthbert B. H. Blundell and Mr R. Farmer (Diocesan Registrar.) Mr W. T. Williams presided at the organ.
>
> Mr Cuthbert B. H. Blundell presented the deed of gift of the church property to the Bishop and Revd E. F. Forrest MA, handed in the petition of the congregation for the consecration of the building. The Bishop in his address took for his text the 7th chapter of St Luke's gospel and the 5th verse, viz, 'For he loveth our nation, and he hath built us a synagogue.' His Lordship said: 'Whenever mention is made of the soldier warriors in the new testament it is always spoken of with the utmost honour and respect. One of the soldiers, originally a pagan, joined the Jewish church. He built a house of prayer for the Jews, and he was a man who not only loved his God but his fellow men. He was a man of rare modesty, and full of faith, and trusted in God. Such was the character of this Roman soldier who of old built a synagogue, and it was a soldier who built this beautiful church of yours, and a soldier has completed it. You know better than I do the work of that noble man. Eighteen years ago, I believe it was begun, for he intended it to be a place of worship for his workpeople, for he desired the spiritual welfare of his people, and now that he has gone, another fills his place, and that person, with a generosity like that of his uncle, has completed the work thus begun. This evening we look with favour

and with hearts full of gratitude on one of the most stately churches, not only of this deanery, but in this diocese, and my dear people of Highfield, this church is yours. I think of your neighbours in the surrounding parishes. I think of Platt Bridge, where the colliers have subscribed almost £3,000 for the church, for the worship of God, and of St Mark's Newtown, and St Luke's Orrell, how loyally and devotedly have the men of those districts worked to achieve their present positions, and this church of yours was given to you without any such work at all. Now you must work, and I know you will work for what you require in the future. I have heard with the utmost delight how you set to work to prepare for a sale of work, and how in the course of six hours raised a sum of £225 and that noble effort gives you the highest credit. This I regard as the first fruits and much has yet to be done. You need a church hall, the hall in which the Revd J. Woods started his ministry will no longer suffice, you require a noble church hall, worthy of this noble church. Your Vicar should have a Vicarage house and a fellow to help him to administer to the needs of this congregation. You cannot raise all the money required, but I know you will raise your share, and you will do it out of gratitude to God, and to the persons who have built you this church. I understand that one of your number, under the disguise of anonymous, has this week sent as a gift the ornaments for the holy table. The second result is that as we step across the threshold we feel the desire at once to kneel down and pray to Almighty God. You have received the gift of a divine Church, and when you worship here let your voices as well as your hearts join in the praises. Nothing is more inspiring than to hear six hundred men and women joining in with spirit and singing together the hymns and psalms. And lastly show how you appreciate it by crowding its seats. Come not only on Sundays, but come on the weekdays, and let this place have such a congregation so that the parishes round may hear of it. Come here to communion and on your saints days. God has given you one after his own heart to administer to you, who has won your hearts, and gladden his heart, by using to the very utmost this great and noble gift thus given to you. It will give, I believe, a mighty impetus to the work of God. In this place you have done much in the past, and now, with the grace of God, you will do more in the future.

The induction of the new Vicar is expected to take place in about six or seven weeks. At a special vestry meeting, held last week, Mr W. R. Richardson and Mr Thomas Barton were appointed Vicar and Parishioners wardens respectively.

Institution of the First Vicar

The institution and induction of the Revd John Woods to the Parish Of St Matthew's, Highfield took place on Thursday 27 October 1910. Again the *Wigan Examiner* recorded the details:

> On Thursday the Right Reverend the Lord Bishop of Liverpool, (Dr Chavasse.) instituted the Revd John Woods MA, L.Th. to be first Vicar of the new Parish of St Matthew, Highfield. The following clergy were present at the service: Revs. D. A. G. Taylor, (Vicar of St George's, Wigan), E. F. Forrest and Charles E. Diggle, (St John's, Pemberton), The Revd J. Hayhurst and Mr J. A. Thompson, (Liverpool), and Mr & Mrs Cuthbert B. H. Blundell. Mr W. Williams officiated at the organ.
>
> The Bishop, in his address took for his text the fourth chapter of Paul's epistle to the Ephesians, 8th and 11th verses: 'When He ascended up on high he led captivity captive

and gave gifts unto men, and he gave some apostles, and some prophets, and some evangelists, and some pastors and teachers; for the perfecting of the saints, for the work of the ministry, for the edifying of the body of Christ.' Before speaking on the text, his Lordship said they had met to institute their Vicar. Institution to a living meant admission to a living. The church gave to the trustees and patrons of the living the right to nominate to that living a clergyman they liked, but it was left to the Bishop to admit him to his work. The Bishop had the right to examine the clergyman to see if he had sufficient learning to teach his flock, but in the case of their Vicar no such examination was necessary. The laity had the right and power to prevent any unworthy clergyman being admitted to a living. He need not say that, they having known their own Vicar had learnt to love him, and found nothing unworthy in him; and now they thanked God from the bottom of their hearts that he was at last to be their Vicar.

Speaking on the text, the Bishop said; St Paul tells us that when our Lord Jesus Christ ascended into heaven he gave gifts to men and that one of these gifts was the gift of the ministry. The thought I want to leave you with today, my dear people of Highfield, is this, that your Vicar is Christ's gift to you. He will bear it in mind himself that God has given him to be your clergyman. He will remember the Church of England contains within her fold men of every political party, and his work will not be to preach politics, but the great principles which our Lord Jesus Christ came upon earth to give, which will help men to be good conservatives, good liberals, good radicals and labour, or to whatever party a man may belong. Your Vicar will think about causes and reasons of many things but he will not preach philosophy that you cannot understand. The very purpose for which God has sent him is, he should try to help you in your Christian lives before men and women so that you can become workers for our Lord. He has worked among you, and now God has owned his own sacrifice and devotion. The thoughts of the great trust that God has committed to him in bestowing such a work upon him, constrains him to devote himself, by his will and spirit, to do the work of God amongst you. Because he is God's gift to you, he will feel that his highest privilege to be ready either to labour or to sacrifice himself for you, the people whom God loves. He will feel that God loves you so much that He has sent him to minister to you. This will clothe with dignity every one of you, and it will make him see, as it were, Christ in each one of you, and make him long to help you as far as he can. Because he is God's gift to you I say receive him and love him. God has sent him to you. Pray for him, do what you can to help him, God has been very good to you, my dear people of St Matthew's, you have one of the most beautiful churches in the Diocese, where you can worship God without payment, after the manner of your forefathers, and God, in his mercy, has sent you a man after his own heart. Receive him as God's gift, thank God for him, and don't forget to pray for him, and work for him. He has a parish consisting of something like seven thousand people in his charge and he will have a loyal helper at Goose Green. You can help, every one of you, men women and children by your prayers, personal services, teaching in the Sunday Schools, by organising open-air services and cottage meetings. God grant that you may help your Vicar, so as to cast such radiance of light over this neighbourhood that many may be attracted to serve God as you do.

The lessons were read by the Revd E. F. Forrest, and at the close of the service collections were taken for the Diocesan Ordination Candidates Exhibition Fund, the proceedings closing with the Benediction.

On 16 January 1911, the Revd Ambrose Edward Buer was licensed to a Stipendiary Curacy of St Matthew's, Highfield, to work in the Goose Green District. His yearly

Girls from school practising on the lawn of Highfield House (now St Matthew's Close) for a concert in the Iron Church building following the annual Congregational Tea Party in about 1911.

stipend was to be £170, and he was to live in a house in Warrington Road, Goose Green. He had previously been licensed to St John's, Pemberton. .

On Saturday 17 June 1911, a Tea Party and Concert was held at St Matthew's Church Mission, Little Lane, Pemberton, Wigan to mark the unveiling of the new Little Lane Banner. Tea was served at 5 p.m. prompt and the cost of admission to Tea and Concert was one shilling each, Under 14 sixpence, and admission to the Concert only, threepence. The Artistes at the Concert were Miss Nellie Hurst, Soprano, Pemberton; Mr Chas. W. Burns, Bass, Poolstock; St James' Handbell Ringers; Mr Chas. Milligan, Humorist and Mr Thos. Arrowsmith, Pianist. Mr Geo. Hampson, of Pemberton presided and during the interval Mrs Jas. L. Little unveiled the new banner. Mr J. L. Little was People's warden at St Matthew's in 1912 and 1913.

During 1911 William Atherton was appointed as Verger at Highfield, an office he was to hold for the next 51 years. He had been secretary to the Men's Bible Class before this. He was a sawyer at Pemberton Colliery.

At the 1912 Vestry Meeting Mr T. Barton resigned as People's Warden and Mr J. L. Little was appointed in his place.

Mr William Williams resigned as Headmaster of the Schools and Organist of the Church from 16 September 1913. He had occupied both posts since January 1896. When the Headmaster's post was advertised, 78 applications were received. Six applicants were invited to attend for interview at Pemberton Colliery Offices, on 27 June 1913, and from these Mr J. W. Brierley, Headmaster of Upholland Moor School was unanimously recommended by the managers. Mr Brierley was to serve the parish faithfully, in many ways, for the next 32 years. He was not, however, an organist, although he had a fine bass voice which he used as a soloist on many occasions. This broke the tradition of combining the position of Headmaster of the School with the position of Organist of the Church. It was necessary then to try to find someone to fill the Organist's position. This was accomplished on 24 July 1913 when Mr A. Harris, late of Chester College, the same College that Mr Brierley had attended, was appointed by the Managers to a vacancy on the School staff, and later as Organist and Choirmaster to the Church. In the next twelve years Mr Harris, supported no doubt by Mr Brierley, was to have a great influence on the standard of Music in the Church.

Tragic death of Mrs Woods

Mrs Woods, the wife of the Vicar had been seriously ill for some months during 1913 and tragically at a young age she died on Tuesday 12 August. Her death was reported in the *Wigan Observer*:

> The news of the death, which occurred on Tuesday, of Mrs Gertrude Woods, wife of the Vicar of St Matthew's, Highfield, was received with heartfelt sorrow and genuine regret not only by the parishioners but by all with whom the deceased lady had come into contact. Mrs Woods had been ailing for a considerable time, and it was with much grief that she was compelled to relinquish the work in the parish in which she had interested herself so earnestly and devotedly ever since she came to Highfield. She had conducted the Women's Bible Class, the Mothers' Meeting, and the Sewing Class, and the members of these organisations particularly will lament the passing away of such a loving leader and instructor, and although her end was not unexpected the grief is none the less poignant. Mrs Woods had endeared herself to all by her kind and sympathetic nature, and the sympathy of everyone will be extended to the bereaved husband in the loss of a devoted wife and to the child who is only three years of age. Mr Woods was a curate at Stockton on Tees prior to taking up his work at St Matthew's. The deceased lady belonged to Darlington, and the body was conveyed by train to that town on Thursday for interment on the following day. At the time the funeral was taking place in the afternoon a Memorial Service was held at St Matthew's Highfield.

Miss M Pattinson, the late Mrs Woods sister, came to live at the Parsonage House to look after the Vicar and his young daughter. She was to become involved in the life of the parish over the next twenty four years.

A New Vicarage

The Gift of a new Vicarage was announced at the Annual Vestry Meeting in 1913. In the January 1914 Parish Magazine the Vicar announced:

> In the early part of the year I hope to be able to move into the new Vicarage, which is nearing completion. Once more the generosity of Mr Blundell has been shown to this parish. He gave first the land, and then offered to pay half the cost of the building. The remainder of the money is to come from the Ecclesiastical Commissioners. When the

house is completed the parish will be in possession of a substantial and permanent house for every vicar who comes. This is not the case as regards the present house of residence. Highfield is again favoured, for almost every other parish is called upon to raise the funds for a parsonage house.

On 9 May 1914, the new Vicarage was dedicated by the Bishop of Liverpool. The Vicar wrote in the June Parish Magazine:

> We were glad to see so many present at the dedication service of the new Vicarage. It showed kindly interest, as well as the desire that by united prayer a blessing might come upon the house and all who might dwell there in the years to come. We hope it will make for the more efficient working of the parish.

It must have been very sad for John Woods to move into the new Vicarage without his wife. They must have had such great plans for the place before she died.

From 1867 the full stipends of the Clergy had been provided, first by Colonel Blundell, and then by Major Blundell. After the building of the Vicarage, Major Blundell made benefactions to the Commissioners, which were then met by them, so that the benefice became endowed to its full amount.

At the annual Vestry Meeting held in April 1914, the Vicar thanked Mr Ollerenshaw who had been responsible for the conducting of the services in the Little Lane Mission for the past three years. Mr J. L. Little had decided not to stand for re-election as Warden and Mr R. A. Southworth who had been a Sidesman since 1894 was elected as People's Warden in his place.

The annual Field Day was held on the first Saturday in July 1914. A note from the Vicar in the Parish Magazine states:

> Arrangements are well in hand for the Field Day, and given a fine day we expect a successful time. If all the scholars would endeavour to be at the schools punctually at 1.30 p.m., a prompt start could be made, and our return to school would be correspondingly early. Then a prompt start could be made for Winstanley Park, and more time could be spent there. It is always felt that the time there is too short, and as we have to leave at 9 p.m., the sooner we can get there the more time we have to enjoy ourselves.'

This was to be the last Field Treat for some time, as the following year the Field Treat was postponed for the duration of the War.

World War I

Britain became involved in World War I on 4 August 1914. Writing in the Parish Magazine in September 1914, John Woods said:

> The one absorbing topic in every mouth at this time is the terrible war which is now going on between nations who are considered to be in the forefront of the civilised and Christian world.
>
> That such a thing as this is possible in our day is a sad comment upon the passions of human nature.

ROLL OF HONOUR

PEMBERTON COLLIERY SCHOOL.

Old Boys who are serving King and Country.

Cavalry:

ASPINALL, ERNEST
    (Lancs. Hussars)
GLOVER, HUGH
    (Dragoon Guards).
LIVESEY, HEZEKIAH
    (Lancs. Hussars).

Royal Horse Artillery:

LOWE, HERBERT.
SHAW, JOSEPH.
WALSH, RICHARD
WYNN, JAMES.

Royal Field Artillery:

ALKER, EDWIN.
BANKS, WILLIAM H.
BELSHAW, ELIAS.
BELSHAW, HENRY.
BROWN, THOMAS.
BROXTON, JOHN
DUNCAN, DAVID W.
GRIMSHAW, MICHAEL.
HEATON, MOSES.
HEATON, RICHARD.
HEATON, STANLEY.
HEATON, THOMAS.
HEATON, WALTER.
HITCHEN, ELIAS
HITCHEN, JONATHAN.
HITCHEN, OSWALD.
HITCHEN, PETER
HOLLAND, HERBERT
HOOTON, THOMAS.
LEA, ARTHUR
NORMAN, WILLIAM.
OAKLEY, BENJAMIN.
SHAW, JAMES.
SHAW, RICHARD.
STATTER, JOSEPH
STATTER, RICHARD.
STRETTON, STEPHEN GEO
TABERNER, HARRY.
TOMLINSON, WILLIAM.
WINSTANLEY, THOMAS

Royal Engineers:

ACKERS, WALTER.
BIRKS, ALFRED.
CARTWRIGHT, HERBERT.
GREEN, WILLIAM
HEATON, ELIAS
HEATON, WALTER H
HITCHEN, JOHN W.
HITCHEN, THOMAS
LEA, JOHN W.
TAYLOR, JOSEPH R.

Grenadier Guards:

CHEETHAM, FRED.
CHEETHAM, THOMAS A.

Coldstream Guards:

ORMESHER, FRED.

Border Regiment:

ATHERTON, HENRY.
CARD, JAMES.
CHADWICK, HERBERT.
GRIMSHAW, ROBERT H.
HALLIWELL, HARRY.
PARKES, THOMAS.
RICHARDSON, THOMAS

King's Own (Liverpool) Regiment:

ALKER, ALFRED.
BURGOYNE, WILLIAM.
GEE, THOMAS
GREEN, JOHN.
LOWE, FREDERICK.
MAKINSON, WILLIAM.

Manchester Regiment:

ATHERTON, ROBERT.
BRYANT, RICHARD.
BROWN, THOMAS.
CHARNOCK, GEORGE L.
CHARNOCK, THOMAS H.
DICKINSON, THOMAS.
FAIRHURST, JAMES.
GLOVER, GEORGE.
GOULDING, JOHN J.
HALLIWELL, THOMAS.
HEATON, WILLIAM.
HENRY, CHARLES.
HILTON, ISAAC.
HUGHES, JOHN T.
JEPSON, HARRY.
RIMMER, WILLIAM.
SHAW, JOHN.
SHAW, THOMAS
STATTER, WILLIAM
TURNER, ARTHUR
WEBSTER, ALBERT
WINSTANLEY, WILLIAM

King's Royal Rifles:

BENNETT, FRANCIS.
HAMPSON, NORMAN
NOCK, SILAS.
STANLEY, JOHN.

Lancashire Fusiliers:

HARRISON, ARTHUR
HITCHEN, DANIEL.
PORTER, GEORGE E.
PORTER, JAMES A.
SMITH, FRED.
UNSWORTH, GEORGE.

Loyal North Lancs. Regiment:

BURGOYNE, JOSEPH.
HIGHTON, JOHN W.
TAYLOR, WILLIAM

South Lancs. Regiment:

HOLDING, GEORGE.

East Lancs. Regiment:

MOORCROFT, JAMES H.
MOORFIELD, HENRY.
MOORFIELD, MARK.

Royal Army Medical Corps.:

AYLES, ROBERT.
BLACKBURN, ROBERT D.
BLINSTON, RICHARD.
BURGESS, SYDNEY.
FOSTER, HERBERT.
HAMMOND, RICHARD.
JEPSON, THOMAS.
PARKES, WILLIAM.
SMITH, SAMUEL.
TRAVENA, WILLIAM.

———

BANKS, JOHN, K.O.Y.L.I.
BANNISTER, THOMAS, Royal Marine L.I.
GASKELL, PETER, Royal Navy.
HITCHEN, WILLIAM, Army Ordnance Corps.
LOWE, ARTHUR, Royal Flying Corps.
ORMESHER, HARRY, Army Service Corps.
SAMMONS, JOHN, Army Service Corps.
MEADOWS, FRED, 1st Canadian Expeditionary Force.

FEBRUARY, 1915.

J. W. BRIERLEY, HEAD MASTER.

ALBERT LEA, PRINTER, WIGAN.

Roll on Honour, 1915, containing the names of all those from the Parish who were serving in the Army and Navy.

Only in the cause of justice can the sword be rightly taken, and never in the course of our history has our nation taken the sword with a clearer conscience than she has in the present conflict.

Now that the conflict has commenced it is for us as a nation to see that our flag is not sullied by any deed of shame, and also that the matter be brought to a satisfactory conclusion as soon as possible. The flower of our manhood has gone forth, and great demands are made upon us to meet the urgency of the case. Many of us cannot go forth to the front, but we have our part to play none the less. In quietness and confidence shall be our strength; we must posses our souls in patience, and be ready to bear what burdens are put upon us. It is useless to expect that we shall escape the burden of sorrow and sacrifice, but the issue cannot fail for our national good. Our sacrifice at this time will win blessings for succeeding generations, even as we have enjoyed the fruits of our forefathers' sacrifices in bygone days. We must hope for the best and be prepared for the worst.

Need we say that we at home can wield a mighty power by prayer. Our God is the God of battles, and can save by many or by few. Let us fall in with the suggestion of the Chaplain-General of the Forces, and remember our soldiers and sailors daily in silent momentary prayer at 12 o'clock noon.

During the continuance of war, prayers and intercessions will be said in Church each Wednesday evening at 7, and each Friday evening at 8. Holy Communion will be administered each Friday morning at 8 o'clock. Half an hour thus spent will surely not be regarded as wasted time by any who know anything of the value of prayer. The call 'to arms' has been magnificent. Will the call 'to prayer' be unheeded?

A working party was arranged in the parish to provide Red Cross and Soldiers' Aid, and parcels of comforts for the troops were sent regularly, the money needed being raised by concerts and efforts in the parish. The parish was 'considerably enlivened' by the presence of some 800 Territorials camping in Winstanley Park, and companies attended services at Church from time to time. In December 1915, the Pemberton Colliery Volunteer Corps. attended service in Church.

An article in the February 1915 Parish Magazine asked for the names of all the men who had gone from the parish to swell the ranks of the army and navy. It was intended to keep a full roll of names and also a roll of all the boys who have passed through the day schools. This was published on a card in February 1915. A copy of this Roll of Honour was sent to Mr Williams, former Headmaster, who sent the following letter in reply:

It might afford some comfort to the parents and friends of the brave lads who have so loyally joined his Majesty's forces, if you would kindly insert a short paragraph in the May number of the Church Magazine, saying how proud and delighted their old schoolmaster is with their noble conduct, and how he hopes and prays for their safe return to their homes and families.

The Parish Magazine for January 1915 announced that this year would see the separation of the Goose Green district from our Parish. It was announced at the Annual Vestry meeting that the Little Lane Mission would be merged into the new Parish of St Paul's. Mr T. Hughes handed over an inventory of effects belonging to the Mission to the Vicar and Wardens. The Parish Magazine for June 1915 announced the Consecration of St Paul's as follows:

The Church of St Paul, Goose Green, will be consecrated on Saturday June 26th at 3 p.m. by the Bishop of Liverpool, and after certain legal preliminaries, a new parish will be assigned to it. Goose Green has only been part of our parish for a short time, and the workers there under Mr Buer are to be congratulated in so soon having a church built. We wish them well as they set forth as a parish, and we hope our people will try and be present at the consecration of the church and give them their support.

Sunday 4 July 1915 was the 21st Anniversary of the Dedication of the Church and it had been intended that great doings should mark the event, but owing to the war things were curtailed. Special services were held and the collections, amounting to £20 9s. 8d., a record, were allocated to a fund for a memorial to Colonel Blundell, the Donor of the Church.

An account of the Choir Trip which the boys had in 1915 was written by one of the choirboys, Arthur Stockley, and published in the October 1915 Parish Magazine as follows:

Our Choir Outing

On account of the war it was suggested that there should be no Choir Trip this year, and that the money should be devoted to the Red Cross Funds. About a fortnight before August our Choirmaster asked us would we like a trip to Rivington Pike and pay our own fares. It was agreed upon at once by all the boys. We paid our fares in advance to the choirmaster. It was decided that we should go on the Tuesday and meet at Wigan at 1.20 p.m. in order to catch the 1.30 p.m. train. Tuesday came and we all turned up and were soon in the train puffing along. Together with the Choir boys was the Choirmaster (Mr Harris), and Mr G. Topping a Choirman. We left Wigan on 'Chorley Bob' and Rivington Hills were soon in sight. The place where we had to get out was Adlington. When we got out we found that Joseph Parkes was without his cap. He had let it blow through the window just before we got to the station. It was soon replaced by one of our noted boys who had a spare cap in his pocket. We had been going along the road for a while when we came to a Church. The Church was not on the road side but it had a beautiful entrance. We went into the Church. It was a fairly big one and was clean and tidy. One thing we all noticed was a small harmonium which Mr Harris said was used for choir practice instead of the large organ. We made our way towards the Pike next. After walking, running and resting we came to the Barn which is at the bottom of the hills. Each boy had brought with him some lunch to eat when we got on the top. At the Barn we had 'drinks' and were refreshed for walking up the hill. There was a kind of race for who could get to the top first. William Taberner was the first to reach the top and Thomas Stockley arrived last amid the cheers of the other boys. We were all ready for our lunch when we got on the top and we enjoyed it very well. Most of us printed our initials on the old tower with a stone and a rusty nail. Of course we all tumbled and fell down the hill like comical Harry Livesey. We had a jolly good time in wrestling and playing about on the Pike. We all looked through Tom Hughes' field glasses. The first place to look for was St Matthew's Church, Highfield. I think we all found it. We started back for home about six o'clock. We all thought it was much easier coming down than going up. We did not come the same way back to Adlington, but came to Blackrod Station. We all had 'drinks' and sweets again at the bottom of the hill. We got along to the station so as to catch the 7.30 p.m. train to Wigan. None of us felt sorry for one of the number when he put his penny in the slot for biscuits and got none. The train came in and we soon left Rivington hills and came nearer home. When we got out at Wigan we remained on the same platform for the train to Pemberton. We had not been riding long before we came in sight of Highfield Church in front of the engine. I think we all enjoyed a fine day just as well as if we had been to the seaside for our Annual Choir Trip.

In November 1915, Miss L. Holland was appointed to the Headship of the Infant School. She was to become very involved in the work of the parish during the next forty years in the Day and Sunday Schools, with the Young People's Guild, and with the Church Missionary Society and the Parochial Church Council.

Memorials to Col. H. B-H-Blundell

The Memorial Fund to Colonel Blundell gained momentum during the next two years and in December 1916, a sale of work was organised which raised the magnificent sum of £166. At a parish meeting early in 1917 it was announced that the parish memorial would be a Reredos, and that Captain Cuthbert Blundell would give a stained glass East Window in memory of Colonel Blundell, his uncle. It was also decided at the same time to place two more stained glass windows in Church in memory of the late Revd John Wood and of Mrs Woods.

The Dedication of the memorials took place on Saturday 29 December 1917, and was recorded in the *Wigan Examiner*:

Another tribute of respect to the late Colonel Blundell was shown on Saturday at St Matthew's Church, Highfield, when a stained glass window and a new reredos were dedicated by the Bishop of Liverpool in the presence of a very large congregation; and also stained glass windows in memory of the late John Wood, for many years curate in charge, and to the late Mrs Woods, wife of the present Vicar. The Bishop was attended by the Vicar of St Matthew's (Revd John Woods), and the Vicar of Pemberton (Revd E. F. Forrest, MA) as his chaplains, and also by the Revs. A. E. Buer (St Paul's), E. J. Wood (Whiston), A. D. Smart (St Luke's) and A. White, (St James'). There was a full choir and Mr A. Harris presided at the organ. For his address, after the dedications, the Bishop selected as his text 1 Samuel 25:11 'And he said, Bring me up Samuel'. Referring to the work of Colonel Blundell, he said a good man was often missed and wanted after he was gone. Samuel had done a great many things in his time and confounded the Philistines. His people did not value him in his day as they ought to have done. The late Colonel was an ideal Christian gentleman, to whom Highfield owed so much. Would to God every man who employed people would care for them as he did. The beautiful church was built by him, so that they and their children, and their children's children might worship God, and the fact that his being asked to dedicate the window and the reredos proved that they missed the Colonel, and had great respect for him. Of the late Revd J. Wood, that dearly loved and lovely man of God, who was ever ready to comfort them in their hour of sorrow, and rejoice with them in their time of joy, the memorial was an appropriate token of their respect for the one who had laboured so long and successfully in that parish. Speaking of the late Mrs Woods, as the sweet young wife of the Vicar, who went down whilst it was yet day, he said they had done right in erecting that memorial, and hoped her life would be an incentive to others. Like Samuel they were all missed, and one day we shall meet them again, and be for ever with the Lord. They had put those beautiful memorials in the Church, and it would inspire them all to follow their example. Like Samuel their work was done; they were missed, and their works were now appreciated. The following are the details of the window and reredos;—The East Window—in memory of Colonel Blundell, has for its main subject 'The Ascension of Our Lord' with a group of apostles in the two side lights. Underneath the main subject are three scenes connected with the Resurrection viz. The Resurrection (centre), The first appearance to Mary (right), and the Scene at Emmaus (left). The aisle windows are in memory of 1. The Revd J. Wood, late curate in charge, and 2. Mrs Woods, wife of the present Vicar. The subjects being 'The Presentation.' and 'The Visitation.' respectively. The whole work has been carried out by Messrs J. Hardman and Co. of Birmingham. The reredos in memory of the late Colonel is from a design submitted by the architects of the church, Messrs Austin and Paley of Lancaster, and has been worked by Messrs Bridgeman and sons, of Lichfield. The design is Early English, in keeping with the architecture of the church. The material consists of yellow Hollington stone, with marble shafts and panels. The reredos, together with the window above, form a fitting memorial to him who built the church, and who in many directions was a generous benefactor to Pemberton. The inscriptions are: The Reredos. The reredos was erected to the glory of God and in grateful memory of Lieut. Colonel H. B. H. Blundell, CB, the donor of the church and generous benefactor to this district by the parishioners and friends. The East Window. To the Glory of God and in memory of Lieut. Colonel H. B. H. Blundell, CB 3rd Grenadier Guards who built this church the east window is erected by his nephew Cuthbert Blundell. Window to the Revd John Wood. This window was erected to the glory of God and in loving memory of the Revd John Wood MA, Curate in charge of this district, 1881 to 1908, by members of his family and parishioners. At rest June 14th 1911. Window to the late Mrs Woods: The above window was erected to the glory of God and in loving memory of Gertrude Dobson, wife of the Revd John Woods, M. A., the first Vicar of this Parish, by her husband and parishioners. At rest August 12th 1913. The dedication service was fully choral, and included an anthem, 'I love the habitations of the Lord', specially composed for the occasion by Mr P. Gilbody, Mus. Bach. of St Luke's, Orrell. After the service the congregation adjourned to the Girls School for the purpose of making a presentation to Captain Cuthbert Blundell in recognition of his interest and generosity to the church. The chair was occupied by the Revd John Woods, Vicar, and on the platform was the Bishop, Dr Chavasse. Captain Blundell was expected to be present but his military duties prevented him from attending. The Chairman, after a tribute of respect to the late Colonel Blundell, referred to the work of Captain Blundell in connection with the church, which was now a separate parish, and his gift of the East Window, and as the church was at last completed, it was considered a suitable occasion to show their gratitude to the Captain for his valuable assistance. He therefore asked the Bishop to present a silver rose bowl in the Captain's absence, to Mr E. Douglas, on their behalf. The Bishop said it was a special privilege to him to be allowed to hand the beautiful gift to Captain Blundell's representative, and also take the part he had in the dedication of the windows and reredos. Referring to a remark of the chairman as to the dusty aspect of the district, he said he had found the kindest of hearts and noblest men and women in that part of south-west Lancashire during an experience of nearly eighteen years. The people of Highfield were most generous, an evidence of that being that within forty eight hours of the presentation being sanctioned, the money was easily raised. It proved their respect for one to whom they were indebted in many respects. They all regretted his absence, but as a soldier it was his duty to do as he was told, and his duties were such as to necessitate his remaining at his post. As to his interest in the parish, the Captain had been responsible for the enlargement of the church, the new schools, the Vicarage, and an increased endowment for the Vicar, and of such a man they had every reason to be proud, and to thank God for his generosity. Concluding, the Bishop said: that with all my heart I ask Mr Douglas to accept for the Captain the silver rose bowl in our names. Mr Douglas, in accepting the present on behalf of Captain Blundell, said he had much pleasure in receiving it, and on behalf of the Captain thanked them for the beautiful gift. The chairman, in the name of the congregation, both of the church and of the presentation, thanked the Bishop for his service, the proceedings closing with the singing of the National Anthem. The inscription on the rose bowl was: 'Presented to Capt. C. L. H. Blundell by the congregation of St Matthew's, Highfield, as a slight token of gratitude for benefactions bestowed by him upon this parish. Christmas 1917.'

The Vicar offered himself for National Service in 1917 to the Bishop, but received the following reply: 'The best National Service you can perform is to look after the Parish of Highfield. It will more than fill your hands. You will be doing a good 'bit' for your country.'

Thomas Barton, who had been one of the first two Churchwardens died on 1 March 1918. The following Obituary appeared in the April Magazine:

We regret to say that we have lost by death one who for many years has been associated with Highfield Church. Mr Thomas Barton passed away on March 1. after a long illness, patiently borne. For some months past we have missed Mr Barton from our midst, as he was not able to get as far as the Church. His interest was maintained in Highfield doings up to the last. Mr Barton had a lot to do with the building of the Church, and it was fitting that when the parish was formed he should have been unanimously chosen as the first People's Warden. This position he held for two years, when failing health compelled him to give it up. Honest to a degree, painstaking in all he did, kindly in disposition, he has left behind him a good example, and we give thanks for his life. The sympathy of all goes out to the members of his family. A token of the respect in which he was held was seen in the large number of people who assembled at St John's Church on March 6th for the funeral service.

Outing on the Canal, 1918

Wartime in the parish was not all doom and gloom as the following report from the Parish Magazine for August 1918 shows:

A most enjoyable afternoon was spent by some of our girls on Saturday July 20th. They embarked on a boat on the Canal at Seven Stars Bridge at 2.30 p.m. and were soon on their way to Gathurst. The weather was good for the voyage, and on arrival tea was enjoyed in a field. Unfortunately rain came on as games, etc., were in progress. We went on board at 6-30, and the rain becoming much worse the shelter of a friendly bridge was commandeered and while it rained on either side we had games and songs in the boat. After an hour or so the rain ceased and the voyage was resumed, Seven Stars Bridge

The canal boat trip, July 1918, from Seven Stars Bridge to Gathurst. The pier-like overhead structure was probably part of the gantry which carried Lamb and Moore's Meadow pit coal trucks, one of the traditional explanations of the origins of Wigan Pier.

being reached at 9 o'clock. All reached home dry and safely and very tired, but it was worth it and a similar outing in the future was spoken of as we separated.

The Mayor of Wigan and Corporation made a visit to St Matthew's on Sunday 29th September. They were welcomed on what was the first occassion on which such a visit had been paid to the Church.

End of World War I

The end of the War was welcomed by the Vicar in the parish magazine in December. He said:

> The eleventh of November is a date which will be long remembered in history as the day when the armistice was signed by Germany and fighting in the great war ceased. The spirit of thankfulness was seen in the thousands who crowded our churches in the land during the week, and on Sunday the 17th. We are rightly proud of our victory, and feel that the King was right when he said that his strength throughout the war had been found in his faith in God and in confidence in his people.

After the war preparations were made to erect a suitable memorial to those who had given their lives and donations came in quickly for the 'Soldiers' and Sailors' Memorial

Fund'. A Welcome Home service and social was given by the members of the Bible Classes to soldiers and sailors from the parish on Saturday 3 May 1919. The Annual Field Day was revived on Saturday 5 July, and two bands; the Pemberton Old and the Standish Subscription Prize Band were engaged. The procession took the longer route via Spring Bank and Billinge Road. It was a real attempt to make up for the omissions of the past years in this first year of peace. There was also, later this month, another walking day for the official celebration of peace.

The Vicar, writing in the October 1919 magazine announced:

> The following information is given for the benefit of those who have reason to see the Vicar on any matter of business. He is generally at home each day at the following hours: Mornings until 10 a. m., noon from 12 until 2 p.m., evening 5 p.m. until 7 p.m. and after 9 p.m. Several people have called lately in the afternoon, but have been disappointed and have had to call again. From 2 p.m. until 5 p.m. the Vicar is generally out visiting, so this time should be avoided, unless it is only intended to leave a message. If requests for sick visiting can be sent before 10 a. m. it would be appreciated, and would help the Vicar in making his arrangements.

Before the Enabling Act of 1919, the government of the Church of England had been in the hands of the clergy. During the next thirty six years the laity were to be given more status in the councils of the Church. In 1920, Electoral Rolls were drawn up for the first time, ready for the first meeting of Electors which was held on the Thursday in Easter week 1920. This meeting decided that the following twelve members should be elected to the first Parochial Church Council: Mr James Berry, Misses Birchall, Holland and Taberner; Messrs G. Ashurst, J. Blinston, J. W. Brierley, A. Harris, G. Melling, R. Roby, Jas. Starkey, and E. Stretton. The *ex-officio* members were the Vicar, Churchwardens, and Miss Pattinson. Mr Richardson and Miss Pattinson were appointed representatives to the Diocesan and Ruri-decanal Conferences.

Parish War Memorials

The War Memorials to the fallen Sailors and Soldiers were unveiled and dedicated on 25 September 1920 as the following report in the *Wigan Observer* of the following Saturday tells:

> On Saturday afternoon the War Memorial at St Matthew's Church, Highfield, was unveiled by Major C. Blundell, OBE and dedicated by the Right Revd the Lord Bishop of Liverpool (Dr Chavasse). The memorial consists of a Tablet, containing the names of the 51 men from the church and parish who made the supreme sacrifice in the Great War, and also four memorial windows, which have been placed in the two double windows of the extended portion of the south side of the church. The subjects depicted on the windows are: 'The Noble Army of Martyrs Praise Thee' (2 windows); 'The Farewell of David and Jonathan'; and 'David's Lament over Jonathan.' This portion of the memorial has been beautifully executed by Messrs Hardman and Son, of Birmingham. The Tablet is made of alabaster, with an inlaid slab of marble, on which is inscribed the following:

This Tablet and the Four adjoining Windows are erected to the Glory of God, and in memory of the following Men from his Church and Parish, who gave their lives in the Great War, 1914–19.

Allen, James H. ; Anders, William; Ascroft, Harold; Atherton, George; Ball, Samuel; Ball, William; Banks, Albert N. ; Barton, John; Bayman, Henry B. ; Bilsbrough, Thomas; Burgoyne, Joseph; Burton, Richard; Card, James; Connor, Harold; Corless, James; Counsell, George; Dean, David; Dean, John W. ; Doran, Stephen; Eden, Joseph; Farrimond, George; Foote, Harold A.; Gerrard, Harry; Green, John; Hampson, Norman; Heaton, Elias; Hodgetts, Samuel; Holland, Herbert; Holland, Joseph; Jackson, Tom; Jepson, Harry; Johnson, Harold; Liptrot, William; Liptrot, Syney H. ; Lowe, Thomas; Monks, Harry; Parkes, Herbert; Parkinson, Thomas; Peet, Peter; Powell, Edward H. ; Rowbottom, William; Rylance, Richard; Stordy, William B. ; Stretton, Stephen G. ; Taberner, William H. ; Taberner, Herbert S. ; Webster, Vincent; White, Joseph; Winstanley, William.

Until the Day Dawn!

The tablet was supplied and installed by Messrs Whippell and Co., of Exeter and London.

In addition to the Revd J. Woods, MA (Vicar), the following: clergy were also in attendance upon the Bishop: Revs. A. E. Buer (St Paul's, Goose Green), A. P. Miller (St Mark's, Newtown), C. R. Slee (St Thomas's, Wigan), A. Smart (Orrell), A. White (St James's, Poolstock), and F. Millward (Liverpool).

The Bishop selected for his text the 11th Chapter of the Epistle to the Hebrew's, part of the 4th verse: 'He being dead yet speaketh.' His Lordship said that on Waggon Hill, outside Ladysmith, there stood a memorial to the memory of the men who fell on that spot fighting for their country. Upon that memorial was inscribed the words: 'Tell England all ye that pass by that we who died to save her, rest here content.' That afternoon a tablet and windows had been unveiled and dedicated to the memory of their 51 brave men who went out, fought, and fell for their country. They could not help but mourn them, they longed for 'the touch of the vanished hand, and the sound of the voice that was still.' The memory of those men often came back to their relatives and friends, and it filled their hearts with sadness, and even when they thought of those men resting with their Lord, the time seemed long before they would meet them again. They had given their lives for others, they had followed their Lord in the path of self-sacrifice; and 'greater love hath no man than this, that a man lay down his life for his friends.' They were reaping today in their Lord's presence the reward of their self-sacrifice. He thought that there came from them to all of us three voices. Being dead, they yet speaketh. They cry: 'Follow us on the path of self-sacrifice.' Many of them at one time never thought that they would wear uniform and be soldiers, but when the call came, however strong the ties that bonded them to their homes, they went forward on the path of self-sacrifice in response to the call of their country. How great was that self-sacrifice many of those present know better than he did. Was there no danger now that the war was over, and things were becoming normal. There was the danger that people were living merely to make money or to have a good time, and were forgetting the noble sacrifice of their fallen heroes. He thought that at a time like the present, they called upon them with a voice not to be forgotten to rise up and follow those who had glorified their nation, and not to lose the victory in the days of peace by forgetting the lesson which had been taught.

The second voice which called was to carry on the work, thereby not letting them die in vain. At present they did not seem to have reaped as they had hoped to reap of the fruits of the great victory which had been won. The whole world seemed out of joint. The financial world was in confusion, and men did not know what was going to happen. Their dead on occasions like that called upon them to step in and carry on their work, not by spending wastefully their increased wages but by economy and by doing their very best to help their country in her day of financial need. The industrial world was out of joint, and once more they called upon their friends to step in and not allow them to be robbed of the fruits of their labours. He urged them to do their utmost to do a fair days work for a good days wage. They should do as the Belgian working men were doing, and put forth their full strength to help their country by their hard and honest work. The moral world seemed out of joint and they cried out that they must not let the country be ruined by impurity which had ruined great empires of old. If they would exercise economy, put their whole heart in their work, produce as much as they could, and live pure and whole lives then they would be responding to the call of those who had gone, and they would be carrying on the work which had been left.

Lastly they should care for the men who had been wounded and blinded—comrades who had come back with their lives but had left behind them their sight and perhaps one or more limbs. They should care for the fatherless, the orphans, and they should comfort the parents who had been left behind. The dead called upon them to get work or to give work to those who had come home and had no work waiting for them. The question was a national one and they should bring to bear upon those in authority all the pressure they could with a view to work being provided for those who had given their best for their country and were now in need. They were pledged as men and women of honour as well as Christians, to do their best to help these men. Those were some of the voices which came to them that day, and he urged them all to follow the examples of self-sacrifice and to carry on the work which had fallen from the lifeless hands of the men whom they were commemorating by the unveiling and dedication of the windows and tablet.

The October 1920 Parish Magazine contained the following Obituary to Mr William Williams:

There passed to his rest on September 26th, Mr W. Williams, late Headmaster of the Schools and Organist at the Church. For 17 years he occupied these positions, and only resigned in September, 1913, on reaching superannuation age. During those years many boys passed through his hands, and he will be remembered by many. Mr Williams was always courteous and gentlemanly, and fulfilled his duties regularly and with acceptation. On retirement he resided at Bolton and was seldom seen in Pemberton, but the School and Church, and people of Pemberton had a warm place in his heart, and his thoughts were often with them. Only a few weeks before his death he sent a very affectionate letter to the members of the Bible Class, of which he had been teacher for so long. We are glad that his closing years were spent in quietness and in the unbroken company of his wife, who passed away a little while ago. The funeral took place on the 29th September, at Bolton.'

The parish was in the middle of a coal strike in November 1920, but in spite of the hardship this must have involved, it was decided to replace the gas lighting in the Church, which was considered 'of a very inferior character', by electricity, which was considered 'more convenient, cleaner and more satisfactory'. The Entertainment Committee took it in hand to raise the necessary amount of money, and started by presenting a sketch entitled 'Proof'. Tickets were to be obtained from Mr W. Atherton, the Secretary, and from members of the Committee.

At the September 1922 meeting of the Parochial Church Council, a Letter of Condolence was sent to the family of the late Mr Richard Atherton Southworth. Mr Southworth was People's Warden from 1914 until his death. Before that he had been a sidesman since 1894. In the 1881 Census he was described as a Coal Agent. Donald Anderson remembers him as 'a pretty tall man. I think that this was the man who was valet to Meyrick Bankes (who died in 1881)'. Mr James Starkey was elected People's Warden to fill the vacancy at the next meeting of the Vestry on 9 April 1923.

Electric lighting was first used in Church on 2 September 1923. A commemorative plaque still remains in the choir vestry recording the fact that the lighting was installed by the Corlett Electrical Engineering Company in 1923 and paid for by the efforts of the Dramatic Society.

New graveyard consecrated

The new Burial Ground at Highfield was consecrated on Saturday 8 September 1923 by Bishop Chavasse. The 1923 Bazaar Handbook says:

> It was fitting that this should be the last occasion on which Dr Chavasse visited the parish, for he had performed all episcopal duties here from the consecration of the church

Dedication of the graveyard, 1923. Mr Arthur Harris and the Choir lead the procession from the graveyard while the Bishop and Clergy, having finished the ceremony, wait to follow back to the Church.

until the present time, and as he goes into well-earned retirement he leaves this parish practically complete for all purposes.

The Consecration was reported in the *Wigan Observer*:

A further development of the Parish of St Matthew's, Highfield, took place on Saturday, when the Right Revd Dr Chavasse, the Lord Bishop of Liverpool, consecrated a portion of land attached to the church for the purposes of a new burial ground. The land, containing about 7,105 square yards, has been given by Major Cuthbert Blundell, OBE, one of the patrons of the living, who has also promised to provide trees and shrubs for the improvement of the site. For some weeks past some of the members of the Young Men's Bible Class and others have been preparing the land for Saturday's function.

A large congregation assembled to join in the Consecration Ceremony. The Lord Bishop was attended by the Revd J. Woods (Vicar), and the Revd A. White (Rector of Golborne) as chaplains, the other clergy included Revd T. A. E. Davey (St Mark's, Newtown), Revd A. D. Smart (St Luke's, Orrell) and Revd J. H. Preston (St Stephen's, Whelley). Amongst others present were Major Blundell, the Mayor and Mayoress of Wigan (Councillor and Mrs J. M. Ainscough), Mr E. Douglas, Mr T. H. Arden (Diocesan Registrar), and Messrs W. Richardson and Jas. Starkey (Churchwardens).

The petition for consecration was presented to the Bishop at the entrance to the ground by the Revd J. Woods, and the Bishop, preceded by the wardens and Registrar, and followed by the clergy, choir and congregation, walked round the site, the appointed psalms being chanted by the choir, under the leadership of Mr A. Harris, organist and choirmaster. The deed of consecration having been read by the Registrar, prayers were said by the Bishop, and the declaration of consecration was pronounced. The whole company then formed into a procession and entered the church, where an address was given by the Bishop in his usual clear and instructive manner.

In the course of his remarks, his Lordship pointed out the meaning of the service. No special virtue had been imparted to the soil by what had been done. A three-fold act had been performed—symbolic, legal and devotional. By proceeding round the ground the people had symbolised their taking possession of it for its sacred purpose. The reading of the consecration deed and declarations of consecration placed the site under the protection of English law for all time, that it might be kept from all profane and common uses, and used only as God's acre for receiving the bodies of the dead. The prayers used contained words of warning, comfort and trust. The concluding portion of the address partook of the nature of a farewell, and many were greatly touched as the Bishop spoke of the impending resignation of his work.

After the service many people waited for the Bishop to leave the church, and he remained for some time shaking hands and giving final words of blessing.

On Sunday afternoon, a special feature was the repetition, as far as possible, of the consecration service for the members of the Sunday schools who had not had the opportunity of being present at the ceremony of the day before. A procession was formed in similar manner, led by the Vicar, choir, wardens and sidesmen, and the scholars in the following order: Infants, Girls, and Boys' Schools. The Vicar addressed the members of the Sunday schools from the vestry steps, and impressed upon them that the ground was consecrated, and must be held sacred as the church itself, and that the site must not be used as a playground or treated in any way in an irreverent manner.

A Grand Bazaar, 1923

The land for the graveyard had been given by Major Cuthbert Blundell who also promised to provide trees and shrubs for planting. It was necessary to build boundary walls and fences, to drain the land, make suitable paths and provide a fund to keep the burial ground in good order. With this object in mind a Grand Bazaar was held in the Girls' and Infants' schools on Wednesday, Friday and Saturday, 10, 12 and 13 October 1923 at 3 p.m. each day. A sixty-two page Official Handbook and Guide was sold which contained the Objects of the Bazaar, a plan of the stalls in the school, a Brief History of the Church in Highfield, which is the earliest written history of the parish, the programme of events for each day, details of stalls and of the Grand Cafe which provided Teas from 4.30 p.m. and Cooked Suppers at 8 p.m. There were also Entertainments each evening at 7 p.m. and 8 p.m. There were competitions and sideshows and the Bazaar Regulations (Strictly Enforced) were as follows:

1. Coming into the Bazaar without paying is forbidden, but paying without coming in is permitted.
2. No charge is made for going out, but if anyone wishes to pay something it will not be refused.
3. There is no limit to the number of articles which may be bought, provided that the purchaser can pay for them.
4. Nobody is compelled to take change on payment for goods, although it will be tendered, when necessary.
5. Any article not deemed suitable after it is paid for, may be given back to the Bazaar without any extra charge.
6. Babies in arms are not admitted alone.
7. Visitors are advised not to leave the Bazaar with money in their pockets. They can then return home with the happy consciousness that they have nothing to lose.
8. Grumbling, fault-finding, and offence-taking strictly prohibited.
9. Those friends who could have improved on the Bazaar, and desire to do so, must write to the Secretary, enclosing an application fee of £5 (or more)—not returnable.

The Official Opening of the Bazaar on the first day was reported in the *Wigan Observer*:

> Having recently had a new burial ground consecrated adjoining St Matthew's Church, Highfield; the parishioners have made a very praiseworthy attempt to raise funds to maintain the ground and its surroundings in a proper state. With this object in view a three days bazaar opened on Wednesday last week, and the amount aimed at was £600. Judging by the well-filled stalls in the schoolroom and the exceptionally large attendance at the opening ceremony, the promoters seem likely to attain their objective. As a matter of fact, the first day's proceedings realised the handsome figure of £373. The land comprising the new burial ground comprises 7,105 square yards, and has been generously

given to the parish by Major Cuthbert Blundell, O. B. E., who has also kindly promised to provide trees and shrubs for planting therein. The proceeds from the bazaar will be used for building walls, additional palisading, draining the land, making suitable main paths, laying out of grounds, and keeping it in decent order.

The Revd Arthur Longden, MC, vicar of St John's, Pemberton, presided, and supporting him were the Mayor and Mayoress (Councillor J. M. Ainscough, JP, and Mrs Ainscough), the Revd J. Woods, (Vicar), Mr James Starkey, (People's Warden), Mr George Ashurst, and Mr Wm. Richardson (Hon. secretary and treasurer).

The numerous stalls were in charge of the various organisations of the Church and Sunday Schools, and were as follows: Sewing Stall; Crockery Stall; Handkerchief Stall; Men's Bible Class Stall; Women's Bible Class Stall; Cake Stall; Refreshment Stall; and Pound Stall. Mrs Gaskell of Orrell was the Palmist, and Messrs Phillips and Son of Wigan, had generously given a Perfumery Stall; and Mrs Pigott of Burscough, a Flower Stall.

In opening the proceedings, the Revd A. Longden remarked that although it was pretty well known he was not in favour of bazaars, he had pleasure in accepting the invitation, because he felt it was a privilege that the Vicar of the Mother Church should take the chair on the opening day. It was a pleasure to him even though the provision of their burial ground was depriving him of a large source of income in fees. He however, felt it only right and proper that a church should have round about it a place of rest for the bodies of those who had identified themselves with that church during their lifetime. (Hear, Hear) After all, it was only right that those who had worshipped all their lives in a church could have their mortal remains laid to rest close by their church, and he was delighted to see from the handbook that it was the desire to raise sufficient money for the upkeep of what they always knew as God's Acre. Nothing gave him greater sorrow in connection with the erection of the church of St John's, Pemberton than that through sheer force of circumstances their churchyard had been laid out in such a manner that it could not be kept as he should like to see it, viz., as a real garden. For that reason he hoped and prayed that in connection with the new burial ground at Highfield it would be possible to so lay it out that it might always be kept decently and be beautiful to look upon, and at the same time be a credit to the church. (Hear, Hear.) He brought with him the good wishes of the whole of the parish of St John's. (Applause).

The Mayoress

The Mayoress, who was the recipient of a beautiful bouquet of flowers, said she was very pleased to have been able to come to their bazaar, especially seeing it was for such a very good cause. As their dear Bishop had said to them in his closing words at the consecration ceremony, she hoped they would always keep it nice and beautiful, and that, she was sure, would always be their endeavour. She had great pleasure in opening the bazaar, and expressed the hope they would more than realise what they aimed at. (Applause.)

The Revd J. Woods, in proposing a vote of thanks to the Mayoress for so graciously opening the bazaar, said he did so with additional pleasure, because Mrs Ainscough so readily accepted their invitation. It was a great encouragement to the organisers of the bazaar when those to whom they wrote for help replied so readily and heartily as the Mayoress did. (Applause.) He added that he was glad of the opportunity of thanking the patrons who had sent them subscriptions, and those who had already done a great deal towards making the present effort a big success. (Hear, Hear.) They were delighted to have the Mayor and Mayoress amongst them, because with the exception of the consecration ceremony the other week that was the first time they had been favoured with the visit of a representative of the civic authority of the town. When he first came to Pemberton, nearly fifteen years ago, they were enjoying a preferential rate. Now that had gone, to their sorrow (Laughter.) In those days he often wondered what the municipal authorities did with the money they got in rates, and he was told they in Pemberton had got a preferential rate and could not ask for much more. Now that they were part of the borough, he really thought they were getting a little bit more attention, and it was only right they should ask the Mayoress to come down and give them a good send-off. (Applause.)

Mr Starkey, in seconding, also extended a hearty welcome to the Mayoress, and said they were all pleased to see her among them. He also paid a deserving tribute to the energetic way in which the parishioners had worked for the bazaar, and hoped when the churchyard was completed it would be a credit to everyone concerned. (Applause.)

The Mayoress briefly returned thanks.

Speech by the Mayor

The Mayor remarked that it was always a pleasure to help those who were attempting to help themselves, and he could honestly say that appeared to be the case at Highfield, for although he had been attending bazaars in this district for a good many years now, he did not remember an opening day at a bazaar when the room was so well filled from end to end. The people of Highfield were evidently determined to help themselves in that matter, and they deserved the help of others outside. After all a churchyard was an inside matter, and one for the parishioners themselves to deal with. They were now connected with the Borough of Wigan, and there would come a time, not far distant, when Wigan would have to make further provision for the burial of the dead. It might be some years hence, and by constructing their own burial ground the people of Highfield were further delaying the arrival of that day. Now that they were part of the enlarged Borough, and, as Mr Woods had remarked, were paying an enlarged rate, he hoped it would cause them to take a deeper and more serious interest in the government of the town. (Hear, Hear.) Turning to the object of the bazaar the Mayor said he noticed from the handbook that the text for the day was in the words of St Paul, Let all things be done decently and in order. It was an excellent text for them, and he also recalled that when the Bishop of Liverpool consecrated their burial ground almost his last words to them were an appeal that they should keep the place in order, so that it might be a pleasure to them when they walked in on week-day or Sunday to see that the graves were decently kept. (Hear, Hear.) There were many churchyards in the district, some of which were not always kept as he would like to see them. He was connected with one of the oldest churches in the district, which had a very large burial ground, and he knew the difficulties connected with it. He also knew Mr Longden's difficulties. Sixty years ago there were such a thing a church rates, and churchwardens could go and get money from the rates to keep the churchyard in decent order. It was not always done, but the money was there if they were willing to do the work. There were no church rates now, so there were no moneys for the upkeep of churchyards beyond the fees which were charged at burials, and any efforts such as that which the congregation might make. He (the Mayor) therefore sincerely hoped that the necessary money would be raised by that bazaar, and that there would be a sufficient sum left for an endowment for upkeep apart from any question of fees. In conclusion, the Mayor proposed a vote of thanks to the Vicar of Pemberton, and in doing so remarked that knowing the determination of Mr Longden

A page from Mr Magraw's Choirboys' register, 1927, showing twenty-one boys with 100 per cent attendance at all services and practices.

Pemberton Colliery, 1929, showing the large complex of operations which dominated the district of Highfield.

in education and other matters, he would not let the people of St John's parish rest until there was an improvement in the churchyard there. (Laughter and Applause.)

Mr G. Ashurst seconded, and said he would like to take the opportunity of thanking those ladies and gentlemen who had so successfully completed their work, viz., those who had been selling thrift tickets. They had been placed under his charge, and he thanked them most sincerely for the work they had done during the past four or five months. The amount of tickets sold was over £160. (Applause.)

The Chairman replied, and the proceedings concluded.

There were numerous side-shows and amusements which were thoroughly enjoyed throughout the day.

In 1924 the PCC decided to hold the Annual Tea Party and Concert ' as in pre-war days'. People bought 'Trays' which were donations to the funds, guaranteeing a table and meal and a reserved seat at the Concert. Admission to Tea and Concert was either 1/6d or 2/– (7½p or 10p) Admission to Concert only was 1/– (5p).

In 1925 Mr Arthur Harris was appointed to the Headship of St Michael's School, Wigan, where he also became Organist and Choirmaster. He left Highfield at the end of the Summer Term. He had been Organist and Choirmaster at Highfield for twelve years and had established an excellent choral tradition. He is still spoken well of by past choristers who were boys in his choir. Mr Joel Magraw, another Chester College trained teacher was appointed to the staff of the boys' school in Mr Harris's place. He was to remain at Highfield as Organist and Choirmaster for the next twenty-six years, and carried on many of the traditions of Mr Harris, including the annual choirboys' camp at Chester College.

A Grand Concert was given in the Parochial Hall on Wednesday 20 January 1926 at 7.30 p.m. by the Orrell Y.M.C.A. Amateur Orchestral Society and St Matthew's Choir, conducted by Mr Joel Magraw, in aid of the Choir Boys' Fund. Included in a full and varied programme the Orchestra played the Overture 'Il Tancredi' by Rossini and other selections. The Choirboys sang 'The Shepherd's Dance' by Edward German. Mr A. Stockley, Tenor, and Mr J. Starkey, Bass, sang solos, and the Choir and Orchestra together ended the Concert with 'Land of Hope and Glory' by Elgar—Highfield's own Promenade Concert in 1926 !!

1926 was the year of the General Strike, which affected the Coal Industry as much as any other. The 1927 Annual General Meeting minutes say: 'Little work required of the Council last year due to the Coal Stoppage', and yet work had to go on in the parish—no doubt John Woods was involved helping his parishioners who were badly affected by the strike, as much as he could. Sally Gaskell remembers Soup Kitchens in the Parish Hall and at Pony Dick during this time.

The old Dossal Frame which carried the curtains behind the altar, and which was no longer needed since the erection of the new Reredos, was given to the new church of St Luke, Orrell, for similar use.

John Woods' father died at the end of 1926, and the Church Council expressed the Condolences of the Parish.

At the 1929 Vestry Meeting, Mr Jas. Starkey resigned, owing to ill-health, and Mr Isaac Massey was appointed People's Warden in his place.

1930 marked the beginning of Guiding in the Parish. The Company was first registered on 26th February 1930 as the '1st Wigan West', with Miss Kathleen G. Woods, the Vicar's daughter as captain, and Miss B. Green as Lieutenant. The Women's Meeting was also founded in the same year.

Revd J. Woods celebrates 21st Anniversary

The Revd John Woods had now been in the Parish for twenty one years, and this anniversary was celebrated on Sunday 2 February 1930. At the evening service he preached to a crowded congregation form the text John 4: 37 & 38,

> One soweth and another reapeth. I sent you to reap that whereon ye bestowed no labour; other men laboured, and ye are entered into their labours'. He spoke on continuity of work in the Church, and gave a review of work in the parish, based on the history of the parish in the 1923 bazaar handbook. He ended by quoting the following statistics concerning his twenty one years ministry in the parish. During that time there had been 1,420 baptisms, 1,049 confirmations, 676 weddings and 204 funerals.

In the March 1930 parish magazine John Woods wrote:

> My dear friends, February 2nd will be remembered by me as long as memory lasts. I cannot adequately express my feelings of gratitude for the wealth of affection which was poured out then, and since, on the occasion of my 'coming of age' amongst you. The early Communion was an inspiration with so many present, and the attendance at the other services of the day were very gratifying. The day ended with the wonderful crowd in the Parochial Hall. The spirit of the celebration has touched me deeply. This found its concrete expression in the generous presentation which was made. To all who subscribed and to those who spoke so appreciatively of my work, I can only say again 'thank you'. If the spirit manifested at this time can be maintained and increased, there is no saying what can be accomplished in the parish in the days to come. On my study shelf there now stands a very handsome clock which was presented to me by the Cubs and Girl Guides on the occasion of the enrolment of the Guides. This will always be treasured by me, coming as it does from another generation of young folk. A man's usefulness continues so long as he can keep a youthful mind, and this gift is evidence that I have not yet lost that touch with youth which is so necessary in the work of a parish. For this I am truly thankful. With friendship and fellowship made stronger by reason of the experiences of the past, may we all go forward to accomplish what we can in the days which are still left for us in this life. I remain,
> Yours sincerely, J. WOODS.

John Woods had worked on his own in a very busy parish. He had a curate for a short time in Revd A. E. Buer, who became Vicar of St Paul's in 1915. In 1932 Mr J. W. Brierley, Head of the Boys' School was licensed as a Lay Reader to the Parish. He was to become a well-loved and valuable leader and adviser to the parish for the next thirty years.

The Women's Meeting, early 1930s.
Back row: Mrs Parkinson; Mrs Atherton; Mrs Lyon; Miss Pattinson;
Mrs Davies; Mrs S. Heaton.
Middle row: Mrs Halsall; Mrs Heaton; Mrs Mawdsley; Mrs Nicholson;
Mrs Ackers; Mrs Heaton; Mrs Heaton; Mrs Barton; Mrs Hall.
Front row: Mrs Tither; Mrs Heaton; Ada Wilcocks; Mrs Gray; Mrs Prior;
Mrs Bimson; Mrs Eden.

New Boys' School, 1932

As a result of the Haddow Report of 1927, the system of Education was being re-organised. This meant the conversion of the Pemberton Colliery Schools into Infants, Junior Mixed, and Senior Boys' Schools. A new Senior Girls' School was provided at St Mark's, Newtown. Major Blundell undertook to make the necessary alterations to the old boys' school and provide additional rooms to preserve Church teaching in Highfield. Plans were submitted to the Board of Education but the scheme was rejected owning to the restricted site. Major Blundell told Revd J. Woods and Mr Brierley that he was determined to preserve the schools at Highfield for Church teaching if they were the last schools in England. By transferring the Infant children to the Boys' school and giving land behind and around the Infants' school on which considerable extensions could be made, and also providing space for school gardens and playing field, he more than met the requirements of the Board. He even told the Managers to instruct the architect to make all rooms larger than then required by the Board, to meet any further requirements for floor space. One of His Majesty's Senior Inspectors told Mr Brierley that the position of Highfield Schools was unique in his experience. He knew of no other case where a private individual had taken similar action and was prepared to do so much for a Church School. The Opening Ceremony on Monday, 19 September 1932 at 3 p.m. was recorded in the *Wigan Observer* as follows:

> The new Senior Boys' Department of the Highfield Church of England Schools was formally opened on Monday by Major C. L. B. H. Blundell, OBE, and hallowed by the Right Revd the Lord Bishop of Liverpool (Dr David) in the presence of a large and representative assembly. The Bishop and Major Blundell, accompanied by the Mayor (Councillor W. A. Hipwood) were escorted from the vicarage to the church (school) by clergy and representatives of the Wigan Education Authority, and they were given a rousing reception by the large crowd which thronged the main school hall. In addition to the Bishop, Major Blundell, and the Mayor, others on the platform were Canon C. C. Thicknesse (Rector of Wigan), Revd A. E. Buer (Goose Green), Revd A. D. Smart (Orrell), Revd A. Hope Johnson (Pemberton), Revd A. White (Golborne), Revd J. Woods (Highfield), Alderman J. McCurdy (chairman of the Wigan Education Author- ity), Alderman J. Cavey, JP (chairman of the Elementary Sub-Committee), Councillor J. Wilcox (vice-chairman of the Wigan Education Authority), Mr L. R. Missen (Director of Education), Mr H. Unwin (architect), Mr I. Massey (builder), Mr W. Richardson (vicar's warden), and Mr G. H. Potter.

Separate Senior Boys' Department

Since 1867, the educational facilities of the parish of Highfield have been gradually improved and extended, chiefly owing to the generosity of the Blundell family, and this year a scheme has been carried out to provide a separate senior boys' department. It is fully equipped for boys from eleven to fourteen years of age, and is complete with class, craft, handwork, and science rooms which have been completely furnished by the Education Authority in the most up-to-date manner. There is accommodation for two hundred and seventy senior boys. The Bishop hallowed and set apart the school for its sacred purposes, and then led the assembly in prayer.

Bishop's Address

Following the singing of the Doxology, Dr David said that according to their good custom they had thanked God for an achievement which marked almost the last stage of their great Wigan enterprise in education. They had nearly secured what they desired for every Wigan child, namely, the chance of being trained, and spending the whole of that training in a school where the faith of Christ was the central thing, and being taught by those who themselves believed it and lived by it. And that desire, the Bishop said, is not merely loved by the leaders of the church in Wigan, it is shared by the people themselves. Parents have remembered in their own experience, and have proved in the experience of their children the value in life of that teaching and that training, and they have made immense sacrifices in order to secure it here. They have realised that nowadays, when people want something very much, they have to provide it for themselves. We shall never get all we want out of the State. It would be a very bad thing for us and the State if we could. The time is passing when we can look for much to be done for the Church, and all its works as used to be done by the gifts of the few. But, thank God that here that time has not altogether passed; there are still, and I think there will always be, men moved by their affection for Church and people to acts of generous and timely help. Certainly we have had large experience of such acts in Wigan, and especially, as most of you know, in Highfield. (Applause). It is the express wish of our present benefactor that we should not be too careful to acknowledge in words today or at any other time what he has done for us here and for Wigan. And that wish only increases, in our eyes, the value of his gift, because it shows the spirit in which that gift was made. He is content with that silent gratitude, which will belong to the memory of this benefaction for many years to come, of those who shall here grow in Christian learning and Christian life, and to God in praise. (Applause).

The Mayor of Wigan, in calling upon Major Blundell to open the school, said, Major Blundell, the people of this district give you welcome. We remember with gratitude the benefactions which you and the Blundell family have bestowed upon this place, and specially thank you for this latest gift. I ask you in the name of this company to declare this school open.'

Major Blundell Performs the Opening Ceremony

Major Blundell, in opening the school, said it was very kind of the Bishop of Liverpool and the Mayor of Wigan to say such nice things about his family, and what they had tried to do for the Church of England education in Pemberton. Their thanks, as managers of that school, were also due to the architect for so ably designing it, and the contractors for so expeditiously building the necessary extensions to make that Senior School. The local education department had helped tremendously by producing the most up-to-date furnishings and equipment for the school, and with such punctuality that not a day had been lost in getting the work done. 'With the religious teaching under the eyes of our Vicar,' he said in conclusion, 'and the teachings in the hands of Mr Brierley, I can only say that so far as I can see we have nothing but confidence in the future of this school.' (Applause.)

The Revd J. Woods declared that as Vicar of the parish, he desired to extend to Major Blundell the thanks of the parents, the present scholars, and the scholars of the future, for his great benefaction, and as a commemoration of that ceremony he handed to Major Blundell a fountain pen as a small memento from the architect.

After the singing of the National Anthem, the new department was inspected.

During the winter of 1934–5 the Graveyard was drained and the paths were covered with tarmacadam and kerbed. At the February 1935 meeting of the Parochial Church Council a vote of thanks was proposed to Mr W. H. Roby for his work in connection with the project.

The Church Lads' Brigade, 1935, with the Vicar and Col. J. W. Holmes TD, and officers 2nd Lieutenant T. Clancy in charge and 2nd Lieutenant W. Nock, assistant.

Church Lads' Brigade formed

Five years after the Guide Company was formed for girls in the parish, a Church Lads' Brigade Company was formed for boys. The Brigade was in charge of Lieutenant T. Clancy, with Second Lieutenant W. Nock as assistant. The first parade was held on Sunday 30 June 1935. The Parish Magazine records the ceremony as follows:

> Despite showery weather the ceremony of enrolling and parading our newly-formed Company of the C.L.B. was well attended. The Enrolment Service, though simple in form, was impressive, and the erect and smartly uniformed men of the visiting Companies, together with our own Company, added much to the dignity of the occasion.
>
> The address, of necessity brief, was very appropriate and much appreciated by those present. We hope that our boys will frequently ponder the thoughts put before them so that when problems arise—as they often do—involving the question of Right and Wrong, and demand a decision, the will to right action will be strengthened.
>
> After the service the Companies, under the command of Col. Holmes, TD, 'fell in' to parade. This called forth much interest all along the route. We should like to see that interest put into terms of respect for, and encouragement of, the boys in their efforts to

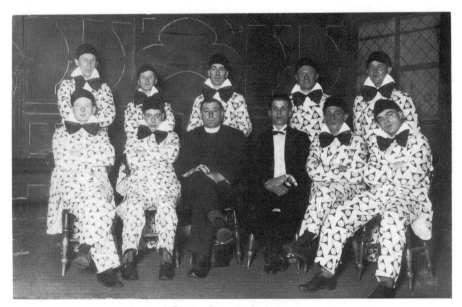

A Concert Party in the late 1930s.
Back row: ? Ashcroft; Bert Stretton; Mr Magraw, Organist; Cyril Prior; Bert Sharrock.
Front row: Tom Derbyshire; Hary Berry; Revd John Woods, Vicar; Harry Stretton; Jimmy
Jones; Noland Lowe.

cultivate Fellowship and Loyalty in Church life. This is what the Church Lads' Brigade stands for, and what its members strive to achieve. T. H.

In 1936 Mr Joel Magraw, Music Teacher in the Boys' School and Organist and Choirmaster, was appointed to the Headship of St James' Junior School at Worsley Mesnes, but continued as Organist and Choirmaster at Highfield.

In the same year the Young People's Union—the Junior Branch of the Church Missionary Society—held an outing to Ashurst's Beacon, Up Holland. The outing was described in the *Wigan Observer* as follows:

Fifty-five children of five to fourteen years of age, members of the Young People's Union of St Matthew's, Highfield, were entertained to an enjoyable picnic at Ashurst's Beacon, on Saturday. It is hoped to make the picnic an annual event. The children were in charge of Mrs J. Miller (General Secretary.), Miss S. Gaskell, Miss Taberner, Miss Marion Jarvis, Miss Holland and Miss Lily Allen. Mr William Miller and Mr Syd. Williams also helped in the supervision. The Party travelled by motor buses to Upholland Monument, and from there walked to the Beacon. Picnic baskets were taken and an excellent meal provided beneath the shadow of the Beacon. Games were organised. The return journey was started soon after 7 o'clock. St Matthew's Young People's Union has been in existence about twelve months, and under enterprising leadership has made great progress. It is a junior organisation of the Church Missionary Society.

Young People's Union outing to Ashurst's Beacon in 1936.

Death and Funeral of Revd John Woods

At the Annual Parochial Meeting held on 21 April 1936, owing to the Vicar's illness, the chair was taken by Mr Wm. Richardson. A Vote of sympathy was sent to the Vicar, but sadly this was the beginning of the end. At the next meeting of the PCC held on 29 September, Mr Richardson announced that the Vicar had died the previous night after a long illness. It was the Vicar's wish for his ashes to be buried in the sanctuary of the church which he had loved and served. Arrangements were made to fulfil his wishes and the funeral took place on Friday 2 October at 2.30 p.m. The service was reported by the *Wigan Observer*:

Affecting tributes to the late Revd John Woods, first Vicar of Highfield, were paid by the people of the district and by his brothers of the clergy at the funeral, which took place on Friday last week. The service was held at St Matthew's Church, where the flag was flown at half mast, and for a long time before the service was timed to commence large crowds thronged the church and the approaches.

The body was carried to the church by members of the Men's Bible Class, followed by family mourners, members of the clergy, members of St Matthew's Church Council, the choir, and other representatives. The procession was met at the Church door by the

Lord Bishop of Liverpool (Dr A. A. David), who was attended by Venerable C. F. Twitchet (Archdeacon of Liverpool), Canon W. O. Hunter-Rodwell (Rector of Wigan and Rural Dean), Canon T. A. E. Davey (Canon Residentiary of Liverpool Cathedral and former Vicar of St Mark's Newtown), Canon J. S. Bezzant (Chancellor of Liverpool Cathedral), Canon C. F. Soulby, Revd S. Bryson, (Bishop's Chaplain), Revd A. D. Smart, (former Vicar of St Luke's, Orrell), Revd A. E. Buer, Goose Green, the Church-wardens (Messrs W. Richardson, vicar's warden and I. Massey, people's warden). Amongst other clergy taking part were Canon A. White, Billinge, Revs. A. Owen, Poolstock, R. O. Shone, (Ashton), A. Dean, (Platt Bridge), I. Keown-Boyd, (Upholland), A. Hope Johnson (Hindley), J. F. Gerrard, (Wigan, St Thomas), E. Troup, (Pemberton), E. B. Bull, (Ince), W. A. Wiffen, (St Stephen's), C. R. Simmons, (Aspull), H. V. Atkinson, (Orrell), T. H. Warne, (Bryn), F. J. Alsop, (St Andrew's), E. O. Beard, (Pemberton), W. R. H. Hall, (Rector of Ashton), D. Gardner, (Hindley), A. E. Hamm and J. Molyneux (St Catharine's), W. H. Vaughan (Abram), T. E. Allen, (Hindley Green), Parker Johnson, (Bickershaw), A. E. Bass, (Rainford), D. A. Smart, (Eccleston Park), J. Howard Preston, (Everton and formerly of St Stephen's, Whelley), and Revd J. N. Davey.

The private mourners were Miss K. G. Woods (daughter), Mr O. B. D. Jones, Miss Mary Pattinson, Miss Margaret Pattison (Darlington), Mr & Mrs Geo. Pattinson (Harrogate), Mr & Mrs Robert Woods (Tunbridge Wells), and Mr & Mrs Arthur Greenwood (Liverpool)

Others present were the Mayor of Wigan (Councillor Tom Smith), the Deputy Mayor (Councillor A. C. Fairhurst), Councillor J. Whitton, JP, Mr A. Royle (Deputy Town Clerk, representing the Town Clerk, Mr W. H. Tyrer, O. B. E., LL. B.). Major C. Blundell, Mr C. D. Gullick, Mr A. E. S. House, JP, Mr A. Harris (St Michael's), Alderman J. Wilcox (vice-chairman), Mr H. Bennett (Assistant Director of Education), and Mr J. Holmes (chief clerk), representing the Wigan Education Authority, Mr H. Caunce (secretary, Wigan Church Schools Association), Mr J. A. Davenport (representing the C. M. S.), Messrs J. Howarth, A. Jackson, S. Major, J. W. Brierley, W. J. Armstrong, T. Barton, T. Gaskell, H. Birch, W. Alleyne (lay readers), Mr W. Atherton, Mr Casson, Mr Chamberlain, Mr Bold, Mr Menzies, and Mr Ramsdale (church vergers), Mr H. Haselden, and Police Inspector Latham. The bearers were Messrs T. Atherton, S. F. Lyon, H. Gee, T. Hesketh, A. Stretton, and J. Stretton.

As the body was received into the church the congregation sang the late Vicar's favourite hymn, 'Crown Him with many crowns,' and other hymns sung were 'We love the place, O God', 'The strife is o'er, the battle done.' Mr Joel Magraw officiated at the organ. The Bishop said: 'We do not think of this as a last tribute, for we make our farewell today, not to him, but to the body he needs no more. We share thoughts and memories which we owe to John Woods, and I will try to give expression to them. In the midst of life and work we do not always reveal our deepest feelings about each other, even to our friends. Some of us are regretting today that we did not say to John Woods what we thought about him, but God has ordained other channels besides words by which such things may pass from one to another. From what he has often said to me of you people of Highfield, and what you have said to me of him I think I know what he was to you—his work and apart from his work, himself. We in the Diocese who knew him and loved him, will always be grateful for the response you made for his affection to you. The heart of his character was love. His greatness lay in the capacity for loving and being loved. We cannot explain or analyse love given or received. If it were possible it would be impossible to imitate it. We cannot counterfeit God's greatest gift. Where love is God is. John

Woods knew it; we saw it in his face. It taught him how to love and how to die. When I saw him last he told me he was looking forward, and I saw quite plainly that he had no fear. I had the privilege that day of going a little way with him down the valley of the shadow, and to be aware of Christ being with us. Now we can still be with him as he passes out, and on to the other side.'

The body was afterwards cremated at Anfield Crematorium, and the ashes were taken to Liverpool Cathedral where they rested until Sunday morning, when they were deposited in the sanctuary at St Matthew's Church, Highfield.

The funeral arrangements were carried out by Messrs Middleton and Wood.

The Dean of Liverpool, Dr F. W. Dwelly, officiated at a special service at St Matthew's Church, Highfield, on Sunday morning, when the ashes of the late Revd J. Woods, Vicar of Highfield since 1910, were interred beneath the sanctuary of the Church.

The funeral of the Revd J. Woods took place the previous Friday, and after the cremation at Anfield, the ashes were taken into Liverpool Cathedral by permission of the Dean, and they remained there until Sunday, when the Dean took them in a casket to St Matthew's, where he was met by Revd J. N. Davey, (Vicar of St Mark's, Newtown), Messrs W. Richardson and I. Massey (wardens of St Matthew's), the verger (Mr W. Atherton), and the choir. A faculty had been obtained for the holding of a service of that nature.

During the committal ceremony the Dean handed the urn to the verger who placed it in the cavity which had been prepared in the sanctuary. The wardens placed their staffs cross-wise over the recess, and after the service the cavity was sealed up, and is to be marked by a marble tile inscribed 'John Woods, First Vicar, 1910 to 1936'.

The Dean said he was privileged to know the late Vicar for many years. He was never tired of talking about Highfield and the little things that made up the pattern of life.' John Woods was my friend,' said the Dean, 'and he was a true friend to you. He possessed rare qualities of mind, and he gave particular attention to the welfare of the young men of the parish. Many times I have met him in Liverpool trying to get one of your young men a job. He did not boast of what he was doing, indeed he tried to conceal it. he chose to believe in God and you must try to do the same. When arguments come to cause doubt, you must face them and choose to believe in God. Nothing will give you more character. When you diligently seek God remember that in your heart you will grow richer. Your life must be one that is not disobedient to the heavenly vision.'

The Dean referred to the late Vicar's visits to the Liverpool Cathedral, and appealed to the parishioners of Highfield to give to their next Vicar the same whole-hearted support they had given to the late Revd J. Woods. More than once, he added they nearly lost their Vicar, and had he taken the opportunities presented to him he might have been in a position of greater dignity. His motto was 'be faithful,' and he worthily upheld it.

At the end of the service nearly four hundred parishioners attended a celebration of Holy Communion, at which the Dean and the Revd J. N. Davey officiated.

Mr J. W. Brierley summed up the feelings of many in the parish when he wrote the following obituary in the November 1936 Parish Magazine:

John Woods
First Vicar
1910–1936

This simple epitaph, chosen by himself, and inscribed on one of the tiles in the sanctuary floor of the Church he loved so dearly, not only marks the spot where his ashes were laid, but is typical of the life of the man.

Father of his people, he shared their joys and their sorrows, rejoicing with them in their happiness, guiding them in their difficulties, and helping them in their perplexities, always inspiring confidence and affection with his cheery smile and his unfailing good humour,

His steadfast faith and his human understanding made him so dependable that his advice was constantly sought, and most valued, by those who knew him best.

His devotion to his parish and his people was proved by his refusal of tempting offers. His decision was always the same- 'My place is at Highfield.' It was this love for his church and his people which made him desire cremation so that his remains could be placed where he had ministered for so long.

Several years ago, he told the writer of this article that, in his opinion, the following words, taken from Micah 6, verse 8, summed up the whole duty of man:

'He hath shewed thee, O man, what is good; and what doth the Lord require of thee, but to do justly, and to love mercy, and to walk humbly with thy God.' The many who knew him and loved him for his unselfish life and quiet devoted service, can truthfully say that John Woods lived up to this ideal.

He has left us many treasured memories.

J. W. B.

Revd Parker Johnson

Second Vicar

1937–1944

PARKER JOHNSON was born in the Everton area of Liverpool on 18 March 1887. He received his early training at St Benedict's, Everton, where he was a Sunday School teacher. On 19 September 1912, he married Mary Ellen Gibson of Everton, most probably at St George's Church, Everton.

He had worked for the Post Office since leaving school, and continued with this work until in 1915 he enlisted as a private in the Cheshire Regiment. He was later commissioned to the Royal Welsh Fusiliers, serving in Ireland, France and Flanders. Whilst an officer–cadet at Christ College, Cambridge, he took a course of theology at Ridley Hall, Cambridge. He was promoted to the rank of Captain, demobilised in 1920, and recommissioned in the rank of Captain in the Royal Welsh Fusiliers to the Regular Army Reserve of Officers.

He was involved in a voluntary capacity at the Mission of St Cuthbert's, Woodland Rd, Clubmoor from 1920 to 1925, and from 1923 to 1925 attended St Aidan's Theological College, Birkenhead.

He was ordained Deacon and Priest in 1925 by the Bishop of Liverpool. Gerald Johnson, his son, says 'I don't know what influenced him, but even from boyhood he seemed to be drawn to Church work, social and missionary work, and regretted he had never been a medical missionary.'

In June 1925, aged thirty-six, Revd Parker Johnson began his first Curacy at St Lawrence, Kirkdale. In 1926 he was a Chaplain to the Royal Welsh Fusiliers. In 1927 he was appointed Vicar of Bickershaw where he served for the next ten years, during which time he was Honorary Chaplain to the Wigan Deaf and Dumb Society.

Induction of Revd Parker Johnson.
Back row: Mr W. Richardson; Dean Dwelly; Mr Tyrer, Town Clerk; Revd Parker Johnson; Dr
David, Bishop of Liverpool; Revd Bryson; Alderman Winstanley, Mayor; Mr I Massey.
·   Seated: Mrs Cuthbert B-H-Blundell; Lady Lethbridge; Sir Wroth Lethbridge.

After the death of Revd John Woods, the Parochial Church Council at a meeting on 12 October 1936 made a request for a 'Liberal Evangelical Churchman, in order that the traditions of the Parish may be preserved, and the continuity of the ministry and teaching of our late beloved Vicar, the Revd John Woods, shall be ensured'.

The news of the appointment, by the Trustees, of the Revd Parker Johnson to the benefice of St Matthew, was made in November 1936, and the Institution by the Bishop of Liverpool and Induction by the Archdeacon of Liverpool took place on Friday 26 February 1937, at 7.30 pm.

In his first letter in the Parish Magazine in March 1937, Parker Johnson says:

My Dear Friends, In this, my first letter to you as your Vicar, let me convey from myself, my wife and family, most cordial greetings and high appreciation of the wonderful tokens of your welcome to us. Such warm-hearted and sincere expressions of welcome have made in our minds an indelible impression of your strong attachment to this beloved Church and parish of Highfield, so faithfully administered for the past twenty six years by my predecessor and friend—the Revd John Woods—whom I am pleased to follow.

Everybody agrees that our service of Institution with its four processions led by the Church Council, The Mayor and Town Clerk of Wigan, Aldermen and Councillors, our splendid Choir of forty-five men and boys, the Lay Readers, Clergy and Canons, the

Patrons—Archdeacon and the Lord Bishop of the Diocese, was a truly dignified and impressive episode in the history of our Church.

The Bishop's kindly reference to John Woods and his work, and the deep concern of the Senior Trustee, Major Blundell, and his family, for the welfare of their parish gave us as much satisfaction, as did the attendance of Mrs M. G. M. Blundell, wife of Major Blundell, and Lady Lethbridge, his sister, who as Co-Trustees, presented me for Institution and Induction, and who so kindly demonstrated their interest by making a tour of each department of our splendid Day Schools.

Our distinguished visitors, including the Trustees and Sir Wroth Lethbridge, complimented us on the excellent rendering of the Service by the Choir.

Now let me thank all who have laboured so faithfully during the interregnum and so successfully held the Church affairs and various organisations intact and almost unimpaired. My incoming is thereby made easier, and for this I am grateful. It will take a time for my wife and I to know all our people by name, but by persistent effort we hope to gain knowledge of you and your work and your homes, and hope that by consideration and determination, there will be an onward march in the path of progress. Please remember us in your prayers, share our confidence and give us yours, that together we may work for the spiritual uplift of Highfield, and the extension of the Kingdom of God.

Ever your friend and Vicar, PARKER JOHNSON.

At the first Parochial Church Council meeting with Parker Johnson, a sub-committee was appointed to consider a suitable memorial for Revd John Woods.

The Church Choir, 1937

In the 20 March 1937 edition of the *Wigan Observer* there is a photograph of the 'New Highfield Vicar with his Choir'. The article accompanying the photograph gives an interesting account of the choir, its members and activities:

The photograph shows the choir of St Matthew's Church, Highfield, together with the newly-instituted Vicar, Revd Parker Johnson, and Messrs I. Massey (people's warden), and J. W. Brierley, (lay reader, and headmaster of Highfield Senior Boys' School). At the time the photograph was taken Mr W. Richardson (vicar's warden) and Mr A. Stockley (a member of the choir for 28 years) were absent owing to illness.

The choir consists of 22 trebles, 8 altos, 7 tenors, and 6 bass, and the aggregate number of years service (excluding the boys) is 438, the average being practically 20 years for each of the 22 adult members. Two additional altos, Messrs J. Ashcroft and A. Parkes, with 22 and 19 years respectively, are now working away from home. The choir has recently lost two of its oldest members by death—Mr J. T. Taberner (43 years) and Mr A. Frankland (34 years). With one exception every member of the choir started in the trebles.

An interesting feature of the choir is the annual summer camp, started some twenty years ago, and established and maintained by the boys' own efforts. On leaving the choir, the boys are catered for by the Old Choirboys' Association, with its many-sided activities, and membership of over 150. In addition to the 'Games' evenings every week, when badminton, billiards, table tennis, etc. are played, the association has formed a nigger

The Church Choir, 1937.

minstrel troupe, a choral society, and a concert party. The names, with years of service in brackets, are, reading from left to right:

Front row, seated.

C. Ashurst, H. Worthington, C. Lancaster, A. Gray, T. Hilton, D. Rowe, R. Parkes, A. Hulme, T. Culshaw, H. Henstead, C. Wilcock, R. Woods, and D. Nicholson.

Second row, seated.

Messrs J. E. Holland (41 years) R. Winstanley (53 years) A. V. Shepherd (33 years) J. Magraw (choirmaster and organist, 12 years) I. Massey (warden) Revd Parker Johnson (Vicar) Messrs J. W. Brierley (lay reader) and W. Taberner (ex chorister and associate organist)

Third row, standing.

Messrs H. Stretton (21 years) W. H. Daniels (41 years) Masters O. Chadwick, J. Melling, D. Shepherd, W. Henstead, M. Matthewson, J. T. Culshaw, H. Prescott, W. Aspey, W. Speakman, Messrs E. Stretton (24 years) A. Darbyshire (21 years) G. Aldington (15 years) T. Prescott (2 years) and J. Jones (15 years)

Back row, standing.

T. Simm (18 years) W. Wilcock (7 years) E. Anderson (12 years) T. Jones (15 years) G. H. Stretton (15 years) J. Heaton (11 years) A. Atherton (7 years) J. Sharples (7 years) T. Stockley (23 years) and D. Ascroft (17 years).

In 1937 Parker Johnson was appointed Chaplain to Pemberton Hospital which was a small Isolation Hospital in Billinge Road on the site of what is now The Spinney.

In September 1937, an article appeared in the *Wigan Observer* announcing that the Iron Church, a familiar landmark for seventy years, was to be demolished. This was not to be the end of the old Iron Church, part of the building was kept as a storeroom which stood through most of the second world war, and was finally demolished in 1944.

Choirboys' Camp, 1937

The 1937 September Magazine contained a full report of that year's choirboys' camp at Chester College:

The Choirboys left Highfield early on the last Monday in July, by motor coach, which was piled with provisions, luggage and boys, the party numbering 35. Arrived at Chester College grounds, they began the work of assembling their equipment, and the first prepared meal was tea. Various unforeseen difficulties had to be overcome before the boys spent their first night in camp, which was quite an adventure for the youngest boys. Games of all descriptions, and a trip up the River Dee to Eaton Hall occupied Monday and Tuesday. But the day of days was Wednesday. spent at Llandudno. The journey was made by road, with a break for the climbing of Little Orme.

On the return journey a break was made at Rhyl. The Vicar was fortunately able to accompany the boys, having arrived the previous afternoon. He was compelled to return on the Thursday to the great disappointment of the boys, who had prepared for him a surprise, which must now wait for another year. The Vicar, we believe, was more disappointed than the boys!! Thursday was visiting day, when a coachload of parents and friends visited the camp and were entertained to tea. On Friday, the boys paid their customary visit to the Cathedral. Later in the day, the annual cricket match between the Cantoris and the Decani was played, to the accompaniment of the usual great rivalry, and it will no doubt provide material for discussion amongst the boys until the next match is played.

Saturday arrived, and with sad hearts but healthy faces, the boys prepared to leave Chester, consoling themselves with the thought that, after all, the next camp was only 358 days off.

Every advantage was taken of the good weather (the rain was left behind at Wigan), the boys being out-of-doors from early morning to sunset. As a result they have returned in excellent health and spirits, ready for another twelve month's service. We heartily thank all members of the Church and parish who by their contributions made the camp holiday possible, and also thank the Vicar's friends who so generously subscribed towards the cost of sports and games gear.—J. M. (Joel Magraw, Organist & Choirmaster).'

Parker Johnson's experience as an officer in the First World War was to be put to good use again in the near future. When Air Raid Precautions were being made he took the lead in the Parish as this article in the September 1938 Parish Magazine shows.

The Dramatic Society, 1937, present 'A Gradely Day in London'.
Back row: Mrs G. Hall; ? ; Mrs Heaton; Mrs Tither; Mrs Heaton, ? ; Mrs M. Atherton; Mrs
Eden; Mrs Gaskell.
Front row: Ada Wilcock; Mrs Parkinson; Mrs Heaton; Mrs Lyon, ?.
A young Mrs Iris Atherton is hidden under the leopard skin.

Air Raid Precautions

We have now heard so much about ARP that its necessity is quite rightly taken for granted. The force in Wigan is already well organised with officers appointed for each department and area.

The Vicar has been appointed Chief Warden with Mr George Millard as Deputy, for Number 11 Area, which comprises roughly slightly more than the ecclesiastical parish of Highfield.

Seventy men from the parish are at work as trained Wardens and fifteen women and girls have also enlisted for service. More are needed and the Vicar will be glad to receive names of any who wish to be trained in this work of self-defence.

Classes will begin within the next few days for those who desire training and since the Vicar is a qualified Instructor, with a Home Office Certificate, it will no longer be necessary to go further than our own schools for this purpose. Details of the work will be published each month and any further information may be had from the Vicar, or the Chief Constable, Wigan.

On Wednesday September 28th 1938, exactly two years after the death of Revd John Woods, a Memorial Window and other gifts were dedicated by the Very Reverend F. W. Dwelly, DD, Dean of Liverpool at 7.30 p.m. The October Parish Magazine records the details of the service:

Church Cleaning and Dedication of Memorial Window and Gifts

Another cause for thankfulness at the close of the past month was the completion of the work of thoroughly cleaning the interior of the Church—its fabric and fittings—by a splendid body of voluntary workers, who verily believe that 'cleanliness is next to Godliness.' Forty worshippers cleaned walls, reredos, marble memorials, floors and pews, all made sweet and clean in readiness for the great service on Wednesday, September 28th, for the dedication of the stained glass Memorial Window and various gifts to the Church. The date was the second anniversary of the passing of the late Vicar, and this, combined with their love for our magnificent Church, encouraged them to work with great zeal. And what a transformation the Church presented when they had completed their labour of love! From all sides they have earned praise—richly deserved and now, by the kindness of one of our trusted friends who visited them at work—these excellent workers are to have a tea party in recognition of their devoted service to the Church, for which we are most grateful.

The Church was crowded for the Dedication Service, and presented a warm and comfortable appearance with the carpets and new furnishings in position, and pews cleaned and polished.

The Very Reverend F. W. Dwelly, Dean of Liverpool, compiled and conducted the service assisted by the Vicar and two close friends and neighbours of Highfield, the Revd J. N. Davey and the Revd A. E. Buer, each of whom took part in the actual unveiling of the window and the dedication of gifts.

The clergy, having robed in the schools, entered the Church by the West door singing the processional hymn 'Come, let us join our friends above.' The Vicar (Revd Parker Johnson) opened the service with the Benedictions, assisted by the visiting clergy, the responses being made by the congregation. The sermon was preached by the Dean who made many references to his friend, the late Vicar, who he described as a keen pastor and one interested in the work of cathedral building. He hoped that the window and gifts of the parishioners would always serve as a reminder of the glory of God, which rested on our ability to share one anothers joys and sorrows, national and international. We must begin that in the home and our church and realm. The Dean concluded: 'Smile where it is appropriate, show sympathy to those in sorrow, give a helping hand where needed, and live to the glory of God.'

THE WINDOW has rich colourings and depicts the apostle St John holding in his right hand the Chalice or drinking cup, whilst in his left hand he carries the Martyr's Palm. Below this central figure is a circular picture of the 'Good and Faithful Steward,' presenting the Keys of his Stewardship well and faithfully done, to his Master. At the foot of the window the inscription reads: 'Dedicated to the memory of John Woods, MA, first Vicar of this parish, 1910—1936. This window is the gift of parishioners and friends.

THE BISHOP'S PRAYER DESK is a massive structure in oak, to match the Bishop's Chair, the Gift of the Mothers' Class.

The last May Queen in the Infant School, 1939, Edna Twigg.

THE CARPETS, also given by the Mothers' Class, tone beautifully with the red sandstone interior of the Church and add warmth to its appearance, as also do the kneelers and cushions all to match.

THE LITANY DESK, in oak, designed by the same architect who undertook the other furnishings, is a replica of the centre panel of the Reredos. It is a beautifully made desk and bears the inscription: 'Dedicated to the memory of John and Margaret Johnson, by their daughters Emily and Edith, 1938.'

THE TWO HYMN BOARDS, in oak, are hung on the main piers supporting the tower and face the Sanctuary, being so placed for the benefit of the Choir and Clergy. They are a much needed addition to our furnishings and are the gift of Mrs Sam Heaton and her son John, one of our Choirmen, who made them himself.

THE PRESENTATION MALLET was originally presented by the Architects to the Revd John Wood, M. A., In white letters on a bronze plate it bears the inscription: 'St Matthew's Church, Highfield. Presented to the Incumbent Reverend John Wood MA, at the laying of the Foundation Stone, July, 1892. The mallet was presented to the Church by his daughter Mrs A. Clough.'

THE ALTAR CROSS, in brass, is solid and of great weight, specially designed to fit the recess in the centre panel of the Reredos, which it now completes. It bears the inscription: 'Highfield Parish Church. The Gift of John Thomas Berry and his wife Mary Elizabeth. 16th June, 1938.'

We are most grateful to the donors of all these lovely adornments for our Church, and also to Mrs Tillotson for re-lacquering and renovating the Font Ewer and its oak stand; and to Mr Gee, Hon. Secretary of our PCC for re-lacquering and renovating the Churchwardens Staves.

Thanks are also due to Mr & Mrs T. Gaskell for cleaning the Reredos and Marble, which now look quite new. At the close of the Dedication Service we retired to the Schools for a cup of tea and the opportunity for our people to chat with the Dean and other visitors.'

Unfortunately, Mrs Clough, who not long before had undergone a severe operation, was unable to be present, but sent her love and kind wishes to all old Highfielders.

The Second World War

The 3rd of September 1939 saw the outbreak of the Second World War. Parker Johnson wrote in the October Parish Magazine:

My dear Friends, The outbreak of War on September 3rd has had its effect upon all of us and our hearts go out to our King—the Prime Minister, and all responsible officers of the state at such a time. Never before have we as a nation, been faced with a situation such as modern warfare thrusts upon us and so we must learn to be patient and forbearing if matters seem to chafe under unaccustomed new conditions.

We must face the facts and do all we can as individuals and good citizens to render the fullest possible service to the state for its preservation, for therein lies our cherished freedom as a people.

Our Church Services will be kept going and every opportunity given for Christian people to commune with God in His hallowed House of Prayer, and especially do we hope that Sunday, 1 October, will find a place in our hearts as we gather together and share in petition to Almighty God for His leading throughout this trying time. We rejoice that in this fair land of ours, our King and his Government recognise the need for God's care by ordering this National Day of Prayer in the Churches. Let us respond whole-heartedly and unitedly, for if God be for us what need we fear, no matter who or what force be against us? Wishing you all God's blessing. Ever your friend and Vicar, Parker Johnson.

The Local Education Committee decided to keep the schools of the Borough closed until Air-raid shelters were provided. Evening Prayer was held at 3 p.m. owing to the 'Black-out' orders prevailing.

Death of Mrs M. E. Greener

The November 1939 Parish Magazine records the passing of Mrs Maria Elizabeth Greener:

All old Highfielders will share our regret at the passing of Mrs Maria Elizabeth Greener, widow of the late Mr W. J. Greener, a former Manager of Pemberton Colliery and prominent official of the old Iron Church where the family worshipped up to the time that the present Church was opened. Mr Greener was present at the Consecration of St

Matthew's and was the first layman to read the lessons there. There are still many worshipping with us who recollect the good old days when Mr & Mrs Greener generously entertained all the Sunday School Scholars at their home 'Wood Cottage' on successive Walking Days.

They will ever be remembered for their generous considerations towards others and for their Churchmanship.

Mrs Greener, who was 84 years of age, died on October 10th, and her passing breaks a link with colliery history for a period of over eighty years. She was the second daughter of the late Mr J. H. Pickering, who sixty years ago was commercial manager to the Pemberton Collieries of Colonel Blundell, CB, MP, being succeeded by her brother, Mr Colin Pickering, who held the position until the formation of the new company in 1929. She was married at St John's Church, Pemberton, in 1878, and on the 1st. February, 1897, her husband was killed by a 'burn' of twenty-four tubs in the Bye Pit. Forty years before that Mr Greener's father, who was Colonel Blundell's mining agent, was killed underground while on a visit to Rainford Colliery.

Mrs Greener lived at Wood Cottage, Highfield, until the death of her husband, when she went to reside at Kirkby, and later at Birkdale. She had seven sons, all of whom served in the Great War, and two were killed. She also had two daughters, the elder being the wife of Mr Geoffrey Gullick, who served his time at Pemberton Colliery, beginning in 1906. Her eldest son, Mr Willie Greener, was manager at Pemberton Colliery under Mr Douglas thirty years ago. Mrs Greener's other brother, Mr Harry Pickering, H. M. Chief Inspector of Mines, was killed while leading a rescue party at Cadeby Colliery, after the explosion there in 1912. His son, Mr Basil Pickering, now general manager of Amalgamated Denaby Collieries, was assistant manager at Pemberton Colliery before the last war. During her long widowhood, Mrs Greener took a great interest in the progress at the Pemberton Colliery.

A service at St John's Church was attended by present and former members of the staff of Pemberton Colliery. Revd E. Troup, Vicar, conducted the service, assisted by Revd Parker Johnson, Vicar of St Matthew's, Highfield, and the hymns 'Abide with me.' and 'Saviour to Thy dear Name we raise,' were sung. The interment followed in the family vault in the Churchyard.

The private mourners were Mr & Mrs W. J. Greener, Mr & Mrs Hugh Greener, Mr & Mrs Harry Greener, Mr & Mrs Geoffrey Gullick, Miss L. H. Greener, Mr C. D. Gullick, Miss I. Gullick, Mr Herbert Greener, Mr B. H. Pickering, Dr & Mrs E. Shirlaw, Mrs J. T. Shirlaw, Mr R. H. W. Cunningham, Mr W. A. Findlay, and Miss E. Walker, (Appley Bridge.)

Pemberton Colliery Officials present were Messrs Thomas Cook, Agent, Edward Lea, Secretary, H. Ashurst, Manager, John Lloyd and R. Finch, under-managers, J. Gaskell, engineer, R. Hurst, coke-oven manager, W. Hickman, surface manager, O. Wooding, surveyor and about 30 other members of the staff.

There were also present a number of men who were working at Pemberton Colliery under Mr Greener in 1897. These were Mr R. Weston (now under-manager, formerly collier), J. Anderson (now foreman-joiner, formerly apprenticed joiner), J. Hitchen (brow foreman, formerly brow hand), T. Winstanley (foreman fitter, formerly apprenticed fitter), G. Pennington, (clerk), R. Preston (pusher-on, formerly haulage hand), G. Heaton (loco cleaner, formerly hooker-on), W. Parkinson (collier), J. Jarvis (now Manager Major Blundell's estate, formerly clerk), G. Hampson (surface manager, now retired, and formerly Mr Greener's personal and confidential clerk), R. Winstanley (under manager, now retired and former collier), and J. Gee (under-manager, now retired and formerly a collier).

It is pleasing to note that a donation of £2 has been acknowledged by Wigan Infirmary 'In memory of Mrs W. J. Greener from a number of old Highfield scholars who have recollections of happy Sunday School Treats at Wood Cottage.'

Mr T. Barton, who for many years had been Headmaster of St John's School until his retirement in September 1939, was ordained Deacon the following year to assist with clerical duties at Highfield, Pemberton and Wigan. The Vicar welcomed him to Highfield in the June 1940 Parish Magazine:

My Dear Friends, The unexpected frequently happens in peace as well as in war, and it is our joy to record that within the past month we have acquired the services of the Revd Thomas Barton, who was ordained on Trinity Sunday, May 19th, in Liverpool Cathedral by the Lord Bishop of Liverpool, with the title of Assistant Curate of St Matthew, Highfield. We were much pleased to be able to lead a contingent of our parishioners to the Cathedral for the Ordination Service, always a most impressive and dignified ceremony, and it is a happy coincidence that the date happened to be the Bishop's 73rd birthday.

Mr Barton comes to us as one who is already well-known and highly esteemed as a keen Church man, who has throughout a long period rendered yeoman service as a voluntary Licensed Lay Reader and has a valuable experience of all branches of Church work. The great welcome accorded him by our parishioners was no surprise and we look ahead to great times together as we share the duties of the shepherding of souls. The prayers of our people are asked on behalf of Mr Barton that God may use him mightily for the work of extending the kingdom.

The Greener family made a gift of the Gates and Communion Rails in oak in memory of their parents Mr W. J. Greener and Mrs M. E. Greener. These were dedicated by the Venerable the Archdeacon of Liverpool, on Sunday 13 October 1940, at 10.30 a.m., along with other gifts which included a new sanctuary carpet and clergy robes from an anonymous donor, a Communion Cruet, Book markers and Altar Linen.

The November Parish Magazine reported that in the Liverpool Diocese twenty-seven churches and eleven vicarages had been damaged by enemy action in the Blitz. It was explained that the Church Tower was used as an Observation Post for civil spotting of lights and fires, not for military purposes.

The Parish Magazine throughout the war years records details of the knitting of Comforts for men and women of the parish who were in the services, and of parcels sent out to men who were prisoners of war. There were letters too, from the men and women themselves, written from many parts of the world, and sadly, there were the reports of those who had made the supreme sacrifice.

Death of Mr James Starkey

Mr James Starkey, who had for many years been involved in the life of the Church in Highfield, and had been involved in the work of the Sunday School, the Men's Bible

Class, a sidesman and later Churchwarden, died on Thursday 17 April 1941. The *Wigan Observer* reported his death as follows:

> The death occurred on Thursday last week of Mr James Starkey of Woodlands Terrace, Highfield. Mr Starkey, who was 71 years of age, commenced his business career as a wheelwright, becoming apprenticed to Mr James Hesketh, late of Wallgate, Wigan. Later he opened on his own account at Pony Dick, the business of wheelwright and smith, in which he was assisted by his brothers Samuel and Joseph. he was very well respected and his courteous manner and sterling character soon worked up a good business.
>
> In his private life he was very interested in the parochial work of St Matthew's Church, Highfield. For several years he was general secretary for the Sunday Schools, He also took a keen interest in the Men's Bible Class and ample evidence of this keenness is manifest and will remain so for many years to come for in his spare time, assisted by his brother Samuel, he provided the material and devoted many hours to the construction of a massive bookcase and cupboard of solid pitch pine which they presented to the Men's Class for their library.
>
> Mr Starkey also interested himself in the church life of the parish, being appointed sidesman in 1918, and he held the office of Churchwarden from 1923 to 1929. It was during this period when he had retired from business life that he spent whole days in the Churchyard, supervising as honorary clerk of works, the laying of the drains, in order to see that the work was performed to the specifications and plans of the surveyor, the late Mr W. H. Roby.
>
> Failing health caused Mr Starkey to retire from active church life, but he never lost interest and for several years he acted as joint auditor of the church accounts. He kept up his attendance at church whenever health permitted. He lived a life which was an example to many.
>
> The funeral took place on Monday, the interment being at St Matthew's Church, Highfield. Revd Parker Johnson, vicar, officiated being assisted by Revd T. Barton, curate. The Vicar paid a high tribute to the fine Christian character of the deceased gentleman. Mr Magraw presided at the organ with the choir in attendance.
>
> The mourners were Mrs Starkey, Mr J. T. Starkey, Miss Alice V. Starkey, Mr & Mrs T. R. Holt, Mr & Mrs Samuel Starkey, Mr & Mrs Jos Starkey, Miss Margaret Starkey, Mr & Mrs Wm. Starkey, Mr & Mrs O. J. Tricket, Mr & Mrs J. Price, Mr & Mrs J. Brooks, Miss Marjorie Starkey, Mr W. Nixon, Mr T. Winstanley, Mr F. Richardson, Mr George Fouracre, Mr C. Holt, Mr Isaac Massey, the Misses Simm, Mrs Grayley, Mr T. Cook, Mr W. Massey, Mr Whittle, Mr A. Harris, Dr K. Fraser, Mr & Mrs B. Jones, Mr G. Monk and Mr R. Winstanley.
>
> Many beautiful floral tributes were sent by relatives and friends including wedding bouquets from Dorothy and Billy, and a wreath from past and present members of Highfield Church Choir.
>
> The funeral arrangements were carried out by Messrs Middleton and Wood, under the direction of Mr Wm. Atherton.

An obituary appeared in the Parish Magazine as follows:

> We share the sorrow of all Church members and residents of our area at the passing of yet another friend, Mr James Starkey, of 416, Billinge Road, who throughout the whole of his life—three score and ten years—had lived in Highfield and taken the keenest possible interest in every department of Church life. He filled all the offices open to the laity and was for several years elected by the parishioners to serve as their Churchwarden.

Mr Starkey's high spiritual character and refined bearing combined with a Christian humility and willingness to serve others, won for him a host of friends and the highest possible esteem of all and sundry. Up to two years ago he held office with us and only gave up through failing health and now that he has been called to higher service and laid to rest in a portion of our churchyard and very dear to his heart by reason of his share in securing its consecration to the Church, he is affectionately remembered by us all as a kind-hearted, sincere Christian gentleman whose life and work remains an inspiration to us all, and for whose honest service we are grateful. 'Well done , good and faithful servant.'

In 1941 William Richardson who had been Vicar's Warden since 1910 stepped down from office due to ill-health. In his place the Vicar appointed Mr Thomas Hesketh who was welcomed to his first Parochial Church Council as Vicar's Warden on 4 May 1941.

William Wilkinson was licensed by the Bishop of Liverpool as a Parochial Lay Reader in 1941 and was welcomed by the Vicar to the Parish 'Staff', thanked for his services already rendered to the Parish and commended to the prayers of the people.

Damages of £90 were claimed for the Little Lane Banner which was lost when the premises where it had been sent for repair were burned down in the Blitz.

At the 1942 Annual Parochial Meeting it was reported that there were 1006 members on the Electoral Roll. Knitting classes were being held for the provision of comforts for the forces. 200 parcels had been sent to parishioners on active service and special parcels to 6 men who were Prisoners of War. St Matthew's Guild of Youth had been formed for young boys and girls aged up to 18 'to provide club life and recreation of a suitable character.' Mrs Miller was in charge of the girls and Mr T. Stockley was in charge of the boys.

The Little Lane Banner, destroyed in the Liverpool Blitz. Photograph taken about 1930.

During the war a company of WAAF and RAF personnel were stationed at Winstanley Hall. They paraded to Church on the first Sunday in January 1943 with their Commanding Officer. It was a bright sunny morning and this added to the smart appearance of the men and women as they marched to and from Church. Parker Johnson, who had not had good health for some time, suffered a breakdown in health early in 1943, recovered for a time but had a relapse in February. At the 13th April meeting of the Parochial Church Council, Mr Brierley was in the chair. In view of the Vicar's prolonged illness the Revd W. Searle was engaged to take the services. At the same meeting, Mr Massey reported that the roof of the Iron Church building was in good condition and was worth repairing as a storeroom. At the August meeting it was reported that the building had suffered wanton damage and the contents had been removed to Massey's works for safety. The demolition of the remainder of the building was finally discussed at the April 1944 Parochial Church Council.

Death and Funeral of Revd Parker Johnson

The Vicar was present at the Annual Parochial Meeting on 29 April 1943, when arrangements to celebrate the Jubilee of the Church was discussed but sadly his health was slowly deteriorating. As the Vicar of St Mark's (Revd James N. Davey) said in his Obituary to Parker Johnson: ' We watched him fade during his last three years but he struggled to carry on even to the last, unwilling to admit what others saw with sadness.'

During the Vicar's last months he continued to plan for the future. A 'Guild of Servers' was announced in the May 1943 magazine, consisting of R. Thomas, J. Balfour, A. Gray, and H. Aspey, and he continued to write his article for the Parish Magazine up to the last.

Parker Johnson died on Saturday 5 February 1944. The sad news was given to the Parochial Church Council on Monday 7 February by Mr William Richardson, Vice-Chairman. A vote of Condolence was sent to Mrs Johnson and family in their bereavement. A plot on the South side of the Church was reserved for Incumbents and Assistant Curates and their wives who may die in office, and the Revd Parker Johnson was buried there. The *Wigan Observer* reported the Funeral which took place on Friday 11 February 1944:

> There was a large attendance at the funeral of the Revd Parker Johnson, Vicar of St Matthew's Church, Highfield, which took place on Friday last week. Parishioners and representatives of various organisations with which the Vicar had been associated were present to pay their last tribute of respect to one who had gained their affections and esteem.
>
> Revd Parker Johnson, who died the previous Saturday at the age of fifty-six, had been Vicar of St Matthew's for the past seven years, and was previously incumbent at St Elizabeth's, Bickershaw, for ten years.
>
> The remains were taken into St Matthew's Church on Thursday evening, when a short service was conducted by the Revd A. Owen (Vicar, St James's, Poolstock) before a large gathering of parishioners.

Canon W. O. Hunter Rodwell (Rector of Wigan) conducted the service on Friday, when a tribute was paid by the Bishop of Liverpool (Dr A. A. David). As the clergy and choir entered the church, Mr J. Magraw, organist, played Chopin's 'Funeral March.' and 'Funeral Music' by Thomas Tallis.

The service which was fully choral, opened with the singing of the hymn 'I heard the voice of Jesus say', followed by the chanting of the 23rd Psalm. Archdeacon C. F. Twitchett read the lesson.

The Bishop said he had enjoyed the friendship of Revd Parker Johnson for twenty years—ever since he (the Bishop) had arrived in Liverpool. Their Vicar was then engaged in a gallant struggle against heavy odds preparing himself for ordination. He was very fortunate in the men who had befriended him at that time—Dr Chavasse, Archdeacon Spooner and the present Rector of Wigan. They were helping a man of firm but simple faith, of undoubted courage and a cheerful outlook which no one could disturb later on. Whilst Mr Johnson was training at the Theological College he worked as a Civil Servant during vacations in order to gain experience and attain his ambitions to serve God in His Church. Their Vicar was a plucky and fair fighter. Once he had made up his mind, even if his decision meant the hitting of other people, he went for it straight and square. If there was striving and someone to be hurt in the striving he knew how to heal the injury. They had watched Mr Johnson growing weaker every month, but still fighting the good fight, and struggling, not for himself, but for the people of Highfield whom God had given into his charge. The Bishop concluded by thanking God for Mr Johnson's service and ministry.

After the singing of the hymn 'Let saints on earth in concert sing ' the Rector of Wigan said the prayers. The hymn ' Jesus lives! no longer now' was then sung followed by the Nunc Dimittis.

The interment was in St Matthew's Churchyard in a place set apart for the clergy, the committal rites being performed by the Bishop.

The clergy present were Revs. T. E . Allen, St John's, Hindley Green, A. Hope Johnson, All Saints, Hindley Green, and W. R. Hall, who acted as marshals. S. Bryson, St Mary's, Lower Ince, (who acted as Bishop's Chaplain), Canon T. E. Davey (Liverpool Cathedral) Canon A. E. White (Billinge), Revs. R. R. Honner, St Andrew's, Wigan, J. Martin, St George's, Wigan, H. Ellis, St Catherine's, Wigan, J. F. Gerrard, St Thomas's, Wigan, A. Owen, St James's, Poolstock, Wigan, J. H. Bartlett, St John's, Pemberton, J. N. Davey, St Mark's, Newtown, J. Taplin, St Paul's, Goose Green, J. Speakman, Bickershaw, R. O. Shone, St Thomas's, Ashton-in-Makerfield, D. Herman, Dalton, E. O. Beard, St Elizabeth's, Aspull, H. Stoneley, Ince Parish Church, A. Dean, St Nathaniel's, Platt Bridge, H. V. Atkinson, St Luke's, Orrell, T. Barton, (Curate), St Michael's, Wigan, H. Senar and S. J. Davies, (Curates, Wigan Parish Church), A. G. Livesley (Curate, St Andrew's), R. H. Dowthwaite (Curate, St George's), R. Thompson, (Curate, St Catharine's), R. G. Young, (Curate, Ince Parish Church), W. R. Searle (Curate, Upholland Parish Church), G. T. Weston (Liverpool and formerly of Ince Parish Church), and T. Gregory, (St James's, Ashton-under-Lyne)

Revs. G. Evans Watson (Wigan Methodist Mission), President, C. Rogers (Scarisbrick St Baptist Church), Secretary, Ernest Jones, (Superintendent, Wigan Methodist Mission), and Bruce H. White (King Street Methodist Church) represented the Wigan and District Free Church Council and the Free Church Ministers.

Masonic Brethren present were Lindsey Lodge, Wor. Bros. Irvine W. Johnson W. M., J. J. Bradley, Dr T. M. Angior, T. Ashton, F . C. Simm, A. Prestt, W. Rimmer, and Bros. J. Fairhurst, A. R. Jackson, G. McCandlish, W. G. Gibson, D. Stuart, Dr J. S.

Mather, and Dr D. N. Mackinnon, Peace Chapter, Comp. W. Webster, G. W. Clough, H. Houghton, A. S. Brunt, P. Wild, P. Glover, A. Melling, ex-Comp. J. Barker, F. W. Boggis, J. Baker, W. C. Taylor, T. Ashton, Dr Oag, J. Seddon, and T. Barton. Crawford Lodge, Wor. Bros. Owen Owen and A. Knowles.

St Matthew's Church were represented by Messrs T. Hesketh (Vicar's warden), I. Massey (People's warden), C. Ashurst, T. Hammond, P. Gaskell, J. Evans, T. Aldington, G. Aldington, members of the Parochial Church Council and the Mother's Union. The day schools were represented by Mr J. W. Brierley (Headmaster, Highfield Senior School), Miss Johnson (Headmistress, Junior School), Miss Holland (Headmistress, Infants' School), and other members of the teaching staff.

There were also representatives present from the 26th Lancashire Battalion (Wigan) Home Guard.

Others in attendance included Sir Wrothesley Lethbridge and Lady Lethbridge, the Mayor of Wigan (Alderman H. Dowling, JP), Mr H. Leather (representing Mr W. H. Tyrer, CBE, LL. M. (Town Clerk), Capt. Johnson (representing Mr R. J. Johnson), Colwyn Bay, and the Johnson family, (trustees of Bickershaw Parish Church), Major C. D. Gullick and Mr E. Lea, secretary (representing Pemberton Colliery Company), Mr C. F. Medway, (representing Major Blundell), Mr T. Cook (former manager, Pemberton Colliery.), Mr H. R. Bennett(Director of Education, Wigan), Mr W. Richardson, Councillor T. Mason (Chairman Abram District Council), and Councillor J. Turner (Billinge District Council).

The bearers were Messrs T. Atherton, R. Gaskell, T. Worthington, A. Dickinson, L. Tomlinson and J. Ashcroft (sidesmen of St Matthew's Church) The funeral arrangements were carried out by Messrs Middleton and Wood, under the direction of Mr C. Brogan. Mr A. Wood was in attendance.

The Vicar of St Mark's wrote an appreciation of the Revd Parker Johnson in the April 1944 Parish Magazine. After detailing the early career of Parker Johnson he went on:

'In 1937 he came to St Matthew's, Highfield. Highfield had basked in the sunshine ministry of the beloved John Woods for over 25 years and it never is an easy task to follow one who has become a real father amongst his people. With his accustomed vigour the new Vicar took reins of office, determined in all things to do what he believed to be right and also for the forwarding of work and life of the Parish. He was very different in temperament as well as in method from his predecessors and the inevitable changes were sometimes difficult to engineer successfully. His courage and devotion, coupled to his enthusiastic conviction, made him accept opposition though he disliked it in Church work, rather than shirk the discomfort it might produce.

There will be many Parishioners, especially the unfortunate inmates of Pemberton Sanatorium, who remember the Revd Parker Johnson for his understanding sympathy, while he shared the constant anxieties and troubles of his people consequent upon the war.

We watched him gradually fade during his last three years but he struggled to carry on even to the last, unwilling to admit what others saw with sadness. He passed into the larger life as a young man, but he had lived fully every day of his 56 years, and continues in that service with those who have heard 'Well done thou good and faithful servant enter thou into the joy of thy Lord.'

In grateful memory of an old friend sincere sympathy with the sorrowing ones and an earnest prayer for God's continued blessing upon St Matthew's. Yours sincerely, Jas. N. Davey.

Revd Canon
W. H. Bullough

Third Vicar

1944–1959

WALTER HERBERT BULLOUGH was born at Bryn Gates near Ashton-in-Maker-field in 1915. His father was the manager of Bryn Gates Cooperative Society, and his Uncle Ernest Bullough was a solicitor, and it was thought that young Herbert would study Law. This hope was not fulfilled but his younger brother Harold studied Law and still practices from a Wigan office.

As a youngster, Herbert attended Bryn Gates Primary School, and on Sundays was taken by his parents to either St Luke's Mission Church Stubshaw Cross, or to St Thomas's Ashton, or to Ashton Parish Church of Holy Trinity Downall Green, which was his mother's home church. On Trinity Sunday all the family went to Holy Trinity to take part in the 'Walking Day Procession of Witness'. They walked from Bryn Gates, across the old Ashton Golf Links, through Bryn Cross to Downall Green.

From Bryn Gates Herbert went to Tideswell Grammar School, Derbyshire. After his Confirmation there, he served at the Eucharist and often a group of the servers were invited to tea at the Vicarage where the saintly Father Edwards had a great influence on them all. As a server in the beautiful 'Cathedral of the Peak' Herbert soon made up his mind to spend his life's work serving the Church and he often felt the guiding hand of God urging him in this direction.

From Tideswell he went to Lady Manners School, Bakewell, and from there in 1934 he entered King's College in the University of London to study Theology.

He was made Deacon on 17 September 1939 by Dr David, Bishop of Liverpool. His first appointment was to be Curate of Widnes Parish Church of St Mary. He remembers well the great care with which Archdeacon Twitchet supervised the careers of the Ordinands in the Liverpool Diocese at this time. After a few months in the parish his

Vicar left St Mary's to become an Army Chaplain and Mr Bullough was left in charge of the parish. He was ordained Priest in 1940 and undertook the responsibility of organising the reception at very short notice of large numbers of refugees from Liverpool.

During his first curacy he kept in close touch with Archdeacon Twitchet and in 1941 the Archdeacon invited him to go to work under the Revd Pryce Jones the Rector of St Peter's Church Woolton, where he would have charge of the Mission Church of St Hilda Hunt's Cross. He found his Rector a very lively and energetic Parish Priest, and although in many ways he was unorthodox everybody loved him. His home was at Betws-y-Coed.

In March 1943 the Curate of Woolton married his dentist wife, Joan, at the Parish Church of St Nathaniel Platt Bridge. The Rector of Woolton was his best man. Canon Arthur White of Billinge officiated.

At Hunts Cross Herbert Bullough had a very happy ministry, and in spite of many problems he established a strong church going community.

In 1944 on one of his visits to see Archdeacon Twitchett the Archdeacon told him that he was going to recommend him for an appointment to a Benefice, and very soon afterwards he received a letter from the Patron of St Matthew's Church, Highfield, Major Cuthbert Blundell of Haywards Heath, Sussex, offering him the benefice, which he accepted. The announcement of his appointment was made to the Parochial Church Council Meeting on the 10th May 1944, the Induction having been arranged for Friday June 9th at 7.30 pm.

Rev Bullough introduced himself to the parish in a letter in the June 1944 Parish Magazine:

> 25 Stuart Ave.,
> Hunt's Cross,
> Woolton, Liverpool.
> 22nd May, 1944.
>
> My Dear Friends,
> I am delighted to have this opportunity of introducing myself to you through the medium of the Parish Magazine. Before long I hope to have the privilege of meeting you and knowing you personally. You will all realise that this may take some time.
> By now you will no doubt have heard that the Induction by the Archdeacon of Liverpool will take place on Friday, 9th June, at 7.30 p.m. I look forward very much indeed to this day when I shall meet many of you for the first time. On Sunday, 11th June, at 8 a.m. I shall be the Celebrant at the Holy Communion Service. It is my earnest hope that a large number of Communicants will prepare themselves and come to this most important Service—my first Communion with my parishioners.

St Matthew's Church

Our Church is beautiful in its proportions, impressive in its size, and inspiring in its bold design and artistic colouring of the great East window. How I look forward to my ministry as Vicar of such a lovely Church. May this beautiful House of God be preserved.

The Jubilee

The Fiftieth Birthday of our Church is fast approaching. I shall do my best to make this important occasion one of the most memorable in the life history of the Church. You will all understand, I am sure, that as a newcomer into your midst much will depend upon you. Provisional arrangements for the Anniversary Services have been made and are set out below. I shall endeavour to obtain special preachers for all Services.

The War

The struggle grows grimmer, but so does our determination to hold on and see things through. The enemy's strength is brutal, but it is also brittle. Even by the time you read this letter great military operations may have begun. I need not dwell on the sadness and suffering of the present time. Let us do our duty manfully, and ask for the strength which God gives to those who trust not 'in chariots and horses', but in the righteousness of their cause. We have much to thank God for.

My Hope

My hope for the future is a single one. We all long to do our bit to serve our times to the best of our ability. I hope, therefore, that we may all become better Christians, with a clear knowledge of what our duty is, and a dependence on God for all the courage and strength which we need. As far as our Church is concerned, this means that we all pull together, and make our Church one keen family of fellow-workers for the Kingdom.

I do most sincerely want to be your friend, and I am hoping to get to know you in your homes and at Church. There is much to be done. Let us 'go to it' with the blessing of God upon us.

Your sincere friend,
W. HERBERT BULLOUGH.

Bishop Albert Augustus David had retired before Revd Bullough was appointed to Highfield, and his successor, Bishop Clifford Martin, had not been enthroned, so the new Vicar of Highfield was instituted privately by the Bishop of Warrington, Right Revd Gresford Jones, who was in charge of the Diocese during the interregnum. Revd Bullough was delighted to return to his native Wigan where he was to serve for fifteen years.

The Induction was reported in the *Wigan Observer* on 13 June 1944:

St Matthew's Church, Highfield, was crowded to its fullest capacity on Friday evening last week, when Rev Walter Herbert Bullough, AKC, was inducted Vicar in succession to the late Rev Parker Johnson. Many people were unable to gain admission. The first portion of the service was conducted by Canon W. O. Hunter Rodwell (Rural Dean), and the induction was performed by the Archdeacon of Liverpool (Venerable C. F. Twitchet).

Amongst those present were the Mayor and Mayoress (Alderman and Mrs H. Dowling), Mr W. H. Tyrer, CBE (Town Clerk), members of Wigan Town Council, relatives and friends of the new Vicar, parishioners from Hunts Cross and Woolton, and a large number of officials from churches in Wigan Rural Deanery.

The clergy present included Canon A. White (Billinge), Revs R. M. Hunter (Rural Dean of Childwall), A. Dean (Platt Bridge), A. Owen (Poolstock), T. Barton (St Michael's), J. Martin (St George's), Philip C. Wells (Upholland), J. H. Bartlett (Pemberton), W. A. Wiffen (Whelley), W. H. Vaughan (Abram), J. Taplin (Goose Green), H. C. N. Lawson (New Springs), M. H. Gaskell (Golborne), J. D. Cook (Hindley), R. O. Shone (Ashton), H. Ellis (St Catherine's), J. N. Davey (Newtown), H. Senar and S. J. Davies (Wigan Parish Church), M. Pryce Jones (Rector of Woolton), H. S. Crabtree (Shevington), L. C. Bradshaw (Curate, Standish Parish Church), E. J. Arnold (Woolton Parish Church), D. M. Ryle (St Paul's, Widnes, who takes up duties at Hunt's Cross in September, in succession to the Rev W. H. Bullough), S. Bundey (Eccleston, St Helens), and Rev T. Clarke (Chaplain to a north-west ordnance factory). Revs E. T. Allen (Hindley Green), and W. R. H. Hall (Ashton) were the marshals. Messrs J. W. Brierley and A. Jackson (Lay Readers) were also present.

The Archdeacon of Liverpool said the service had been limited to the induction of the new Vicar, who had already been instituted privately by the Bishop of Warrington, who was in charge of the See during the vacancy. Seven years ago, Rev Parker Johnson had been given charge of St Matthew's but for a considerable time he suffered from ill-health and in the end, after a brief ministry, God took him to fulfil his ministry in His nearer presence. His successor, Rev Walter Herbert Bullough, who was one of their own candidates, trained for the ministry, was ordained to the diaconate only five years ago. He was licensed to the curacy of Widnes Parish Church of St Mary, where after only one month, he was called upon to shoulder heavy responsibility, the Vicar being released for service as chaplain to the Forces. Mr Bullough's work there and devotion to duty brought him to the notice of the Rector of Woolton, and with the permission of the Bishop, he was appointed to the curacy with charge of St Hilda's, Hunt's Cross, Liverpool. In that sphere he gained the capacity for leadership, and he had been chosen by the Patrons of the Benefice of St Matthew's to assume that solemn and responsible task. The Archdeacon said he was thankful that the patrons had selected one of their own clergy from the diocese. Mr Bullough took up his charge at a time of great crisis in the affairs of the church and nation. They would soon be welcoming in their midst the fourth Bishop of Liverpool, the appointment having been announced that day, and they would look to him for such leadership as would inspire them to strengthen the forces of spiritual religion in the Diocese. To their new Vicar, the service that day must be a landmark in his life. The church in that parish and deanery expected great things, and with the Grace of God he would succeed. They commended him to the prayers of the people in his charge, and they would pray that God would abundantly bless his ministry as he began a new page in the spiritual history of the parish of St Matthew, Highfield.

After tolling the church bell, the newly inducted Vicar concluded the service.

The new Vicar was immediately involved in the arrangements for celebrating the Jubilee of the Church. Special Services and preachers were arranged for the Sundays before and after the anniversary, and on the day itself, Tuesday 4 July there were Celebrations of Holy Communion at 7 a.m., 8 a.m., 10.30 a.m., and a Jubilee Service at 7.30 p.m., when the preacher was the Venerable Archdeacon of Liverpool, C. F. Twitchett, FKC. There was also a Parish Social and Concert held in the Schools at 7.45 p.m. on Wednesday 5 July.

Formation of Boys' Brigade

From his early days at Widnes Parish Church the Vicar had been a strong supporter of the oldest uniformed boys' organisation The Boys' Brigade. Revd Bullough was successful in the formation of the Boys' Brigade Company and Life Boys in the parish. In the November 1944 Parish Magazine he wrote:

> On Wednesday evening, October 18th 1944, the first meeting of the boys interested in the formation of a Company of the Boys' Brigade was held. There was a splendid turn up both of younger boys and boys over 12 years of age. For six weeks we shall be hard at drill, after which enrolment can take place and the Company will be attached to the Wigan Battalion. We welcome all boys who belong to our Church to come along on Wednesday evening at the following times: Boys 12 years and over come at 7.30 p.m.; Boys of 8 years and over come at 6.30 p.m. I am pleased that Mr N. Mills has offered his services and also Mr W. Winstanley. Mrs R. Stretton will become leader of The Life Boys.'

The Guides and the Brownies were also flourishing due to the hard work and enthusiasm of Miss K. Atherton and Miss B. Green to get the company and pack re-started after the loss to the parish of Kathleen Woods who had done so much together with Miss Green to establish the group in 1930.

An early photograph of the Boys Brigade and Life Boys, founded in 1944. The Highfield Company will celebrate its Golden Jubilee soon after the Centenary of the Church in 1994.

1944 and 1945 were momentous years in the history of the world. In June 1944 Normandy was invaded by the Allies, and the Germans were steadily driven back until on 7 May 1945 the German forces surrendered and the war in Europe came to an end. The devastating effect of the atomic bombs on Hiroshima and Nagasaki forced the Japanese to surrender three months later on 14 August. The parish had been sending parcels to all members of the parish on active service. Only the prisoners of war had been denied these comforts and so a Prisoner of War Fund had been set up to save for gifts on the return of the prisoners, seven in Germany and two in Japanese hands. Some of the prisoners were officially welcomed home at the Garden Fete in 1945.

After the war Revd Bullough became involved in several organisations outside the parish. He was appointed to be Honorary Secretary of the Bishop of Liverpool's Advisory Committee on Religious Films. This was in a way, a considerable advantage to the parish in that many of the films were shown to various organisations within the parish. He was appointed as Honorary Secretary for the Wigan Deanery to the Society for promoting Christian Knowledge. He was appointed Honorary Chaplain to Wigan Hippodrome (A.C.U.) and to the Wigan Deanery Branch of the Northern Provincial Guild of Vergers. He was also appointed District Chaplain to the Lay Readers in the Wigan Deanery.

At the end of 1945 Mr J. W. Brierley, who had been a well-loved and respected Headmaster of the Boys' School since June 1913, having seen the school through thirty two years of its history, including two world wars, retired, though he was to continue to serve the Church as Lay Reader, Treasurer, and School Governor for another sixteen years. In his place Mr E. Davies, BSc., of Holywell, was appointed to commence duty

The Rose Queen Ceremony was started in 1946. This picture of the 1950 ceremony shows Shirley Nicholson as Retiring Queen and Audrey Martin as the newly crowned Rose Queen.

at the beginning of January 1946. He also was a Lay Reader and he and his wife and their two daughters were to become involved in the life of the Church.

In November 1946, it was announced at a meeting of the Parochial Church Council that Major Cuthbert Blundell had 'gifted the Recreation Ground to the Vicar and Churchwardens for all time, to be known as St Matthew's Recreation Ground'. A letter of gratitude was sent to Major Blundell and in 1952 a parish appeal raised the sum of £412 to pay the death duties on the Major's magnificent gift.

After the war, plans were made for a suitable memorial to those who had given their lives. A War Memorial Fund was set up and it was decided to work towards the raising of funds to furnish a Memorial Chapel in the North transept.

Death of Mr W. Richardson

Mr William Richardson, a faithful servant of Highfield Church for over fifty years, died on 6 March 1947. His death was reported in the *Wigan Observer*:

> We regret to record the death, which occurred on Thursday, of Mr William Richardson, of 375, Billinge Road, Highfield, in his seventy sixth year.
>
> Mr Richardson was a former director and secretary of Messrs William Park and Co. (Forgemasters) Ltd., of the Wiend, and also director and secretary of English Tools Ltd., retiring on 31st July, 1944, after forty four years service. In his early days, Mr Richardson was in the office of Mr Preston, builder, of Church Street, Wigan, and he left the North Western Railway in 1900 to join William Park and Co. as an accountant.
>
> A keen Churchman, Mr Richardson had a long and active association with St Matthew's Church, Highfield. He was a sidesman from 1898 to 1910, and since the latter date, when St Matthew's was made into a Parish Church, he had been a churchwarden, apart from a break of two or three years. He was superintendent for thirty three years of St Matthew's Girls' Sunday School. He was a member of the National Church Assembly until last year, when he retired from that position, and he had served on various Diocesan sub-committees.
>
> Since 1935, Mr Richardson had been honorary arbitrator to the Lancashire and Cheshire Miners' Permanent Relief Society. At one time he was a teacher of book-keeping at the Wigan and District Mining and Technical College. Predeceased by his wife eight years ago, Mr Richardson is survived by two sons. The eldest son, Mr Frank Richardson, is headmaster of St Paul's C. E. Primary School, Goose Green, and the younger son is Canon Alan Richardson BA, of Durham Cathedral.
>
> The funeral takes place on Tuesday, a service at St Matthew's Church at 10.30 a.m., preceding cremation at Anfield Crematorium.

In his address at the funeral, recorded in the April 1947 Parish Magazine, the Vicar, Revd W. H. Bullough said:

> Here we are today in the Church he loved, to remember before God, with thankful hearts, the life and work of William Richardson. Few men have won the affection of so many people in such varied walks of life. That was not because of any easy, indulgent, hail-fellow-well-met address (on the contrary he was always forthright, so that on every side we hear the comment, 'He was always straight') but because of his sincerity, because

of his willingness to bend his mind to the affairs of his friends and the community in which he lived, because of the essential goodness of the man.

His outstanding characteristic was a desire to serve his fellow men. I have heard how terribly keen he was on his job, how he valued his connection with Messrs William Park and Co., and, of course, the honour of holding the position of director and secretary of English Tools Ltd., and how he treasured the present given to him on his retirement. I know from various 'asides' what a real personal interest he took in all those with whom he worked, especially those who took particular care of him at the office. He was absorbed with his work, but never so immersed but what he could take the keenest interest in all that was of human concern.

His later years were especially happy because of the work of his two sons. He missed greatly his son Alan, working as Canon of Durham Cathedral, but was cheered by frequent records of his work and an occasional book.

It is no coincidence that the very backbone of that life so respected and beloved was a living faith in God, and a staunch practice of his religion. He knew where to turn for strength and guidance, and he proved as well in joy as in sorrow that God never fails those who come to him in humility and faith. He gave himself wholeheartedly to the service of God through the Church. He served faithfully as one of the lay representatives from this diocese on the Church Assembly, and for many years he was a member of the standing committee of the Diocesan Conference, and lay secretary of the Ruri-Decanal Conference. The Bishop has asked me to say how sorry he is not to be present this morning, and also how very much the Diocese will miss this faithful servant. The Bishop also added; 'I shall never forget the warmth of Mr Richardson's welcome on my first visit to St Matthew's, Highfield'.

We mourn the loss of a very great hearted gentleman. I do not say that we mourn his death. No one could have wished for the prolonging of a life fraught with weariness and suffering. His strength had indeed become 'but labour and sorrow.' It is the loss of his presence with us that we feel. He loved Highfield to a remarkable degree, and it will scarcely be Highfield without him. So vivid and so vigorous a personality, such courage and such large heartedness, such practical sympathy and service, are not so common that we can lose a friend who displays these qualities without realising our loss. But here in this Church which he loved so dearly and so well, we shall always remember him, and his influence will be greatly felt for a long time.

I have never had the privilege of knowing anyone to whom the Church meant more or whose faith was more complete.

I bid you give thanks to God for the life and example and memory of William Richardson. Let us give thanks for the gifts of counsel and strength with which he guided and encouraged the people of this parish as a faithful and wise steward. In the name of the Church to which he gave his loyalty and service, from the laying of the foundation stone fifty three years ago until the morning of March 6th 1947, we bid farewell in love and gratitude to this noble-minded and great-hearted Christian gentleman.

Death of Major C. L. B-H-Blundell

The end of an era came to the parish on Wednesday 16 April 1947, with the death of Major Cuthbert Blundell. For eighty years he and his uncle Colonel Henry Blundell had provided all the buildings and much of the maintenance of the parish. In his Obituary in the Parish Magazine the Vicar writes:

> The hoisting of the flags of the Church and Schools to half mast on Wednesday, April 16th, announced to Highfield the death of our great friend and Patron, Major Cuthbert Blundell. He passed away on the Wednesday morning at his residence in Sussex. What a sad blow this is to Highfield, and how we shall miss our great benefactor. We give thanks to God for his wonderful generosity and for the great interest he took in all matters affecting our Church and our Schools. The Church Officials attended the funeral which took place at Halsall on Saturday, April 19th. Floral tributes were sent by the Parochial Church Council on behalf of the parishioners; by the managers and staff of the schools and also by the scholars of the schools. A simple memorial Service in which all the scholars took part was held in Church on Friday morning, April 18th. The children will remember this for a very long time. The Parish Memorial Service was held on Sunday evening, April 20th. It was a simple service (the family wished it to be so) modelled on the form of service used at Halsall on the Saturday. Many friends have told me how very much they appreciated this service 'which,' to use the words of one parishioner, 'will live in our memories until we join him.'
>
> So there has passed the great friend to St Matthew's. After the generous examples which have been shown to us by the Blundell family we cannot fail now to play our part in the maintenance of our Church and Schools. Let us resolve before God that we will not shrink from our great responsibilities and pray for His guidance and help day by day.

Major Blundell's Obituary in the *Wigan Observer* reads:

> The death occurred at his London residence on Wednesday last week of Major Cuthbert Leigh Blundell Hollinshead Blundell, OBE, late of the Grenadier Guards, of La Mancha Hall, Halsall, Ormskirk, in his 66th year. Major Blundell was a member of the Blundell family who owned and operated the Pemberton Colliery Company for many years, and he was Chairman of the Company when it changed hands in 1929, and became the Pemberton Colliery (1929) Company Ltd. Major Blundell was the younger son of the late Canon Blundell, Rector of Halsall, and he was a nephew of the late Colonel Blundell, CB, who was Conservative MP for Ince, from 1885 to 1892, and from 1895 to 1906. Well known in sporting circles, he was a staunch supporter of the Waterloo Cup Coursing Meeting. He never won the trophy however, although on one occasion one of his dogs reached the last four. He had had forty successive nominations for the cup. He served with the Grenadier Guards in South Africa, 1900 to 1902, and in the European War, 1914 to 1918. He leaves a widow and two daughters. Lady Lethbridge, of La Mancha Hall, is his sister.

Before his death, Major Blundell had given the Reredos for the new War Memorial Chapel. The Parochial Church Council decided that the Memorial to the late Major Blundell should be a carved oak screen to be placed in the North-West Transept Arch of our Church. This screen would also complete the War Memorial Chapel. The carving was to be carried out by the same firm who were constructing the War Memorial Chapel. A Fund was opened for the Blundell Memorial as well as the Fund for the War Memorial.

Memorials Dedicated

The War Memorial, the Blundell Memorial and the Pemberton Colliery Memorial were all dedicated by the Bishop of Liverpool at a Special Service in St Matthew's Church on Sunday 16 November 1947. The following report appeared in the *Wigan Observer*:

> In the presence of a crowded congregation, three memorials, the War Memorial, the Blundell Memorial (to the late Major Cuthbert L. B. H. Blundell OBE), and the Pemberton Colliery Memorial, were dedicated by the Bishop of Liverpool (Dr Clifford A. Martin) at the evening service at St Matthew's Church, Highfield, on Sunday.
>
> For the War Memorial, a side chapel has been created in the North Transept in memory of the men of the Church and Parish who laid down their lives in the 1939 to 1945 War. The Reredos has the figures of St Michael, St Uriel, St Gabriel and St Raphael beautifully carved in oak, the Memorial Tablet having fourteen regimental badges carved around it. The lectern has been presented by the 'D' Company of the Home Guard. The Blundell memorial consists of a carved oak screen erected under the North Transept arch dedicated in memory of Major Blundell, Patron of the Church and generous benefactor to the Parish on behalf of the Parishioners. In the cornice is carved the Blundell crest coloured in the Blundell colours. The Pemberton Colliery Memorial given by the owners of Pemberton Colliery (1946), is also a carved oak screen erected in the South Transept arch, to the memory of all those who for many generations have worked in the Coal Mines near the Church. The interesting feature of this screen, and probably a unique feature of any oak carving in England, is the inclusion in the carving of the cornice of six emblems illustrative of the mining industry. They consist of a pit headgear, a pony and loaded tub down the mine, a miner's lamp, a canary and cage, a pick and shovel, and a fossil. The oakwork of all three memorials has been executed by Messrs R. & J. Boulton, of Cheltenham, at a total cost of £2,000. The architect was Mr J. Terney, of Morecambe, who was the architect of the Church and is 80 years of age. Before the commencement of the service, which was conducted by the Vicar (Rev W. H. Bullough), Mr J. Magraw played the following music at the Organ: March Funebre by Chopin, Prayer in Bb by Guillemant and Thomas Tallis's Funeral Music.
>
> The Bishop said it was a wonderful sight to see a church as crowded as that church was that night. The people, he added, had come in such large numbers because it was a very great occasion, an occasion on which they would all look back over many years; and an occasion when they had come to dedicate such beautiful gifts in memory of people whom they held dear.'That lovely chapel and those beautiful screens,' said the Bishop, 'have been most tastefully designed and beautifully carried out. They were gifts of which the Church ought to be proud and they would add to its beauty and dignity. The gifts were to keep alive in their memory the real love and honour of those who had passed on.' The Bishop said he supposed there were a good many in the Congregation who were linked with the names of those commemorated—those who were killed in the recent war or who worked in the coal mines, and Cuthbert Blundell, Patron of that Church. Some people, Dr Martin added, endowed a bed or gave a sum of money, etc. to keep alive the memory of those whom they had loved and lost awhile.'It is a good thing,' he said, adding, ' but I can think of no better way than having a memorial in a church—doing as you have done today.' There were three reasons why he would choose to put, or help to

put something like those memorials in the House of God, for his loved ones. Firstly, because he wanted to remember their names and their places in the family. Secondly, because in the Church, they came to Holy Communion, and it was in Holy Communion, above all other services, that they found the ground for their acceptance in the Heavenly Family. The third reason was that a Church was, or should be, a place of quietness. In this rush and hurly burly life the thing they needed was somewhere where they could be peaceful and quiet. The service concluded with the singing of the Hymn 'O Worship the King' and the pronouncement of the blessing by the Bishop.

At the Annual Parochial Meeting held in April 1948 Mr Thomas Hughes was elected People's Warden in place of Mr Isaac Massey. Mr Hughes had been involved in the Little Lane Mission in the early days. He had been a Sidesman for over thirty years, a Sunday School Teacher and member of the Bible Class and was very much involved with supporting Missionary work in the Church through the Church Missionary Society. He was also a member of the Parochial Church Council and Treasurer of the Day School Fund .

Change of Headteachers

Another chapter in the History of the Junior School ended on Tuesday, 31 August. 1948, when Miss Edith Johnson retired from the Headship. The Vicar paid tribute to Miss Johnson in the Parish Magazine:

> Miss Johnson finishes her job as Headmistress, a position she has held for 23 years. (She had been Head of the Girls' School from August, 1925 until April, 1933 when the Junior Mixed School came into being.) This is a great loss to our Junior School and we shall miss her very much indeed. Miss Johnson has given of her best for the benefit of the children committed to her charge, and no small number of them, now old scholars, owe their present positions to the fine training they received when under the watchful eye of our grand Headmistress. Parishioners and friends will join in wishing Miss Johnson a long and happy and healthful retirement. It is a source of deep satisfaction to know that Miss Johnson will still retain her very close connection with our Church, and we hope that she will be 'one of us' for very many years. W. H. B

In the same magazine the Vicar welcomed Miss Johnson's successor:

> On September 1st next, Mr Edward George Elliott will begin his duties as Headmaster of our Junior School. He comes to us with a very wide experience. At the present time he is the first assistant master at the Waterloo Church of England School, at Ashton-under-Lyne. He will reside at Hindley Green for the present along with his wife (also a teacher) and his two small children. I can assure Mr and Mrs Elliott that they will receive a real Highfield welcome when they arrive. We are all looking forward to having them with us and our united good wishes go out to Mr Elliott as he commences his work as Headmaster of our Junior Schools. W. H. B.

Mr Elliott was appointed Vicar's Warden in succession to Mr T. Hesketh at the Annual Parish Meeting in 1949.

The parish lost another faithful servant in August 1948, when Mr T. Atherton died. Mr Atherton had been for many years a member of the Dramatic Society, Secretary of the Men's Bible Class, Bellringer, Sidesman and member of the Church Council. His brother William was Verger of the Church. In his Obituary in the Parish Magazine the Vicar wrote:

> We are still labouring under the shock at the suddenness of the death of our great friend Mr T. Atherton. We are already missing him very much indeed and as time goes by we shall realize more fully what we owe to him. For over forty years he has served St Matthew's in so many ways. Whenever the bell rings we think of him, and his position as secretary of the Men's Bible Class, which he held for twenty three years, will be difficult to fill. Few men serve their Church as he did, and we give thanks to God for his life and work, and with one voice say: 'Well done, thou good and faithful servant.' Thanks be to God for the sure and certain hope of resurrection to eternal life through our Lord Jesus Christ.

In 1948 the Vicar was appointed to the Chaplaincy of Pemberton Hospital. Over and above his normal duties he involved himself with others, in the showing of films to the patients, and each year on Walking Day, many of the older patients were brought out to the gate and the procession stopped to sing a hymn and pray for the inmates. The children of the Infant Sunday School also took their Harvest Gifts to the Patients in the Hospital.

A reorganisation of the Archdeaconries in the Liverpool Diocese in 1949 meant that the Wigan Deanery, which had, since the formation of the Diocese in 1880, been in the Archdeaconry of Liverpool, was to be transferred to the Archdeaconry of Warrington. This was agreed to at a meeting of the Parochial Church Council on 16 May 1949.

Dedication of Memorials

After her brother, Major Cuthbert Blundell's death, Lady Lethbridge, who then became Patron of the Parish of Highfield, promised to give the Altar Ornaments for the Memorial Chapel in memory of her brother and of the men of Highfield who gave their lives during the Second World War. These, together with the Font Cover and the South Chancel Screen were dedicated by the Bishop of Warrington at a Special Remembrance Day Service on Sunday 6 November 1949. The *Wigan Observer* reported the event as follows:

> In the presence of a large congregation, the Bishop of Warrington, the Right Rev C. R. Claxton, on Sunday night dedicated a silver cross, candlesticks and altar vases, given by Lady Lethbridge (Patron of the Benefice) for the Memorial Chapel in St Matthew's Church, Highfield. They are in memory of Lady Lethbridge's brother, Cuthbert Blundell, and of the men of Highfield who gave their lives during the Second World War.
>
> The Bishop, who gave the address, also dedicated a carved oak font cover given by Mrs Kathleen Jones, as a memorial to her father, the late Rev John Woods, the first Vicar of the Church (1910 to 1937) and a carved oak chancel screen, presented by Mr C. D. Gullick, a former Director of Pemberton Collieries. A special form of service for

Remembrance day was used, the Vicar, Rev W. H. Bullough officiating. Mr J. Magraw was at the organ, and the hymns sung were: 'We love the place, O God.', 'O God our help in ages past.', 'Great God to Thee our hearts we raise.', 'Thy Kingdom come, on bended knee.' and 'For all the Saints.' The lesson was read by Mr E. Davies, Lay Reader and the Roll of Honour for the two world wars were read by Mr J. W. Brierley, Lay Reader. Wreaths of Poppies were placed near each War Memorial. After the Choir had rendered John Goss's anthem 'I heard a voice from heaven.', the Last Post and Reveille were sounded by Mr T. Gaskell, Band Officer of the 14th Wigan Company Boys' Brigade attached to St Matthew's Church.

The Bishop began his address by telling a story of the brilliant and gallant soldier, General Wolfe, the hero of the great Victory won by the British army at Quebec. As the General lay dying on the field of battle, news was brought to him that the enemy were in complete rout and his last words were 'The Victory is ours, O keep it'. General Wolfe's men kept that Victory and the speaker took those words as they were gathered, to remember in honour before God those men who gave their lives in the two world wars and won the Victory over the forces of tyranny and oppression that sought to dominate the world. 'We must see that the Victory which they won is not lost,' he said. 'It was a Victory that could only be won at a very great price and it is fitting and right that every year we should gather on Remembrance Sunday to pay our tribute and express our gratitude to those who died that we might live in freedom. As the years passed it was quite possible for us to forget the mortal danger in which this country was placed particularly in the last war, the Bishop continued. Many in that Church knew nothing or very little of what we went through in 1940 when we stood alone to face the fury of a desperate and unprincipled enemy. It was all brought back to him so forcibly when he heard Sir David Maxwell Fyfe speaking about the Nurenburg Trials. 'Never have I been so moved,' said the Bishop. 'Hardly have I ever been so horrified at the revelations which he made of the utter callousness of those leaders and the Nazi party with their complete contempt for human life.' We might be inclined to grumble about our lot these days, saying. These are not the conditions for which we fought, but if we had not won the Victory our conditions today would have been ten times worse; we should be the slaves of people without any kind of principles at all. That was why we should do well to remember those who fought and died for us. Evil still existed in the world; it still attacked us in our own lives. We must stand and fight for those things for which they gave their lives—for righteousness, for justice, for truth, for love and for mercy. That was the call which came to us. We lived in a world that was grievously troubled and the peace we had inherited was an uneasy affair. At root, there was one main conflict. He believed there were two issues, two conflicting ideas. One concerned those people who believed in a material conception of life—that that was the only thing that mattered and God was irrelevant to the situation. It was material things which governed our affairs. Over and against that was the Christian conception that this was God's world, and that every man, woman, boy and girl had his place in it and was as important in that world, and that civilisation could only be built on those fundamental principles of truth, justice, and righteousness. 'Without them,' said the Bishop, there could be no peace in the world. 'Do we really believe that it is in God we are going to find the answers to the world's problems and our own, and are we prepared to act on that faith?' he asked. It was only as we overcame the evil in our lives that we should be able to overcome the evil that was all around us in the world, he added, and it was only as we made the Church strong not only in this country but throughout the world, that we should see peace established throughout the Universe.

The Annual Christmas fair was held on Saturday 10th December, 1949 in the Schools. The Opening Ceremony was held at 3.45 p.m. The Matron of Billinge Hospital performed the opening ceremony. Teas were served at 5 p.m., Films were shown at 6 p.m. and a Grand Social was held at 7.45 p.m. Parish organisations were responsible for the following: Teas and Suppers—Mrs T. Atherton and the Women's Meeting. Linen Goods Stall—The Working Party. Pound Stall—The Boys' Brigade. The Christmas Tree—The Boys' Brigade. Cake Stall—The Guides, assisted by the Brownies. The White Elephant Stall—Mr A. Atherton and the Bible Class. The Grotto—The Young People's Guild. The Bran Tub—The Life Boys. Hoopla—The Young People's Guild. Advertising and Ticket Secretary—Miss H. Hughes. Social—Mr H. Gee, Mr E. G. Elliott, Mr E. Davies, Mrs E. Davies, and others. Admission to Christmas Fair and Films was 1 shilling. Admission to the Social was 1 shilling. The proceeds, which amounted to £121 15s. 10d., were for Church Expenses and the Church Missionary Society.

Death of Mr Isaac Massey

Another faithful stalwart of the Church, Mr Isaac Massey, died in January 1950. He had been involved with the Church for many years and was Churchwarden from 1929 to 1944. His death was reported in the *Wigan Examiner*:

Mr Isaac Massey, of Sommerville, Highfield, a director of Messrs Massey Bros. (Pemberton), Ltd., coach builders and builders and contractors, died, we regret to record, on Sunday, at the age of seventy.

Mr Massey, as a boy, attended Pemberton Colliery Schools. He afterwards served as a clerk with Messrs J. E. Peck and Co. Ltd. and subsequently was in the employ of Mr W. H. Baker, brassfounder, Wallgate, and in later years he became a director.

In 1904 he went into partnership with his brothers Thomas and William as Massey Bros. Under his supervision many large public buildings, cotton mills, schools and cinemas were completed, amongst the foremost of which were: Extensions to Electric Light Dept., Wigan, Out-patients Dept., Wigan Infirmary, Earlestown Technical School, Sandbrook Mills, Orrell, Enfield Mill, Pemberton, All Saints' Senior School, Wigan, St Mark's Schools, Newtown, West Park Grammar School, St Helens, St Patrick's School, Wigan, County Playhouse, Wigan, and cinemas at Atherton, Tyldesley, Platt Bridge, Pemberton and Whelley Council School.

In 1920 his enterprise developed the firm's activities to the building of charabanc bodies owing to the great slackness in the building trade. This has since developed into the manufacture of double decker and single decker omnibuses for many large municipalities and omnibus undertakings and the firm is well known throughout the country. From the employment of a few hands in the early days the firm now has a staff of approximately 150, which at present is largely engaged in motor coach body building.

Mr Massey was prominently identified with St Matthew's Church, Highfield; he was for many years churchwarden, but relinquished the position a few years ago owing to ill health. A Freemason, Mr Massey was one of the founders of Heber Lodge. His wife pre-deceased him in August last year and he is survived by one daughter and four grand-children.

The Funeral

There was a large and representative congregation at the funeral service which took place at St Matthew's Church, Highfield on Thursday. The staff, workpeople and choir lined the entrance to the church, and as a mark of respect, a flag was flown at half-mast on the tower of the church.

The Rev W. H. Bullough (Vicar) conducted the service, and Mr J. W. Brierley (lay reader) read the lesson. Psalm 23, the hymn 'The strife is o'er' and Nunc Dimittis were sung. Master Keith Magraw was the organist.

In a tribute, the Rev J. N. Davey (Vicar, St Mark's, Newtown) spoke from the words 'The steps of a good man are ordered by the Lord' (Psalm 37, verse 23). He said Mr Massey found his spiritual home in that church, where he had hold of joy that came to him in that work with the conviction that life had its richness in the service given. The reverend gentleman went on to refer to his friendship with Mr Massey for twenty five years, and the great deal of happiness he had found in that friendship. He was a good man and in his life he had all those characteristics of those who follow in the steps of the Man of Galilee. Mr Massey first of all learned what it was to be a friend—he was a faithful friend—and then he sought day by day to give himself to those with whom he lived. He never counted the sacrifice because it was the expression of his friendship. He was generous, and never at any time refused to help those causes which made demands upon him. He asked for no recognition, sought no public admiration but found a joy in serving others which was his reward. Mr Massey was a good neighbour, and was at all times moved by the difficulties which came into the lives of people. Day by day he tried to express by his friendliness his concern for them, which was a characteristic of a follower of the Lord Jesus. They thanked God that he had made life richer for his having been in it, and they could truthfully say that he had entered into that higher service where there was fulness and joy for evermore.

The interment followed in the churchyard, where the committal rites were said by the Vicar, who also read the Masonic Burial Service.

In addition to the family and private mourners those present included Masonic brethren representing Heber, Holmes, Corinthian, Crawford and the Pemberton Lodges, The Wigan and District Building Trades Employers' Association was represented by Messrs H. Speakman, (president), N. Cunliffe, (vice-president), J. Livesey, E. Matthias, J. E. Oakley, W. H. Lester, J. P. Glover (Messrs Farrimond & Glover).

There were also in attendance Messrs J. Hopwood Sayer and S. Baron, (solicitors), H. P. Greener (Messrs M. A. Peters & Co. Ltd.), T. L. Lace (Messrs Lace & Co. Ltd.), E. Gaskell (Messrs Clough and Gaskell Ltd.), W. Benion (Messrs R. A. Naylor Ltd., Warrington.), A. V. Forster (Messrs R. G. Tickle & Son Ltd., Liverpool.), G. F. Ibbotson (manager, District Bank, Wigan.), F. Wardle (clerk-in-charge, District Bank Pemberton.), T. Winstanley (Messrs Webster & Winstanley), F. W. Coleclough (Norley Quarries Ltd.), T. C. Robinson (Eagle Picturedromes), G. Melling (NCB Pemberton Collieries), R. G. Taylor (Messrs Lathom & Taylor), and Mr F. Winstanley and T. H. French.

St Matthew's Parochial Church Council was represented by Mrs Clark (secretary), Mrs Hughes and Messrs G. Elliott and T. Hughes.

The bearers were Messrs E. Dawber, J. Blackwell, W. Gee, C. Derbyshire, L. Sutton and E. F. O'Dwyer, employees.

There was a profusion of floral tributes from the family, relatives and friends, staff and workpeople Messrs Massey Bros., Masonic Lodges, firms and organisations. The funeral arrangements were in the hands of Messrs Middleton and Wood, under the direction of Mr G. Wood.

Formation of Communicants' Guild

The 1950 February Magazine reported the formation of the Communicants Guild:

The newly formed Communicants' Guild has got off to a grand start and the members are all very keen indeed. The Guild formed at the request of the Confirmation Candidates themselves, has one aim and one aim only: TO BRING HOME TO THOSE WHO ARE CONFIRMED WHAT IT MEANS TO BE A MEMBER OF CHRIST'S CHURCH AND TO ENDEAVOUR TO KEEP THEM WITHIN THE FELLOW-SHIP OF THE CHURCH.

Every year a vast number of young folk who are confirmed drift away from the Church in a very short time. Here is the opportunity to hold them and help them. I am grateful to all those who have encouraged me in this new venture and to the many offers of help which have been made. The following are the names of the Leaders. Leaders in charge. The Vicar, Mr E. G. Elliott, Mr E. Davies, Mr W. Nock, Mr W. Hooke, Mrs W. Nock, Miss M. Atherton.

. Leaders in charge of craft work. Mrs Bullough, Mrs Hitchen, Mrs Corless, Mr H. Aldridge.

Guild Leaders. Norma Langton, Keith Berry. Hon. Sec. Eric Moore.

Assist. Sec. Audrey Martin. Treasurer. John Berry. Hostesses. Jean Halliwell, Dorothy Simm. Committee. Eric Schofield, Geoffrey Nuttall, Dorothy Sharrock, Jean Rowbottom.

Meeting Night. Thursday evening, Senior Hall, at 7.15 p.m.

I am grateful to the parents of candidates who have offered to help in various ways and for the many expressions of thanks for what has been done for the candidates. The service of welcome will long be remembered by all who took part in it. W. H. B.

The Annual Congregational Tea Party was a long established tradition in the parish, having been started in the 1870s. In 1950 it was held on Shrove Tuesday with Tea at 6 p.m. and an Evening Entertainment at 7.30 p.m. The children were entertained to a Grand Film Show on the previous evening at 6 p.m. Admission was ninepence (including refreshments.)

The Schools Problem

Following the death of Major Cuthbert Blundell, the solicitors administering his estate sent the following letter to Lady Lethbridge, one of the executors of the estate, and one of the Patrons of St Matthew's, Highfield:

> You will, no doubt have been informed that the Judge ordered that the property, Highfield Schools, Pemberton should be sold forthwith. In this connection we have instructed Messrs Bevan, the leading Estate Agents and Auctioneers to try to effect a sale. Yours W. P. Barrell.

Lady Lethbridge immediately telephoned Revd W. H. Bullough and there began one of the most intensive series of meetings involving the Diocese, the Wigan Education Committee and the Finance Committee of the Town Council, the Ministry of Education, the School Managers, the Parochial Church Council, and the Patrons.

The Vicar tells the story of the events in the June 1950 Parish Magazine:

My Dear Friends,

During the past months events of major importance have taken place. The future of the Highfield Church of England Schools has been decided. The Secondary Modern Boys' School has become a Controlled School, and the Junior Mixed and Infants' (The Primary School) has become an Aided School. The question which many of you will be asking yourselves is this. Why has this decision been made so suddenly? The answer is a lengthy one.

It was the intention of Major Blundell to hand over the Schools to the Church, but before this was accomplished he died. The School buildings and sites therefore became part of his estate. The executors of his will hoped to carry out the wish of Major Blundell, but because two of the beneficiaries under the will are young children and cannot speak for themselves a Judge in Chancery Court ruled that the property should be sold. Things came to a head when it became known to the Managers that the Schools were to be sold by auction. Swift action was taken by the Local Education Authority in consultation with the Managers and the Ministry of Education in London. The outcome of the many and various consultations has resulted in the Local Education Authority placing a Compulsory Purchase Order on the Sites and Buildings, which means that no one else can buy them.

An agreement has been made with the Local Education Authority whereby the School Managers will buy back again, through the Diocesan Board of Finance, that part of the School which has been granted Aided Status—namely the Junior Mixed and Infants' Departments (The Primary School.) The Local Education Authority will be responsible for the cost of that part of the School which has become a Controlled School—namely the Secondary Modern Boys' Department.

So the decision was made—very reluctantly but with courage and hope that the parish will wholeheartedly support the Managers in the great task that is before them. We have made a magnificent start through the Day School Fund, and again on behalf of the Managers I say thank you. If there are any readers who are not members of this Day School scheme will they please think carefully about joining the great band of Church people who are determined to keep the Highfield Church of England Schools as Church Schools for ever.

The Parochial Church Council at their last meeting passed the following resolution unanimously:

'That the Parochial Church Council approves the action of the School Managers in their efforts to preserve the Highfield Schools as Church Schools and supports the application of the Managers to the Ministry of Education for the recognition of the Primary School (Junior Mixed and Infants) as an Aided School and the recognition of the Secondary Modern Boys' School as a Controlled School.

The Parochial Church Council undertakes on behalf of the Parish to accept its share of the financial responsibility for the purchase of the said Primary School by the Diocesan Board of Finance and also the financial responsibility for the future maintenance of the School as an Aided School.'

To sum up. The Parish will now work to raise the money to pay back to the Diocesan Board of Finance the amount (not yet fixed) of the purchase price of the Primary (Junior Mixed and Infants) School, and will continue to work to maintain the Primary School as an Aided School.

Another question that is sure to be asked now that the Senior Boys' School has become a Controlled School is this. What difference will this make to the Parish in respect of the use of the buildings for parochial purposes? I am happy to be able to answer—practically no difference at all.

It is my intention to call a Special General Meeting in the Parish at the earliest possible date and to explain the whole situation fully and answer any questions. The meeting will take place as soon as it becomes known how much we shall have to raise to buy the Primary School.

In the meantime let us go faithfully about our duty as members of the Church and by every appointed means strive to extend the Kingdom of God.

I ask for your prayers, as we face together this new but challenging opportunity of witnessing for Jesus Christ.

Your sincere friend,
W. HERBERT BULLOUGH.

Following this letter an account of the meeting of the Wigan Education Committee was reprinted from the *Wigan Observer* of 19 May 1950 'for historical purposes':

The future of the Highfield C. E. Secondary Modern School and the Highfield Primary School was discussed at a special meeting of Wigan Education Authority on Tuesday last week. After a Chancery Court ruling given on April 27th, a solicitor in charge of the estate of the late Major C. B. H. Blundell, who built and maintained the two schools, informed the school managers that the schools were to be sold by auction.

Councillor E. Maloney (chairman) told the members that at the last meeting of the Authority the chairman and vice-chairman (Councillor S. Taylor) were empowered to deal with any urgent business which might arise prior to the formation of the new committee. 'Last week,' said Councillor Maloney, 'something arose of such a character that it was impossible to be dealt with by myself and the vice-chairman and that is the reason this special meeting has been called.'

Changed Situation

The chairman went on to say that last week, Mr Edwards (Director of Education) received information that an auctioneer had been to the Highfield schools in order to value them with the intention of selling the schools. The Highfield Primary and Secondary Modern Schools were built and maintained by Major C. B. H. Blundell. Under the Education Act, 1944, a changed situation arose, particularly as regards voluntary schools, and in consequence Major Blundell decided to transfer the school sites and buildings to the Highfield Church authorities. He instructed his solicitors to undertake the necessary conveyances, but, unfortunately, twelve hours before he should have signed the deed of assignment he died.

The executors made investigations to discover whether it would be possible still to complete the gift. The solicitors in charge of the estate obtained a decision from a Chancery Court judge that the gift was not a valid one and that the schools should be sold. 'It was clearly the duty of the executors to realise the estate to the best possible advantage,' said Councillor Maloney. 'Unless they did so, they were not doing their duty.' The sale of the buildings was put into the hands of a Liverpool firm of solicitors, and the school managers were informed that the schools were to be sold by auction.

School Managers' Decision

Councillor Maloney described the conversations which took place regarding the future of the schools and detailed the discussions of the complicated issues involved. As a result of these discussions the school managers decided to apply to the Wigan Education Authority for the Authority to acquire the schools and land, if necessary by compulsory purchase, and for the land and buildings later to be re-transferred to the managers. The price would be fixed by the District Valuer and failing acceptance, by arbitration. After pointing out that 520 children attended the two schools, Councillor Maloney added 'If the schools were disposed of privately, responsibility for making provision for the scholars would fall on us. The continuity of these schools must be preserved and the fairest way of doing so would be for compulsory purchase orders to be made.' Councillor Maloney went on to detail a series of resolutions passed at a meeting of the school managers. The resolutions of the managers will result in them becoming responsible for the payment of all expenses in connection with the acquisition of the Secondary Modern School, which has now been designated a 'Controlled' school. The managers are willing to reimburse the Education Authority in respect of any portion of the 'Controlled' school premises which ultimately are required for the purposes of the Primary Department. The Minister of Education has made orders directing that the Primary School shall become an 'Aided' school and the Secondary Modern School a 'Controlled' school.

After discussion, the Authority unanimously decided that application be made for compulsory purchase orders in respect of the land and buildings. These orders were made at the monthly meeting of the Town Council held the following evening.

At the end of 1950 Mr J. Magraw, who had been Organist and Choirmaster for over 25 years resigned. He had maintained the high standard of choral tradition at St Matthew's throughout this period. The Choirboys' Camp and the Old Choirboys' Association had flourished. The last of the Choirboys' camps at Chester College took place from the 29th July to the 12th of August 1950 and was enjoyed as much as all those in previous years. Mr Magraw had also been involved in other work in the parish including Magazine Secretary and work with the Dramatic Society and Socials, including at one time a Pierrot Group of Singers.

Mr R. Kay from Ashton-in-Makerfield was appointed Organist and Choirmaster in his place from the beginning of 1951.

The Barn Social

Harvest 1951 marked the beginning of another event which became an annual feature over the following years: The Barn Social. The October 1951 magazine gave details of the first social which was organised in those early days by the newly formed Communicants' Guild:

> This year at St Matthew's the Festival of Harvest will not end at Evensong on Sunday, September 30th. We are going to bring the spirit of Harvest Thanksgiving into a grand parish social on Saturday, October 6th.
>
> At 7 p.m. on this day the Social will be opened by 'The Squire' and he will be accompanied by 'The Duchess.' There will be instrumental and vocal items and the old tyme dances and Barn Dances. The Junior Hall will be transformed into a barn and supper will consist of Hot Pot and Jam Tart and Currant Cake all 'home made'. The tickets are on sale in all parts of the parish at two shillings and sixpence. You are asked to get your ticket early to avoid disappointment. Here is a rough outline of the arrangements.

> Hymn 'Come ye thankful people, come.'
> Squire's opening remarks.
> 'Arken to the Duchess.
> Instrumental item.
> Barn Dances.
> Solo Country Song.
> Game for the younger ones.
> Country dress parade.
> Old Tyme Dances.
> Solo Country song.
> Dancing.
> Epilogue. Solo 'Bless this House.'
> Hymn 'Crimond.'
> Benediction.

I hope as many of you as possible will come to the social attired in Country Dress. Valuable prizes will be awarded for the best costumes.

The Barn Social was in later years organised by the wives of some of the farmers in the parish. Mrs Halsall of Worthington Fold Farm will long be remembered for her performance of the clog dance at these socials.

The Rogationtide Procession

The 1950s marked the beginning of another parish tradition, the Rogationtide Walk round the farms of the parish.

Rogationtide, the fifth Sunday after Easter, is the time when we ask for God's blessing on the fruits of the earth. We were following an old custom of the church in making our procession round the farms of the parish, to join with the farmers and their families at this critical time of the year to acknowledge our dependence upon God.

In Mr Bullough's day we began with a short service outside the church when we sang the hymn 'All people that on earth do dwell' followed by a short prayer, and the procession, led by the choir, walked up Billinge Road followed by the Infant Sunday School, the Junior Sunday School and as many parents and other adults who came along to enjoy the pleasant walk through the farms of the parish. In later years, the procession sometimes began from outside the Parish Hall.

The first stop was at Ackers farm on Billinge Road, situated between what is now Clevedon Drive and Culcross Ave. The farm was demolished in May 1969. Mr and Mrs Ackers and their son Jim were there to welcome us. Here we assembled in the farmyard and read:

> The chief thing for life is water and bread and a garment and a house. Health and a good constitution are better than all gold: and there is no gladness above the joy of the heart. O all ye works of the Lord, bless ye the Lord: Praise him and magnify him for ever.

Then we sang the hymn 'Praise, my soul, the King of heaven' and the Vicar ended the short service by blessing the farm and all who worked there.

We then processed along Billinge Road, as far as Pony Dick. The ruin of the old pub was still standing up to 1954 when it was finally demolished. Here we crossed the road and entered the grounds of Winstanley Hall and called at Rylance Mill farm—the home of the Fouracre family. There was a lovely pasture in front of the farmhouse, sometimes with horses in it. Here we said an appropriate prayer:

> O God, who hast given us the beasts to share with us the burden and heat of the day: Grant that we may show our gratitude to Thee, who art the giver of all life, by treating with gentleness and consideration all living creatures entrusted to our care; through Jesus Christ our Lord. Amen.

Then we sang the hymn 'The King of love my Shepherd is', the Vicar pronounced the blessing and the procession moved on, up Hall Lane towards the Hall, to be met by Captain and Mrs Bankes and members of their family. Sometimes we stopped near a plantation of trees and sometimes at a cornfield and read:

> Thine eye shall desire grace and beauty: and above both the green blade of corn. Sow to yourselves in righteousness: reap in mercy. Man shall not live by bread alone: but by every word that proceedeth out of the mouth of God. O all ye green things upon the Earth, bless ye the Lord: praise him, and magnify him for ever.

Then the hymn 'God of mercy, God of grace' was sung and the blessing ended the visit.

From here the procession turned round and returned to Pony Dick, crossed the road again and went through Blundell's Wood, and followed the footpath round the edge of the fields to Holmes House Farm which stood around the Southery Avenue area. Here the Kearsley family lived. It was one of the highlights of the walk because they had a pond—and the ducks may even be out swimming! This was the nearest that the parish could provide to a 'well, stream or river' and so we read:

> Jesus said, Whosoever drinketh of this water shall thirst again: but whosoever drinketh of the water that I shall give him shall never thirst; but the water that I shall give him shall be in him a well of water springing up into everlasting life.

> O ye showers and dew, bless ye the Lord:
> O ye wells, bless ye the Lord:
> O ye seas and floods, bless ye the Lord:
> Praise him and magnify him for ever.

We then sang the hymn 'Lead us, heavenly father, lead us', a prayer was said for all who work on the sea, and the Vicar ended the service with the blessing. From here, the Infants returned to church. It was usually as much as they could manage to walk.

The rest of the procession then walked along past the area which is now occupied by St Aidan's church and school, and turned left down what was then part of Clapgate lane, now Highfield Grange Avenue, to Harvey House Farm, (now demolished, but

Rogationtide. The Infants' Sunday School at Holmes House Farm in the 1950s.

which stood near the large tree in front of no. 94, Highfield Grange Avenue), where the Ashall family lived and worked. Here the service may have been for a field of corn or of roots, depending upon what Mr Ashall was growing. We read:

> O God, who by the hidden growth of roots dost supply food for man and beast, and bringest sweetness out of the strong earth: Grant that we may lift from the soil an abundance of wholesome food; and when the work is wearisome and the soil is heavy, yet give us strength to persevere till the whole crop is safely lifted; through Jesus Christ our Lord. Amen.

We sang the hymn 'Love Divine, all loves excelling' and the Vicar ended the the service with the blessing.

We had to turn back again from here. The road ahead went down to Goose Green, and we made our way to the Tan Pit Cottages where we stopped and said the service appropriate for gardens and allotments. We read:

> O God, by whose dispensation each one of us may share in the cultivation of the land: Give us also such skill and patience in digging and sowing and planting, that fruit and vegetables may come forth to nourish our bodies, and flowers to gladden our eyes; through Jesus Christ our Lord. Amen.

We sang the hymn 'Lord, thy word abideth', the Vicar gave the blessing and we moved on again.

Rogationtide at Langley House Farm. The row of cottages in the background were part of the 'New houses' off Pemberton Road, demolished to make way for the new bungalows on Pemberton Road.

The next stop was a very welcome break at Worthington Fold Farm, a very old building, now sadly demolished. Here we again said the service for a farmyard, and then Mrs Halsall had refreshments waiting for us. There were orange and lemon drinks for the youngsters and tea and cakes for the adults to enjoy, home baking by Mrs Halsall in the old farmhouse.

Suitably refreshed we set off on the remaining part of our journey back to the church, calling at Tan House Farm (still standing in 1991), where Miss Wadsworth lived. Next we called at Melling's farm (now demolished) where the Alkers lived and worked, and our last call was at Langley House farm where Mr and Mrs Johnson and their three daughters lived and worked. Mr Johnson is still living here (1991) but the farm land has been covered with new houses. At each of these farms we read a service appropriate to them, sang a hymn and the Vicar pronounced the blessing on the families and their work.

From here the journey was back again along Pemberton Road, down the hill and back to church where the final prayers and blessings were said outside the church.

Before the actual walk started, the Vicar and choir went by car to three farms which were too far away to include in the walk: to Windy Arbour farm where Mr and Mrs Turner lived with their two daughters and two sons (now a busy farm shop); to Sandyforth farm, beyond what was Windy Arbour Colliery, where the Smith family lived and worked, and to Jamieson's farm (now called Cherry Tree Farm, off Pine View) where the Dierden family lived and worked.

The collections taken on the Rogation walk were always good. The farmers were very generous in their contributions and thank-offerings for this visit to their farms. The weather was usually very kind to us, and the walk was a most enjoyable afternoon outing, but I can remember occasions when we took umbrellas and raincoats, 'just in case !'

First Baby Born at the Vicarage

A very happy event occurred in the lives of the Vicar and Mrs Bullough in November 1951 when a son, John Martin Bullough was born to them at the Vicarage. This was the first child to be born at the new Vicarage; Herbert Lancaster Laidman and Kathleen Woods were born at the old Vicarage, now Iona. So far, up to 1992, John Bullough is the only child to be born at the Vicarage in nearly 80 years. John Bullough is now a Dental Surgeon in Scarisbrick.

Mr Paul Gaskell was appointed Church Treasurer when Mr Brierley decided to resign the post in April 1952. Mr Gaskell had been a member of the Parochial Church Council, a Sidesman and an Auditor of the Church Accounts. He had been involved in Church life for many years, being a member of the Tennis Club when there were courts on the Recreation Ground.

Mr Thomas Hesketh, who, in the words of the Vicar 'Would do anything for you, he was always willing to step in and do something' died suddenly while on holiday. He had been at various times Churchwarden, Sunday School Superintendent, Vice-Presi-

The Church Choir about 1952, with Revd W. H. Bullough, Mr R. Kay, Organist and Choirmaster, Mr J. W. Brierley and Mr E. Davies, Lay Readers.

dent of the Men's Class and Treasurer of the Church Finance Scheme. His death was reported in the *Wigan Observer*:

> The death occurred on Saturday, whilst holidaying in Cleveleys along with his wife, of Mr Thomas Hesketh of 'Woodside', Pemberton Rd, Winstanley. Mr Hesketh, who was 65 and commenced his vacation the previous Saturday, collapsed suddenly whilst walking along Fleetwood promenade and was taken to Fleetwood Cottage Hospital, where he died shortly after admission.
>
> A native of Pemberton, Mr Hesketh had resided in Pemberton Rd for eighteen years. For thirty-one years he had been employed by Messrs Baxter Bros. retail grocers of Upholland, formerly as a traveller and latterly as a book-keeper. Mr Hesketh served in the Royal Field Artillery during the 1914–18 War. He was a prominent member of the congregation of St Matthew's Church, Highfield, holding the office of Churchwarden and Sunday School Superintendent during the period 1940–47. He was also vice-president of St Matthew's Men's Bible Class. Mr Hesketh leaves a wife, son and daughter.

The funeral took place yesterday, (Friday), a service at St Matthew's Church, Highfield, preceding the interment in the churchyard.

At a meeting of the Parochial Church Council in March 1953, Mrs Clark, who had been Secretary to the Council for fourteen years, tendered her resignation due to ill-health. In her place Mr Ernest Stretton, a member of the Council and a member of the Choir as man and boy since 1915, was appointed Secretary.

In April 1953, Mr G. A. Cooke, a Lay Reader from St Thomas's, Golborne, married Miss M. M. Houghton, who was involved in Sunday School and Youth work at

Highfield, and moved into the area. His Reader's Licence was transferred to Highfield, and he too became involved in the work of the parish in the Sunday School and Communicants Guild, and also later that year, as a member of the Parochial Church Council.

The Coronation of Queen Elizabeth II

In 1953 the whole country was excited about the Coronation of the young Queen Elizabeth the Second. The Coronation took place on Tuesday June 2nd. A Special Order of Service was issued by Royal Command for use in all Churches on the previous Sunday, which was Trinity Sunday. Highfield decided to celebrate the Coronation by holding a Coronation Party on Saturday 30 May at 6.45 p.m. The party was held in the Infants' School which had been elaborately decorated for the occasion. A Special Edition of the Parish Magazine—Coronation Issue, June 1953—was published which contained details of the party as follows:

> On Saturday, 30th May, over 300 parishioners will assemble in the Infants' School which has been transformed by beautiful decoration. After the reception in the Junior Hall at 6 p.m., the guests will proceed to the Infants' School to dine. Naturally the 'Roast Beef of Old England, will be on the menu. After the tea the first toast—the most important one—to Her Majesty the Queen, Duke of Lancaster will be proposed by the Vicar. The National Anthem will then be sung. The second toast, that to the Ancient and Loyal Borough of Wigan, is in the hands of Mr E. Davies, and the Town Clerk of Wigan will reply. The third toast to the Diocese of Liverpool will be proposed by Archdeacon A. White, and the response will be by the Bishop of Warrington. Then follows the toast to the Parish of St Matthew, Highfield, to be proposed by Mr Brierley, the Vicar making the response. Finally the toast to the Guests will be proposed by Mr T. Hughes, and Miss Janet Lowe will reply.
>
> A wonderful programme of entertainment has been arranged by the entertainments committee, and as the evening goes on joyful sounds will issue forth from the School Room. At a suitable place in the evening's entertainment we shall pause to partake of the Coronation Cake. All the guests will have a souvenir menu card. All parishioners who have handed in their name for a ticket should by this time have received them. If any person has not yet received their ticket, they should get in touch with the Churchwardens at once. WHB, EGE, TH.

The Master of Ceremonies for the Party was Mr E. G. Elliott. The Chief Stewards were Mr S. Woods and Mr R. Thomas, and a Vote of Thanks at the end of the Evening was proposed by Mr Paul Gaskell.

Mr E. Davies resigned as Headmaster of the Boys' School at the end of the Summer Term. The Vicar wrote in the Parish Magazine:

> It is with mixed feelings that we learn of the resignation of Mr E. Davies. We congratulate him most heartily on his appointment to the Headship of Deeside Modern Secondary School. We wish him well and hope he will be very happy. His going will be a great loss to the parish and we shall miss him very much indeed.—W. H. B.'

Two stewards at the Coronation Dinner, 1953: Mr Stanley Wood and Mr Roy Thomas.

Mr A. Coates was appointed Headmaster in his place.

At the end of 1953 Mr T. Lea resigned from the position of Bellringer. Mr W. Atherton pointed out the difficulty of ringing the bell which was the heaviest in the Wigan Deanery. It was decided therefore to install a mechanism to ring the bell by the hammer rather than by swinging the whole bell. It would then be possible to ring the bell from ground level in the Church.

At a meeting of the Vestry held in 1954, Mr Thomas Hughes was appointed Vicar's Warden and Mr Herbert Gee was appointed People's Warden. Mr Gee had been closely involved with the life of the Church for many years. He was Secretary to the Parochial Church Council from 1929 to 1940, He was involved with the social and sporting activities—Dramatic Society, Football Club and Bowling Team, and his abilities as a pianist involved him in many activities in the parish.

July 1954 marked the Diamond Jubilee of the Church but owing to the fact that the date coincided with the first week of Wigan holidays, it was decided to hold the Special Thanksgiving Services from Sunday the 19th September to Sunday the 26th September including the Patronal Festival.

The Revd W. H. Bullough was appointed to be the Church of England Representative on the Wigan Education Committee in 1954. A position which he held until he resigned the living of St Matthew's in 1959.

Miss L. Holland, who had been Headmistress of the Infants School for almost forty years retired at the end of 1954. She had been Teacher and Superintendent of the Infant Sunday School for over forty years. She was a member of the first Parochial Church Council in 1920, a leader of the Young People's Union and Church Missionary Society

*Children of the Infant Sunday School take their Harvest gifts to Pemberton Hospital,
Billinge Road, in the 1950s.*

Secretary for a time. She was followed as Head of the Infants' School by Miss L. Waddington.

Mr R. Kay, Organist and Choirmaster, resigned at the end of 1954 to take up a position at St Peter's, Hindley. Mr Kay had maintained the tradition of Choral Music at St Matthew's during the short time he was in charge. One of the Highlights of the period was a performance of Handel's 'Messiah' on Sunday 29 November 1953 at 2.15 p.m. by the Church Choir which was augmented by members of Ashton-in-Makerfield Choral Society. Among the soloists was Highfield's own Arthur Stockley who sang the Tenor solos.

Miss Ruth Turton, LRAM, FRCO, from Parr, St Helens, was appointed organist and Choirmistress from January 1955.

The New Parish Hall

The Second Bishop of Liverpool, Dr Chavasse, had said in his sermon at the Consecration of the Church in 1910, listing the needs of the Church: 'You need a church hall. The Hall in which the Revd J. Woods started his ministry will no longer suffice, you require a noble church hall, worthy of this noble church.' It took over sixty years for the hall to come into being, but it was appropriate that the plans for this task were to be put forward in the Diamond Jubilee Year of the Church.

Builders of the Parish Hall in fancy dress for the Barn Social in 1955.

At a meeting of the Parochial Church Council on 16 June 1964 the Vicar put before the Council plans for a Parish Hall, drawn up by Mr Lucas of Liverpool. These were examined and discussed and finally the necessary resolutions were passed to make the first preliminary steps. At the next meeting of the Council on June 22nd, after discussing estimates of the cost of the building which were £4,800 using contractors, and £3,700 by voluntary labour, it was decided to build the hall by voluntary labour. At this stage the male members of the Council were elected to a Church Hall Building Committee, the first meeting of which took place immediately after the Council meeting had finished its business. At this meeting Mr G. Taylor and Mr A. Martindale, both experienced building contractors, volunteered their services to guide the project. An appeal for labour was made and a meeting of volunteers was held. The Vicar made a report of this meeting in the August 1954 Parish Magazine:

> What a grand meeting we had on Thursday, July 15th. It was wonderful to see so many of our menfolk keen to get going on the great task of building the new Parochial Hall. A start was made immediately after the meeting and some grand work has been put in since then—alas sadly interrupted by bad weather. The whole parish is thrilled that the job has begun and the watchword now is 'stick at it.' If there are any men who feel a little shy at starting NOW, just forget your shyness and roll up, there is plenty of work for all of us.

Alongside the building of the hall there went the effort of raising money to pay for it. The Church Council had £1,970 11s. 11d. in the Parochial Hall Fund which had been worked for over many years, and all the current efforts of the parish were put towards the Parochial Hall Fund. The Target set to raise in 1954 was £1,000 and by the end of the year over £1,050 had been raised.

Work on the hall proceeded well and the walls were built during the Summer and Autumn. The Vicar laid the Foundation Stone at a service held on the site on Saturday 23 October 1954 at 3 p.m. This was reported in the *Wigan Observer*:

> The foundation stone of the new Parish Hall of St Matthew's, Highfield, was laid by the Vicar (Rev W. H. Bullough) on Saturday afternoon. The stone bears the inscription: 'In commemoration of the great voluntary effort by the people of St Matthew's Highfield. This stone was laid by the Vicar, Rev W. H. Bullough, AKC, Saturday, 23rd October, 1954. A Coronation five-shilling piece was placed under the stone by little John Bullough, and copies of the July, August and September Parish Magazines were also placed there.
>
> After the Vicar had led the Choir from the Church to the Site of the Parish Hall to the singing of the Te Deum, Mr J. W. Brierley, Lay Reader, asked the Vicar to perform the Ceremony. As the rain steadily fell, parishioners, members of the Church Council, the Churchwardens and the Choir, heard the Vicar declare the stone 'well and truly laid' and saw him place it with a small mallet which was later presented to him to commemorate the occasion.
>
> During the afternoon, parishioners had come to the site to lay bricks into the foundation. They paid anything from one shilling upwards to lay a brick, and the money will go towards the cost of erecting the new parish hall, which is £4,000. The money and labour is all being given voluntarily by parishioners and friends, and men of the parish have given up much of their free time to building the hall which adjoins the cricket pavilion.
>
> The pavilion is being turned into kitchens and small ante rooms, whilst the one storey hall will have a permanent stage and dressing rooms and a wood blocked floor. Under the stage will be a cellar containing heating equipment. The workmen, including the Vicar, have even erected electric lights around the site to enable them to work during the dark nights of the coming months. Amongst those present at the ceremony were Mr Alan Royle (Town Clerk) and Mrs Royle, and Mrs Haworth Hilditch, Wife of Wigan's Medical Officer.

The work on the Parish Hall was remembered by Mr John Berry, Senior, written some time before he died:

> Some time ago, my son John, a member of the above Church asked me did I remember the building of the Parish hall at Highfield, and would I write of what I did remember. This I promised to do as this was one of the happiest times of my life, and I would regret now if I had not been a member of the gang.
>
> My first memory is of the great leader we had in the Revd Bert Bullough. He inspired a collection of men of the Parish, young and old, to spend night after night and week-ends to help in any way they could to assist. I thought at the time that if a Vicar of a Parish wished to get chaps to go to Church who'd stopped going, he should build a Parish Hall by voluntary labour from the chaps of the Parish. I remember that the Vicar put on his overalls during the daytime and put his cassock over these when he had to attend to his Church duties.
>
> It was my job to take Mr Bullough to Manchester on numerous occasions to my place of work (Samuel Gratrix Ltd.) to purchase equipment etc. The managers of the different departments looked after him very well and he usually got goods at a favourable price.

There was only one drawback, Mr G. Cooke mentioned this on the menu he produced for the Dedication Dinner. He said that the firm's motto was 'Goods would be delivered tomorrow, never today!'

A percentage of the men were tradesmen and the majority not. The tradesmen had their own tools and the rest a variety of tools of all descriptions. These were borrowed from one another but always returned to their owner at the end of the day. Mr George Taylor, who was the foreman, 'got his rag out' on occasions when work had not been done to his liking during his time away, blew his top, and then got on with the job.

Mistakes were made, for instance, I remember a wall was built about four feet high, and some heavy equipment had to be lifted over it. I remember two chaps building the flue chimney, when they had got halfway up the sky, saying to one another 'Dus think wur far enuf up ?' It was very nice to drop down to the Railway Pub for a pint at the end of the day.

It is such a long time ago, and my memory is not as good as it was, only to say it was a very happy time, and I expect some of my gang have gone to a Parish Hall above, they will always be remembered and their relatives and children can always say 'My Dad helped to build the Parish Hall.'

We should not forget the ladies and wives who sacrificed many nights out, made tea and coffee and encouraged their husbands to get to work at the Hall when they felt like having a night off.

J. Berry.

In May 1956 the news of the building of the Parish Hall was reported in the National Press with the following article in the *Manchester Guardian*:

The parish church of St Matthew, Wigan, which was built and enriched by the owners of a now-closed local colliery, has not only flourished but grown in the economic drought of nationalisation. Its new recreation hall, to be formally opened on June 12, has been built almost entirely by the voluntary work of parishioners and was recently insured for £18,000 although its cost was considerably less than that sum.

The Vicar, Rev W. H. Bullough, had the inspiration for this venture after a local joiner had carved the planking for a war memorial out of some derelict pews in the church. He thought then that it might be possible to harness such voluntary enthusiasm to a larger purpose, and in July 1954 he announced a public meeting to discuss plans for building a new hall.

The response to this appeal in the parish magazine was so encouraging that the meeting would not wait to discuss ways and means but rushed to the site and began cutting the turf. By evening this preliminary work was completed.

Lent £3,000

Mr Bullough then called on an architect friend to draw up a plan for the building. Other friends in Wigan business quarters lent £3,000 interest free, and a further £2,400 was raised by local subscription. The hall was built beside a six-acre playing field, also the property of the church, and it incorporates the former pavilion.

The labour for this enterprise was provided by the parish. Every night during the last two years an average of twelve men have contributed their skilled or unskilled labour. Since the first service in this area was held more than a century ago in the joiner's room of the old Pemberton colliery, it was appropriate that present day joiners should have worked among the hardest, and outside help was only called in to fit the oak block flooring to the concrete. Other skilled craftsmen, such as bricklayers, plumbers, electricians, and heating engineers have attended regularly. Among the regular gang of unskilled helpers are a bus-driver, an income tax official, a schoolmaster, a baker, the manager of a cotton mill, and several miners. 'Every evening they would come at 7 and work till 9. 30,' Mr Bullough explained, 'and then they go off to the pub—and I go with them.'

A visitor who inquired for Mr Bullough at the new hall yesterday afternoon was warned not 'to go near him or you will find yourself painting the wall.' He is a man with the kind of initiative and nervous energy more frequently found among successful business men than in priests, and he enthuses about the hall with typical Wigan frankness.

Greater Significance

He believes firmly that the hall has a significance far greater than its use for 'plays, concerts, dances, whist drives and domino drives,' He felt it was necessary to come down to the level of the parishioners rather than simply expect them to come to church, and that there was no better way of getting to know a parishioner than by working with him.

Many of the most enthusiastic helpers were those who had never visited the church except at harvest festival and 'walking' ceremonies. Now they are regular attenders and the congregation for evensong on Sunday is seldom less than three hundred.

However there were, disappointingly, few young people among the workers on the hall, a fact that provoked some slightly ironic comment, since they are not loth to use the playing fields which adjoin it. There were also more 'tradesmen' than workers, although the area is predominantly working-class.

Opening of Parish Hall

After two years of hard work and dedication by the loyal team of men and women who all played their part, the Opening and Dedication of the Parish Hall took place on Tuesday evening, 12 June 1956 at 6.30 p.m. when Lord Derby came to perform the Opening Ceremony. The *Wigan Observer* caught the excitement and atmosphere of the special occasion in the life of the parish:

> The Union Jack fluttered proudly from the spire of St Matthew's Church, Highfield, on Tuesday evening, and a hundred yards below it stood a large, imposing building, the result of nearly two years of hard work, often in rain and wind, by the parishioners of St Matthew's. Now, after long and arduous labours and a task that at times seemed just a little too large, stood at long last a fine, parochial church hall. On Tuesday the new hall was opened by the Earl of Derby, M. C., Lord Lieutenant of Lancashire, and about four hundred people, many of whom had helped in the building of the hall, packed the church for the short service before the opening ceremony. Outside the church many hundreds more gathered to await the arrival of Lord Derby, who was accompanied by the Mayor of Wigan (Alderman Albert Horrocks) and the Town Clerk (Mr Alan Royle). Before the service began a programme of organ music was played by Miss Ruth Turton, FRCO,

The Opening of the Parish Hall, 1956: Lord Derby; Revd W. H. Bullough; Alderman Horrocks, Mayor; Mr Allan Royle, Town Clerk; Mr G. A. Cooke and Mr J. W. Brierley, Lay Readers; Mr H. Gee, Churchwarden.

LRCM, This included 'Toccata and Fugue in D Minor' (Bach), 'Largo from the New World Symphony'(Dvorak),'Grand Choeur in D'(Guilmant), 'Gothic Suite' (Boelmann), and 'Hornpipe and Air' from Handel's 'Water Music'.

Rev W. H. Bullough (Vicar) who was the leader of the building party during the erection of the hall, and who first proposed the idea, delivered a short address in which he said that he had received messages from the Bishops of Liverpool and Warrington which contained the following passages: 'This great enterprise ... A magnificent achievement of which the parish can be justly proud ...' He explained the reasons for the building of the hall, and said that ever since the first meeting, when forty men attended, he had no doubts about the completion and the quality of the hall. He wished to thank all those who had helped directly in the building and also those who had no connection whatsoever with the parish, but who had willingly done all they could to help.

The Vicar led the clergy, choir and congregation, singing 'Te Deum', to the Hall where they were met by Lord Derby. Mr T. Lucas, in asking Lord Derby to open the Hall, said: 'The people of St Matthew's have worked together in building this hall by voluntary labour, and on their behalf I ask you to open it, that we may proceed to the ceremony of dedication'. The architect, Mr Michael Law, presented the key to Lord Derby, who then unlocked the door and led the way into the hall. The Vicar dedicated the building, there followed the Lord's prayer, and the singing of the Doxology, and the Vicar gave the Blessing.

Major Victor Blundell proposed a vote of thanks to Lord Derby, and also thanked the people of Highfield for conferring on him the honour of being present at the opening of their new hall. He knew that a great many people had helped in the building work, but he was sure that no-one would take exception if he specially mentioned one man—the Vicar. Mr Bullough's enthusiasm and leadership had been an inspiration to all those connected with the building of the hall. Major Blundell said that a sum of £5,000 was still needed, but he was sure that the parishioners would soon 'knock a large hole in it'.

Lord Derby said he considered the proposing of a vote of thanks for his presence there was entirely unnecessary. Indeed it was he who was privileged to attend such a function. He congratulated the people of Highfield on their achievement and said that as long as there were people who would give up their evenings and Saturday afternoons for the benefit of others, there was no need to worry about the future of this country. He hoped that all who used the hall would remember the time and effort which had been given to its construction, and that the parishioners would always be proud of their hall.

The proceedings inside the hall were relayed to hundreds of people outside.

The new hall has cost about £6,000, and measured 72ft. by 30ft. The accommodation includes a large assembly hall, a tea-room, a kitchen, ladies' and gentlemen's toilets, separate dressing rooms, a stage, a cellar, and a boiler-house.

The following is an extract from the July 1956 Parish Magazine:

The Builders

We honour the following men who gave their spare time to build the New Church Hall:

Leader: Revd W. H. Bullough
General Foreman: Mr G. H. Taylor

T. Ashcroft	J. Evans	H. Pouncey
J. H. Atherton	G. Fairhurst	W. Peel
J. Ackers	J. H. Foote	R. Parks
D. Ascroft	J. Flemming	W. Parkinson
J. T. Ascroft	W. Green	T. Parkinson
W. Ashurst	T. Gaskell	H. Parkinson
W. Atherton	H. Gee	H. Preston
E. Alker	H. F. Gaskell	J. Ratcliffe
A. Atherton	P. Gaskell	A. Richardson
H. H. Burrows	A. Gibbons	J. Roughley
F. Birks	G. Greenall	E. Schofield
J. Berry	J. Heaton	H. L. Stockley
N. R. Brown	A. M. Hughes	A. Stockley
R. O. Butts	A. Houghton	E. Stretton
A. Brown	J. Hitchen	J. Silcock
A. Brown	G. C. Hall	H. Sharrock
S. Barlow	B. Jones	G. H. Stretton
W. Boyd	E. Jones	J. Shaw
H. Brighouse	G. Kenyon	E. Stockley

A. Banks	J. Livesey	E. K. Stockley
C. J. Benson	W. O. Millard	T. Stockley
E. Buckley	J. Muldoon	B. Stretton
D. Beardsmore	A. Myers	E. Twigg
G. A. Cooke	N. Mills	R. Thomas
A. Coleman	A. Martindale	T. Topping
J. Clarke	J. G. Lee	T. Winstanley
F. H. Critchley	W. Nicholson	H. Walker
G. Davenport	W. Nock	S. Williams
J. Daniels	G. D. Peel	R. Winstanley
F. Dodd	G. Perrin	S. Wood
A. Derbyshire	J. D. Peel	N. Whitter
E. G. Elliott	T. R. Philps	K. Wright

At a meeting of the Parochial Church Council held on 27 June 1955, the Vicar paid a special tribute to the late Mr Arthur Stockley, a most respected member of the Church who passed away on 30 April, at the Wigan Infirmary. Mr Stockley who had been a member of the Council, had also served as a member of the Choir for 46 years, a large share of this as tenor Soloist. He had also taken a leading part in the production of Concerts and Drama for the benefit of the younger people, and for the parish as a whole.

Some of the builders of the Parish Hall, 1956.

A hymn was sung and prayers were said at the entrance to Pemberton Hospital on Walking Day.
This picture was taken about 1956.

He was a true and loyal servant who had left a good example of service, and now went to the Higher Service.

At the Annual Parish Meeting in May 1956, Mr Paul Gaskell announced his resignation as Church Treasurer. The Vicar thanked him for his loyal service. At the following Parochial Church Council Meeting Mr G. A. Cooke was elected Church Treasurer. The first meeting of the newly formed Parish Hall Committee was held two weeks later and Mr G. Perrin was subsequently appointed Treasurer of the Parish Hall Committee and Mr H. Gee was appointed Secretary.

Formation of Women's Fellowship

From very early days in the parish there had been two or three women's organisations in existance, and sadly, over the years, support for them had declined. Mr Bullough announced at a meeting of the Parochial Church Council on 15th October, 1956, that he had decided to invite Mrs W. H. Morton of Greenhill, Wigan, who was well-known in Highfield as a great Church worker to be the leader of a Women's Fellowship. The first meeting was called for Thursday the 1st of November. This was the beginning of an organisation which has grown from strength to strength over the years, and has played its part in the life of the parish in so many ways. Each year it makes gifts to charity and to the Church, and has supported all the efforts of the parish in which it has been involved.

In December 1956, Miss Ruth Turton resigned from her position as Organist and Choirmistress. Mr G. A. Cooke took over on a temporary basis until in May, 1957 Mr Fred Ashcroft of Wigan was appointed

At the January 1958 meeting of the Parochial Church Council, the Vicar outlined the targets and commitments for the future. He hoped that the debt on the Church Hall would be cleared by the end of the year. He reminded the Council that the Schools would have to be purchased, but here, we should receive assistance from the Diocese. The Infants' School needed re-roofing, the Church spire needed attention, the organ was in need of a major overhaul and the graveyard needed to be put in decent order. In view of all this it was decided to appoint a committee to consider an electoral roll appeal and report back to the Council.

At the March meeting the committee reported back with the proposition that the whole parish should be broken down into groups of about twenty houses, which would be visited by a volunteer collector with an appeal letter asking for regular weekly support via the team of collectors. The suggested appeal letter was read to the meeting and the scheme was approved with the name 'St Matthew's Church Fund.' Sunday 18 May 1958 was the date approved for a special service to commission the collectors for their work. This scheme was to be a great success over the following years in putting the finances of the Church on a sound basis.

At the same meeting, the Vicar announced that the Bishop of Liverpool had invited him to become Rural Dean of Wigan in succession to the Rector of Wigan, Canon A. Finch. Mr T. Hughes offered congratulations to the Vicar on what, he said, was a well-merited appointment. These sentiments were received with acclamation by all the members present. The Vicar suitably responded, and said that his Installation would be held at a service in the Wigan Parish Church on 24 April.

In 1958 Mr H. L. Stockley—a younger member of the family, who, in the words of Mr Bullough 'were all died in the wool Highfielders, who were totally active and involved in the life of the Church at Highfield'—was licensed as a Lay Reader. He had been involved in the Choir from an early age, and also in Sunday School and Youth work, and was to become more involved in the work of the Church.

At the Annual Parochial Meeting held on 13 April 1959, the Vicar paid tribute to another member of the Stockley family who had passed away. Mr T. Stockley had been a member of the Choir for 45 years, and had been leader of the Sunday School, the Youth Groups and the Men's Bible Class for many years.

At the same meeting the Vicar announced that the debt on the Parish Hall had been completely cleared, 'It now stood,' he said, 'as a glowing tribute, and a memorial to the men of the Parish who built it, they could look on this building with pride.'

Revd W. H. Bullough to Move to Halsall

The Revd Bullough's days at Highfield were rapidly coming to an end. He announced to the Parochial Church Council on 9 June 1959, that he had accepted the invitation of Major Victor Blundell to become Rector of St Cuthbert's, Halsall. The members of the Council were very sorry to learn that the Vicar was to leave Highfield, but they were unanimous in extending to him their congratulations and very good wishes on his preferment.

A New Organ

From early in 1959, discussions had been held with a view to overhauling the Church Organ. After considering several schemes it was decided to put before the Parochial Church Council at a meeting on 29 June, a scheme from Messrs Rushworth and Dreaper of Liverpool to install a re-built Lewis organ, which they had obtained from a church in Scotland, for the sum of £3,650. After a long and interesting discussion it was passed unanimously that we accept the scheme as tendered.

At the Vicar's last meeting with the Parochial Church Council, held on 30 September 1959, he detailed the final arrangements for the installation of the new organ, and announced that it would be dedicated at a service on the afternoon of Sunday 25 October. In his closing remarks to the Council at this meeting, Mr Bullough said how happy he had been here and how he had enjoyed the mutual confidence of the Council. He thanked the Council for their wonderful support during his ministry here, and hoped that the same sort of confidence would be given to their new Vicar when he arrived. Thanks and good wishes were extended to the Vicar by Mr Brierley and Mr Hughes and endorsed by all present.

Sunday 25 October was also the last Sunday of the Revd W. H. Bullough's ministry at Highfield.

The Dedication and Opening of the new Organ took place at 2.30 p.m. The Organ was dedicated by the Vicar, Revd W. H. Bullough, AKC, the Recital of Organ Music was played by Mr K. Long, BA, Mus. Bach., FRCO, Organist of Wigan Parish Church, and the Sermon was preached by Revd Canon G. Jones, MA, Rector of Aughton.

The Churchwardens invited the Vicar to dedicate the Organ and after prayers and responses he did so in the following words: 'In the faith of our Lord and Saviour Jesus Christ, We dedicate this organ, that therewith the worship of this Parish Church may be enriched and beautified, to the Glory of God and the inspiration of His faithful people. In the Name of the Father, and of the Son, and of the Holy Ghost. Amen.'

After prayers, the Organ was heard for the first time during the singing of the Hymn 'Praise to the Lord, the Almighty, the King of Creation'.

The first part of the Organ Recital followed. It consisted of:

Prelude and Fugue in F minor by J. S. Bach.
A group of Chorale Preludes by Bach, Kellner and Vogler.
Early Italian Organ Music by Martini and Zipoli.

Then followed the Address by the Revd Canon G. E. Jones, M. A., Rector of Aughton, after which the second part of the recital consisted of:

Introduction and Passacaglia by Max Reger
Chorale Prelude—How brightly gleams by Karg Elert
Paean by Herbert Howells
Song to the Mountains by Flor Peeters,
Toccata, from Symphony No. 5 by Widor.

The Final Hymn 'O Praise ye the Lord!' was sung, during which a collection was taken for the Organ Fund as a thank-offering for the 70 years service of the old organ, and a fitting contribution towards the cost of the new organ.

The service ended with the blessing pronounced by the Vicar.

A description of the organ was printed on the back of the Service Sheet as follows:

The new organ is a Two-Manual and Pedal instrument of 24 speaking stops with 6 couplers and a tremulant, being controlled by Stopkeys. Thumb and Pedal pistons are also provided for easy registration, and the entire instrument has been designed on the Rushworth electro-pneumatic system. There are in all 1499 pipes.

Pedal Organ

1. Open Diapason	16ft.
2. Sub Bass	16ft.
3. Octave(Extension of No. 1.)	8ft.
4. Bass Flute(Extension of No. 2.)	8ft.
5. Open Flute(Extension of No. 3.)	4ft.

Great Organ

6. Open Diapason	8ft.
7. Lieblich Gedeckt	8ft.
8. Dulciana	8ft.
9. Octave	4ft.
10. Flaute Traverse	4ft.
11. Twelfth	2⅔ft.
12. Fifteenth	2ft.
13. Mixture	III Ranks
14. Trumpet	8ft.

Swell Organ

15. Geigen Diapason	8ft.
16. Rohr Flute	8ft.

17. Viol D'Gamba	8ft.
18. Geigen Principal	4ft.
19. Lieblich Flute	4ft.
20. Nazard	2⅔ft
21. Piccolo	2ft.
22. Mixture	III Ranks
23. Contra Oboe	16ft.
24. Horn	8ft.
25. Trumpet (From Great No. 14)	8ft.
Tremulant.	

Couplers

1. Great to Pedal	4. Sub. Octave
2. Swell to Pedal	5. Unison Off
3. Swell to Great	6. Octave.

Revd W. H. Bullough's Farewell

The Vicar preached his farewell sermon at Evensong on that day. Presentations having been made to Mr Bullough and his family before they left for Halsall, Mr Bullough wrote in the December 1959 Parish Magazine:

Our Dear Friends,

I have asked to be allowed to express to you all the very sincere thanks of Mrs Bullough and myself and John for all the wonderful kindness and generous gifts you have given to us. The many gifts will find honoured places in our new home and your great generosity in the gift of the cheque for £100 will enable us to purchase something which will always remind us, although this is not necessary, of your love and affection.

The farewell services will remain a vivid memory for the remainder of my life and I am grateful to you all for making them so.

It was grand to see a representative group from Highfield at St Cuthbert's Church for the Induction. I had to carry out the Bishop's instructions and only permit one coach, and I very much regret that the numbers had to be so small.

Once again please accept our thanks for all your kindness. We particularly appreciated the gifts which our little boy has received.

We remain ever your sincere friends,

Herbert, Joan and John Bullough.

Mr Bullough was to remain at Halsall for thirty-one years. He was appointed Rural Dean of Ormskirk from 1969, Honorary Canon of Liverpool Cathedral from 1971 and was for some years Chairman of the West Lancashire District Health Authority and for many years a member of the North West Area Health Authority. He served on many Diocesan Boards and Committees. He celebrated fifty years in the Ministry in 1989, and finally retired in 1991 and now resides in Churchtown, Southport.

Revd Canon Robert James Smith

Fourth Vicar

1960–1974

ROBERT JAMES SMITH was born in the Anfield area of Liverpool on 5 April 1909. His parents were Robert and Gertrude Smith. Later, a younger brother, George, and a sister Muriel, completed the family. In 1916 they all moved to Edge Hill where Robert James attended Earle Road School. In 1922 the family moved to Wavertree, and the following year Robert James left school at the age of fourteen and was recommended by the Headmaster to a firm of West African Shipping Agents with offices in the Pier Head. During this time in the shipping offices he attended various evening classes in Office and Business studies.

He became involved in the work of the Church when, as a boy, he joined the choir of St Mary's, Wavertree. In about 1931 he was licensed as a Lay Reader at St Mary's and also became involved in Boys' Brigade work. The shipping agents for whom he worked closed down in 1932 and Robert James started serious study by a postal course for his Matriculation Certificate with a view to Ordination.

From 1934 to 1937 he attended St Aidan's Theological College, Birkenhead and in 1937 he obtained a Durham L.Th. and Exhibition. He was ordained Deacon by the Bishop of Liverpool, and began his first Curacy at St Catherine's Edge Hill in the same year. In 1938 he was ordained Priest by the Bishop of Liverpool and in 1939 he began his second Curacy at St Anne's Aigburth. On 2nd September 1939 he married Doris Pearson, and the following day, 3 September 1939, the second World War began. Bob Smith used to relate this fact with a wry smile on his face.

From 1941 to 1946 the Revd R. J. Smith was a Chaplain in the Forces. He spent his whole service abroad in the West African 8th Army, twice being mentioned in Dispatches. After the war he returned to the Diocese of Liverpool and from 1946-47 he was Curate at St Mary's Prescot.

In 1947 he became Vicar of St Michael, Hough Green, Ditton and ministered there until 1952. From 1949 to 1950 he was Chaplain to the Mayor of Widnes and was a member of Widnes Committee for Education from 1950 to 1952.

In 1952 he became Vicar of St John the Baptist Burscough, and in the same year he was appointed Chairman of the Diocesan Board of Dilapidations. In 1953 he was appointed a Surrogate for Marriage Licenses. From 1958 to 1964 he was a Proctor in Convocation and Member of the Church Assembly for the Diocese of Liverpool. In June 1959 he was invited by the Patrons to become Vicar of St Matthew Highfield, and at a meeting on the 29th June 1959, he was introduced to the PCC by the Vicar, Revd W. H. Bullough, who is one of the Patrons, who informed the PCC that the Revd R. J. Smith had accepted the invitation of the Patrons to succeed him as Vicar of St Matthew Highfield. The Revd Smith had a general discussion with the members present, and then retired from the meeting. There was no objection raised by any member of the Council to the recommendation, by the Trustees, of the Revd R. J. Smith to the Benefice.

The Revd R. J. Smith was Instituted and Inducted to the Benefice of St Matthew Highfield, on the Feast of the Epiphany, 6 January 1960, by the Bishop of Liverpool, Clifford Martin, and the Archdeacon of Warrington, Venerable Eric Evans. The Bishop's Mandate reads as follows:

CLIFFORD ARTHUR BY DIVINE PERMISSION LORD BISHOP OF LIVER-POOL TO OUR BELOVED IN CHRIST THE REVEREND ROBERT JAMES SMITH CLERK L.TH. GRACE AND BENEDICTION WE DO BY THESE PRE-SENTS DULY AND CANONICALLY ADMIT AND INSTITUTE YOU IN AND TO THE CHURCH AND BENEFICE OF THE NEW PARISH OF ST MATTHEW HIGHFIELD WIGAN IN OUR DIOCESE OF LIVERPOOL NOW VOID BY THE CESSION OF THE REVEREND WALTER HERBERT BULLOUGH CLERK ASSOCIATE OF KINGS COLLEGE THE LAST INCUMBENT THERE TO WHICH YOU HAVE BEEN PRESENTED UNTO US BY ELIZABETH ALICE HEDLEY CHRISTIAN VICTOR RICHARD BLUNDELL-HOLLINSHEAD-BLUNDELL GENTLEMAN EDWARD WILLIAM JERVIS BANKES GENTLE-MAN JOSEPH WILLIAM BRIERLEY GENTLEMAN AND THE REVEREND WALTER HERBERT BULLOUGH CLERK ASSOCIATE OF KINGS COLLEGE TRUSTEES OF THE PATRONAGE OR RIGHT OF PRESENTING A MINIS-TER TO THE SAID CHURCH AND BENEFICE AS IT IS ASSERTED AND WE DO DULY AND CANONICALLY INSTITUTE YOU VICAR OF THE SAID CHURCH AND BENEFICE AND INVEST YOU WITH ALL AND SINGULAR THE RIGHTS MEMBERS AND APPURTENANCES THEREUNTO BELONG-ING (YOU HAVING FIRST IN OUR PRESENCE MADE SUCH DECLARATIONS AND TAKEN SUCH OATHS AS ARE BY LAW IN SUCH CASES REQUIRED) AND WE DO BY THESE PRESENTS COMMIT UNTO YOU THE CURE AND GOVERNMENT OF THE SOULS OF THE PARISHIONERS OF THE SAID PARISH AND AUTHORISE YOU TO ADMINISTER THE HOLY SACRA-MENTS AND TO PREACH THE WORD OF GOD IN THE CHURCH OF THE SAME PARISH SAVING ALWAYS TO OURSELF AND OUR SUCCESSORS

OUR EPISCOPAL RIGHTS AND THE DIGNITY AND HONOUR OF OUR CATHEDRAL CHURCH OF CHRIST IN LIVERPOOL.

IN WITNESS WHEREOF WE HAVE SET OUR HAND AND CAUSED OUR EPISCOPAL SEAL TO BE AFFIXED THE SIXTH DAY OF JANUARY IN THE YEAR OF OUR LORD ONE THOUSAND NINE HUNDRED AND SIXTY AND IN THE SIXTEENTH YEAR OF OUR CONSECRATION.

(signed and sealed) Clifford Liverpool.

The Archdeacon's Certificate of Induction reads as follows:

I, the Venerable Eric Herbert Evans Clerk, Archdeacon of the Archdeaconry of War-rington do hereby certify and make known that by virtue of Letters Mandatory of the Right Reverend Father in God, CLIFFORD ARTHUR by Divine Permission, Bishop of Liverpool, bearing the date the Sixth day of January 1960 to me directed, I did duly and properly Induct and place the Reverend Robert James Smith into the real actual and corporeal possession of the Church and Benefice of the New Parish of St Matthew Highfield in the Diocese of Liverpool, and did invest him with all and singular the rights, members and appurtenances thereto belonging on Wednesday the Sixth day of January in the year of our Lord One Thousand Nine Hundred and Sixty.

As witness my hand this Sixth day of January 1960 E. H. Evans.

Witnesses Thomas Hughes Herbert Gee Churchwardens.

On the Sunday after his Institution and Induction, 10th January 1960 the Incumbent, following the traditions of the Church, was required to 'read himself in' by reading the Thirty-nine Articles of Religion from the Book of Common Prayer, and making the following declaration:

I ROBERT JAMES SMITH Clerk, L. TH. do solemnly make the following declaration:

I assent to the Thirty-nine Articles of Religion, which I have now read before you, and to the Book of Common Prayer, and the Ordering of Bishops, Priests, and Deacons. I believe the Doctrine of the Church of England, as therein set forth, to be agreeable to the Word of God; and in Public Prayer and Administration of the Sacraments, I will use the form in the said Book prescribed, and none other, except so far as shall be ordered by lawful authority.

The Churchwardens, Thomas Hughes and Herbert Gee witnessed and signed this declaration.

The Vicar introduced himself in the January/February edition of the Parish Magazine:

The Vicar's Message

The Vicarage, Highfield.
25th January 1960

My Dear Friends,

First of all may I take this opportunity of expressing my grateful thanks to you all for the welcome you have extended to us on our coming to Highfield. My family and myself feel very happy here and in no small measure this is due to you because you have made it perfectly plain that this is what you want for us. We are very conscious that you intend to help us to get to know you, and your friendly attitude and ever ready offers of help are much appreciated.

The Institution on January 6th was a very wonderful thing. The atmosphere outside was bad and it could hardly have been a worse night, but inside the Church there was a very reverent and dignified atmosphere which contrasted greatly. The service was excellently conducted and it was obvious that all who had had a hand in it had prepared for it. Nothing went astray, no hitches, no awkward moments, everything just right. All this greatly helps a new vicar and makes him feel that here are people who care very much and want only the best they can give. I know that the people of this parish have a very high regard for their parish church and for those who minister in it. I will do my best to be worthy of your support.

At the beginning of a new ministry the poor vicar does not quite know where he is. There are so many people he meets right away so many strings to pick up which his predecessor has laid down, and for a while he is in a sort of maze. But it soon sorts itself out and then he gets down to the business of the parish. I hope that it will not be very long before I get everything sorted out, and I look forward very much to visiting you in your homes. I intend every month to tell you in the magazine where I hope to be visiting—I say hope—because the best laid plans often go astray and there are many things which crop up in a parson's ministry to upset his plans, but at any rate it will be some sort of guide. Naturally this task of house to house visiting will take a long time. It took me 3½ years to visit every home in my last parish but I know you will understand. Some home has to be the first and another the last and in between will come all the rest. But so long as you know that I am on the job I know that you will bear with me in the task, and will not worry if your home is not amongst the earlier visits.

Greetings to you all, Yours sincerely, ROBERT J. SMITH.

In the April 1960 Parish Magazine the Vicar gave details of his Parish Visiting:

Parish Visiting

The Vicar promised to give details in the magazine of the streets in the parish which he hoped to visit each month. He has already made a start as you know, and during April he hopes to finish off Enfield Street and maybe get on with the smaller streets off Enfield Street. It is not always easy to keep to the time-table for there are so many unexpected things which turn up to thwart the plan but he will do his best.

It had for many years been traditional to give the Easter Offering to the Vicar. On Easter Day cards were placed in the Church pews to remind the congregation of this tradition. In the May Magazine the Vicar acknowledged the gift handed to him by the Church-wardens on behalf of the Parishioners.

The Vicar took part in his first Rogation Walk in May and the Parish Walking Day in June 1960. This was his first experience of a Walking Day and he wrote in the Parish Magazine:

Whitsunday, June 5th is Walking Day and we look forward to a grand day with our children leading the walk around the parish. The Vicar has never seen a Wigan Church on its Walking Day but from what he has heard it is something worth seeing. He hopes that the day will be regarded as a day of Witness to the fact that we are members of the

Church and are not afraid to let it be known, and that not only our Sunday School children but all of our parishioners who can walk will join in the procession. Let this really be a grand witness to the Faith.

Annual Parish Events

In the July 1960 Parish Magazine, the Vicar presented an Appreciation of all the efforts of those who had been involved in the many Annual Parish Efforts which traditionally went on year by year. 1960 had been typical of the summer efforts of so many years past:

During the past month or so a number of our Annual functions have taken place and all have gone off with success.

The Garden Party on a grand day was a very happy affair and although intended as a social get-together and not as a money-raising occasion we did in fact end up with a nice little credit, which will help in getting rid of some of our debts. We were very happy to invite Mrs Pardy to open the party and we thank her for coming.

Next came the Walking Day and the Procession of Witness. We were fortunate in having a good day for the Walk and even when we got to the Recreation Field for our service the winds blew and the storms threatened but we managed more or less to hold our service, and we hope everyone got home before the storm broke.

The Sunday School Field Day again was fine and warm. We were a bit disappointed because quite a number of our children did not turn up—whether they had forgotten about it with there being no Sunday School on the previous Sunday we do not know, but anyhow, those who did come enjoyed themselves and had twice as much to eat, so it's an ill wind that does not do somebody good.

The Bowling Club had its day out to Fleetwood and other places on the return, and there is no doubt but that everyone voted it a good day. It was even threatened, now that the Vicar has discovered that you don't play bowls with a cricket bat, he might even be roped in as a spare body for the team. Do they want to lose every match? Congratulations to those who carried away the prizes.

The Secondary Modern and the Junior Schools have each held successful sports days and it is obvious that amongst our boys we have sportsmen of the future. We expect to see some of them turning out for the bigger teams in due course.

Have we left anything out? No. The point is that all these affairs have to be arranged and a lot of people have worked to make them successful. A word of thanks therefore is very necessary. All too often the people who work in the background are forgotten and their efforts taken for granted. To list names of the many helpers would be wrong but we do want all who have helped in any way at all to know that we are grateful to them for their faithful service and willing help. Many thanks to you all. VICAR.

22 July 1960 was the 50th Anniversary of the Consecration of the Church, the Golden Jubilee. On the Anniversary day, which was the Feast of St Mary Magdalene, the Anniversary was remembered at the celebrations of the Holy Communion at 7 and 9.30 a.m.

Crown Green Bowling had long been a popular pastime among the men at St Matthew's, and in 1956 a team had been re-started after many years in abeyance. The following report in the October 1960 Parish Magazine records the successes of this team.:

> The members of St Matthew's Bowling Team have this year excelled themselves by bringing to Highfield the Championship of Division 'C of the Wigan and District Churches Amateur Bowling League. This is a particularly praiseworthy achievement as the team has only been in existence for the last four years. Well done all you bowlers.
>
> Special mention must be made of one of the bowlers—Mr Bob Belcher—who throughout the whole season has not lost one game, thus qualifying for the League prize awarded to the individual best performer. Congratulations Bob!

At a meeting of the PCC held on 18 September 1961, the Vicar stated that with the approval of the Bishop, the Lay Readers in the Diocese would wear blue scarves to their present robes as from October 1961. It was unanimously approved that the Council purchase the scarves and present them to our two Lay Readers, Mr G. A. Cooke and Mr H. L. Stockley. Mr Cooke tendered his thanks for the gifts.

Following the death of Mr J. W. Brierley in February 1961, Mr W. H. Morton was appointed manager of Highfield Schools in his place.

Missionary Notes

St Matthew's have supported the Church Missionary Society for many years through efforts and contributions. In recent years many of these contributions had been give to support the work of Mr K. Ogden who was our 'Link' Missionary, and who, from time to time visited the Parish when home on leave. Such a visit was recorded in the July 1961 Parish Magazine:

> We were very glad to have the opportunity of a visit from Mr and Mrs Ken Ogden last month. Mr Ogden, a local man, (from Ashton-in-Makerfield) is well known to many but his wife (Betty) we had not met before. Both of them gave us a most interesting and illuminating (in more sense than one) evening. Mrs Ogden, who is a nurse, told us of her work in her part of Africa and her beautifully coloured slides helped put us in the picture. Ken, who is officially a technician in the service of C. M. S., gave us a pictorial edition of his work as a builder of churches and schools and also as an evangelist. It was all new to some who never thought of missionary work in this way. It all went to point out that there is no trade or profession that cannot be used in the service of Christ in the work of the Church.
>
> The Ogdens warned us of the urgency of the situation in their part of the field saying that although they are booked to return to their station in July they had not yet received their visas. Christianity is not having the road made easy and the rival religions are being encouraged and supported in many cases by official sources.
>
> We must remember these good people and their work in our prayers and in our gifts. We cannot all go overseas but we can all help those who do go.

The PCC on 18 September 1961 confirmed the appointment of Mr N. Knowles as Organist and Choirmaster from July 1961, in place of Mr F. Ashcroft who was thanked for his services over the past four years.

Parish Organisations

The place and function of all the Parish Organisations was detailed in the September 1961 Parish Magazine:

At this time of year when our organisations are beginning their Winter's activities, it might be useful to newcomers to know what we have to offer.

For The Youngsters—Sunday Schools held in the Day Schools and Parish Hall 2.45 p.m.

Life Boys each Thursday in Junior Schools 7.15pm. (Ages: 8 to 12)

Boys' Brigade each Friday in Junior Schools 7.30 p.m. (Ages: 12 to 17)

Youth Club—mixed group for teenagers who have been confirmed—each Tuesday in Parish Hall 7.30 p.m.

Ladies—The Women's Fellowship each Thursday in the Parish Hall 7.45 p.m.

Men—The Fortnightly Group to commence in October, 2nd and 4th Tuesdays in Junior School 7. 45pm.

In addition, our regular Sunday worship in the Parish Church and our weekly celebration of Holy Communion on Thursday mornings at 7 a.m. and 9.30 a.m.

No-one is left out and new members will be very welcome. We would particularly ask that those who are free will try to make a mid-week Communion. If you can make the 7 a.m. before you go to work, do so regularly, or perhaps you could join with the faithful members who come each Thursday at 9.30 a.m. At this service we especially remember the needs of the parish as well as for the world-wide Church. Here is afforded a quiet time for thought and prayer in the middle of the week. Why not regularly join us?

The Schools Problem

The Schools Problem which started with the death of Major Cuthbert Blundell in 1950 (See Chapter 7) had taken eleven years of meetings and correspondence before the final solution was arrived at. It was now sorted out and the Church, honouring the decision of 1950, was now required to pay back the money for the two schools. The amount was £3,500, plus legal fees. A grant of about £1,400 had been promised by the Diocese and the Vicar succeeded in borrowing the balance from the Diocesan Board of Finance over a number of years. This loan cost the parish about £200 a year for the next ten years and then about £50 a year for the following ten years. In addition, the Parish had to put aside between £200 and £300 a year for the future development of the schools to bring them up-to-date. One of the most urgent needs was new toilet and cloakroom accommodation for the Junior Girls. This had to be put right quickly and the Church's share of this job was to be round about £700.

The Vicar wrote in the Parish Magazine in October 1961:

The Church Council honestly believes that it has done the right thing. It believes that if it had been possible to go around and ask all the parishioners the question—'Are we to keep our schools or lose them?'—most people would have answered 'Keep them'. Is the Council right?

So you can see what we are facing in the name of the Church. You will see that all this is going to mean sacrifice and giving, but if we accept the fact that we have done the right thing then it is up to everyone who would agree with us to help.

Now you can see why we need the regular giving of everyone. Please help your Church in her great task.

Early Building Developments

One of the earliest building developments in the Parish which took place during Revd Smith's ministry was in the Tunstall Lane area. The Vicar referred to this in the February 1962 magazine:

Week by week sees new parishioners taking up residence in their new homes in the Tunstall Lane area. We do want to make them feel welcome in our parish and within a short time of their settling down either the Vicar or one of our Church workers visits them. Mrs Albert Taberner, who herself now lives in one of the new houses, has been very good in visiting her new neighbours on behalf of the Church, and the Vicar is most grateful to her. A number of our magazines are circulating in this area and quite a number of our new parishioners have joined our Church Fund Scheme. We do hope that 'ere long they will find their way to our beautiful Parish Church and join in our worship week by week. Details of our services are always to be found on the back page of the Magazine.

1962 was CHRISTIAN FAMILY YEAR, when efforts were made throughout the Church to bring the family more into the life of the Church. Lay-people were encouraged to visit aged and infirm parishioners. The Vicar was grateful to some of the members of the Women's Fellowship who had undertaken this work. In May the first Family Communion was held, and was greatly appreciated. This service was planned for the third Sunday of each month, and it was hoped that many would make the effort to attend as families together.

There had been an Association Football team in the Parish, connected with the Church, for many years in the past and in 1962 a Parish team was re-formed. Mr Albert Taberner, an ex-professional footballer, trained and coached the team. The Membership fee was £1 and 1s. per player per match. The football ground for home matches was the 'Pony field' at the corner of Foundry Lane.

In October 1962, Mr N. Knowles, who had been Organist and Choirmaster for just over a year, resigned. Mr G. A. Cooke offered to take over on a temporary basis. The Vicar wrote in the Parish Magazine announcing the change and said:

Mr Gordon Cooke has offered to carry on as our Organist, so if he has some time to pop off the Organ stool into the Pulpit we shall quite understand.

The Parish Magazine at this time was a 'duplicated' publication, produced entirely by a small group of Church members and issued free of charge, since May 1958, to all who contributed weekly to the Church Fund. The Vicar wrote about this in the January 1963 Parish Magazine:

The monthly circulation is just on 700. We should always be happy to give a copy of our Magazine to anyone who is interested, and if they should not wish to join our Church Fund Scheme (details of which will be given in the magazine in the next month or so) then we hope a small donation to cover our costs would be welcome.

In what was his fourth Annual report to the parish at the 1963 Annual Parochial Meeting, the Vicar referred to the

considerable building programme during his ministry, and what were empty spaces in 1960 now contained new property within the parish.

At a meeting of the PCC on 28 March 1960 the Vicar read a letter from Mr F. Richardson, offering on behalf of himself and his brother, the Rev Professor Alan Richardson, two brass candlesticks, to the memory of their aunt, Miss Moss. This offer was given very careful thought and after much discussion a proposal to accept the offer was carried by a very large majority in favour of accepting this gift, only three members of the Council voted against. At the Annual Parish Meeting on 27 May 1960, Mr J. W. Brierley spoke against the candlesticks and a resolution from the Annual Parish Meeting was sent back to the PCC to reject this offer. The next PCC meeting on 29 June 1960 was undecided. The Voting was 11 for and 11 against, but at a meeting on 12 September 1960 the offer was finally accepted 14 for and 11 against.

Following the original offer by the Richardson brothers, the Vicar, at a meeting of the PCC on 24 April 1962, informed the meeting that they now desired to offer a Processional Cross in addition to the candlesticks. After a full discussion by the Council the offer was accepted unanimously. On Mothering Sunday, 24 March 1963, at the Evening Service, the Revd Professor Alan Richardson, DD, Professor of Theology, University of Nottingham, came to preach and dedicate the Processional Cross and Altar Candlesticks which he and his brother Frank had given to the Church in memory of their parents and Miss Moss. Mr Richardson, their father, who died in 1947, was Churchwarden for thirty-two years.

At a PCC Meeting on 10 June 1963, Mr E. G. Elliott on behalf of the PCC extended to the Vicar congratulations and good wishes on his celebrating twenty-five years in the ministry.

Whitsunday 1963, was the first occasion when a new Lectern Bible, the gift of the Stockley family in memory of Arthur and Thomas Stockley, two faithful servants of the Church and Choir, was used for the first time.

At the September 1963 meeting of the PCC, Mr Ernest Stretton, who had been Secretary of the PCC for over ten years, resigned. He had recently celebrated fifty years as a Chorister and had been very involved in many aspects of Parish life, for many years organising the New Year Parish Dance. Efforts were made by the PCC and the Vicar to persuade him to stay, but in the end, after many months of efforts, his resignation was finally accepted.

At the PCC meeting on 9 September 1963, the Vicar referred to the proposal for a new CE Secondary Modern School for the Wigan Deanery to replace the existing CE Secondary Modern Schools, including Highfield Boys' School. The PCC, after some discussion, expressed their concern at the proposed closure of their school and the problem in accepting any financial responsibility for the new school.

The Women's Fellowship continued to meet regularly on Thursday evenings in the Parish Hall. The January 1964 Parish Magazine reported:

> A friendly gathering of prayers and carol singing took place on December 19th. Mrs Morton expressed her gratitude to all who have worked with her, and particularly to Mrs Elliott who retired from her position as secretary, which she had held from the beginning. Mrs Morton spoke of the great work done by Mrs Elliott, of her loyalty, excellent judgement and many services. Her position as secretary had been a very full one and at all times she had been efficient and ready. A gift was presented to her, and Mrs Elliott replied that her service had been happy, and spoke of the help she has received in the doing of it.
>
> At Evensong on December 15th, the Women's Fellowship Anniversary Service, the Vicar received a gift of 200 hassocks from the Women's Fellowship.

At the Annual Vestry and Church Meeting held on 10 April 1964, Mr T. Hughes, who had been the Churchwarden for sixteen years, officially resigned. Mr Hughes felt that the time had come when he should make way for a younger man. Appreciation was made of the work Mr Hughes had done in the parish over many years and in many capacities. It was hoped that he would continue to enjoy the rest that freedom from office would permit.

Mr H. Gee was appointed Vicar's Warden in place of Mr Hughes, and the Vestry unanimously elected Mr J. G. Taberner as People's Warden. Mr Taberner was welcomed to this position with confidence that he would fill the office of warden with diligence and zeal.

In his report at this meeting the Vicar commented on the steady growth of housing development within the area, and of the new property being built in the Tunstall Lane and Valley Road sections. He also said that future and extensive development would probably take place in the area behind Pemberton Road and extending across towards Goose Green. Although not officially in Highfield Parish the Vicar was being pastorally responsible for the new property in the Baxter Pit district.

Since Mr E. Stretton's resignation, the Vicar had acted as PCC secretary, but at a meeting of the PCC on 15 May 1964 Mr W. O. Millard was appointed secretary to the Council.

At this meeting Mr A. Coleman asked if some ground in the Churchyard could be put aside for the burial of ashes. It was agreed that a petition for a faculty be presented to the Consistory Court for the reservation of a piece of land in the churchyard. In 1968 an area beside the path on the south side of the Church was set aside for this purpose.

Mr G. A. Proctor the Headmaster of the Senior Boys' School from 1956 to 1964 emigrated with his family to Tasmania and his service at Highfield terminated at the end of the Summer Term. A presentation was made to him at the end of August expressing the gratitude of the parish to him for his services to the school.

*Mrs Ethel Hall leads St Matthew's Brownies in the St George's Day Parade
through Wigan in 1965.*

The Wigan Corporation had been widening Billinge Road in front of the Church, and the fence which had stood for many years was removed, and the PCC had proposed a scheme to build a wall and Lych-gate at the front of the Church. At the PCC Meeting of 26 October 1964 the Vicar reported that the Diocesan Advisory Committee had rejected the proposed designs. Permission was granted for the road-widening only. At subsequent meetings of the PCC further discussions on the wall took place and it was decided that the front be left open for an experimental period.

At the Annual Parochial Meeting of the Parish held at the end of April 1965, Mr G. Perrin was elected Vicar's Warden in place of Mr H. Gee, recently deceased, and Mr G. Taberner was re-elected as People's Warden. Mr Perrin was welcomed and thanked for this and his many other services to the Church. Mr J. H. Foote and Mr N. Boardman were re-elected Deputy Wardens.

At the same meeting the Vicar reported that the parish continued to increase with many regular worshippers from the new built-up areas, who were his responsibility to visit. This brought up the matter of Parish Boundaries. They were in the process of revision and a petition would soon be presented to the Crown. Sincere thanks were expressed to Captain E. Bankes who had undertaken the whole of the work involved.

Twelve months after the first plans for the widening of Billinge Road the state of the Church approaches was still upset but the new 'U turn' would eventually be an advantage for cars at funerals and weddings by keeping them off the narrow road.

On Sunday evening, 19 December 1965, the Choir sang excerpts from Part 1 of the Messiah. Solos were sung by Mrs E. Gaskell, Soprano, Miss M. Anderton, Contralto, Mr H. L. Stockley, Tenor, and Mr E. Stretton, Bass. The Choir sang five choruses from Handel's wonderful musical account of the Christmas story.

Alternative Services

During the next few years many alternative services were to be tried as alternatives to the 1662 Prayer Book Services which had been used at Highfield from the beginning. The Vicar in his letter of February 1966 said:

> Instead of my usual form of message this month I would like to say something about the new forms of Services which have recently been published, and which will come up for discussion in the Church Assembly at a special meeting this month.
>
> The only legal prayer book used in the Church of England today is over 300 years old (1662) and is the Prayer Book that so many of you know and use Sunday by Sunday. An attempt was made to introduce a more up-to-date book back in 1927/28, but this proposed book was not accepted by Parliament, and although it is not legal, much of it has, in practice, been used in the Church since it was proposed. At the time there was not much controversy on the new ideas and prayers for Morning and Evening Prayer, Holy Baptism, the Marriage Service and other 'occasional offices', but there was some controversy about the new Holy Communion Service, and it was this part of the new book that caused it to be rejected by Parliament. So it has come about that many of us have, in fact, used much of this book, and this without objection, generally speaking.
>
> But now, by the passing of Church Assembly motion in Parliament recently, the way was made open for the Church to make some new suggestions and alterations in her forms of Services, and liturgical experts have been working away on these new ideas, with the result that a few weeks ago their proposals were published—and then immediately went out of print—and a reprint is expected very shortly.
>
> If these new proposals are accepted by the Convocations of the Church and the Church Assembly, then they will become lawful and may be used in our Parishes, if a majority of the Parish Church Council agrees. It will thus be seen that there is no intention of thrusting upon Churches services which they do not prefer. The date suggested for these new services is May 1st, but it remains yet to see how the Councils of the Church will react to them when they are debated.
>
> It is not possible to go into any detail of the form of these new services in this article, but briefly I may say that there are two books of Services. One contains Services for Morning and Evening Prayer, something similar to what we have now, but new forms of Confession and Absolution and new prayers. Psalms and Canticles remain, but in different places in the service. Much in this first book is familiar to us, and should not find much, if any, objection. The second book contains some new ideas for the Service of Holy Communion, and some of the 'Occasional Offices' (Burial Service, The Thanksgiving of Women after Childbirth, etc.) Here there might be varying opinions, but for my own part I cannot find anything that should trouble us.
>
> The idea is that these services should be tried out for an experimental period of some years and see how we get on with them. Considering that so many people have often complained that the Church is 'old-fashioned' in her services, that she ought to bring them more up-to-date, this serious attempt to do something should, at least, receive the serious and considered attention of our people and be given a trial.
>
> I propose, therefore, that during Lent we might give some thought to these services, that those who would like to know something more about them, and perhaps go into

them in more detail should meet together in Church on the Wednesday evenings during Lent. This will mean that if we give permission to use them later on in the year we shall have familiarised ourselves with them to some extent and be ready to try them out.

At the moment of writing this letter to you I have not, in fact, been able to get copies of the new services myself, but I have had a quick look at them and I hope I will have copies when Lent comes around.

Bishop Clifford Martin retired at the end of November 1965 after 21 years as Bishop of our Diocese of Liverpool. On Thursday 23 June 1966, Stuart Blanche, the new Bishop of Liverpool came to conduct the Confirmation Service at Highfield.

The income of the Church is a continually recurring subject in Parish life and in June 1966 an appeal was made to increase the income by asking members to covenant their direct giving to the Church:

With Income tax at the standard rate of 8s. 3d. in the £, people can help the Church if they will sign an agreement to pay the Church a fixed sum (£1 upwards) to the Church for a period of at least seven years. For example, a subscription of £1 1s. a year under Covenant means that the Church is able to recover 14s. 8d. repayment from the Inland Revenue thus making the value of the Subscription to the Church to £1 15s. 8d., while £10 10s. becomes £17 16s. 8d. We already have a few people in the parish who are helping in this way and last year we received back about £35 from the tax man.'

Revision of Parish Boundaries, 1966

The Vicar had reported on the revision of Parish Boundaries in 1964 and 1965, and in the July 1966 magazine the details of the new Parish Boundaries were published:

We have now heard that the alteration of the Parish Boundaries have been approved and was officially published in the London Gazette on May 19th 1966. For the information of parishioners our Parish boundaries are as follows:

Take as a starting point the junction of (Little) Billinge Road and Ormskirk Road. The boundary line runs up Ormskirk Road to the corner of Smethurst Lane (even numbers only) then turns up Smethurst Lane (again even numbers only) out at the top and across the Lamberhead Works estate to the railway line to the junction of the line and the M6. The boundary then proceeds along the M6 southwards passing under Slackey Brow to the point where an old footpath meets the motorway.

It then follows the footpath to the old and now disused railway line, then it follows the old line, crosses Little Lane and continues along the old line to the junction of this old line and the existing line. It then follows an imaginary boundary across the allotments to Melling Street. Then crosses Billinge Road into (Little) Billinge Road back to the starting point. A map of the new boundaries can be inspected in the Church Porch.

From a practical point of view this revision means that the persons living in Little Lane Nos 12 to 28 and in Billinge Road Nos 94 to 194, hitherto in St Mark's, now come into Highfield parish. Those in Pemberton Road beyond No 152 on the even side and all on the odd side, together with those living in Winstanley Park, hitherto in either Billinge or St Luke's Parish, also come into Highfield. All the new property behind Pemberton Road

A group of Parish catering ladies led by Mrs Lucy Chadwick in the 1960s.

(Sunnyfields, Beech Walk, Sycamore Drive and Pine View), together with the new property now being erected on the Langley Farm Estate all come into our parish.

Banns of Marriage from the whole of the new area will henceforth be published in our Church and, of course, all within this area will have parochial rights of burial in the Churchyard.

Miss M. Barton, who had taught in the Junior School for many years retired at the end of August 1966, and a presentation was made to her on Wednesday 31 August in the presence of parents, old scholars and friends.

In December 1966 the Women's Fellowship gave a new carpet to the Church on the occasion of their Anniversary. The Vicar expressed the thanks of the Parish for this generous gift:

> We want to thank the Women's Fellowship for its marvellous gift of new carpets for the Church. The ladies have made a practice of giving something to the Church on their anniversary each November, but this year the gift far surpasses anything we could have imagined. We do sincerely thank Mrs Morton who inspired the idea and the many members of the Fellowship who so generously set themselves out to turn the inspiration into a fact and in so short a time. What more can we say but 'Thank you all very much'.

Things did not always go according to plan, even at the usually well organised Women's Fellowship meetings as the following account of a social held on 16 February 1967 shows:

> Thanks are offered to Mrs Chadwick and Mr G. Taylor who rose to the crisis when refreshments ordered failed to be delivered, and hungry women were awaiting food, long overdue. Mr Taylor gallantly drove Mrs Chadwick to a chip shop, and they transported 110 fish, cooked in batter, steaming and fragrant in his car. Many thanks from the hungry.

Parish Hall Extension

On 12 May 1967 it was exactly 100 years since the Iron Church School was opened. An article, written by Mr T. Hughes, about the old Iron Church School and a brief History of the Church, based on the 1932 Handbook History, appeared in the May 1967 magazine.

The Parish Hall had been built for and used by the various parish organisations from its building in 1956. The Women's Fellowship on Thursday evenings, Men's Groups on Fridays, Youth Groups and organisations all had their times. On Wednesday evenings a dance class had been run for many years by Mr and Mrs Ted Topping. On Sundays the Hall was used by the Sunday School. From early days the hall had been let for wedding parties on Saturdays and many of the Parish Organisations held their own dances and socials. Very often the catering for these functions was done by the Hall Catering Committee, run in the early days by Mrs Lucy Chadwick and a team of ladies from the Women's Fellowship. Parish Dances were very popular and well-attended. They were run by the Parish Hall Committee on such occasions as New Year, Patronal Festival, Valentine's Day and the evenings of Parish Efforts. The Hall was crowded with the numbers attending, and it was felt that an extension would help with accommodation on these occasions. The Centenary was celebrated by the building of an

Revd W. H. Bullough opens the Parish Hall extension in 1967,
one hundred years after the building of the Iron School Church in 1867.

extension to the Parish Hall which was officially declared open on Saturday 9 September 1967 at 3 p.m. by the Revd W. H. Bullough. A varied programme of entertainments had been prepared and afternoon teas were served. A Parish Dance followed in the evening at 7.30 p.m. In the October Magazine the Vicar wrote:

> How fortunate we were on Saturday September 9th to have such a grand day for the official opening of the extension to our Parish Hall. Everything was just lovely. Mr Bullough was in good form and came to do the honours on this occasion. We know that he was very happy to do this, and we were glad to see him.
>
> We do want to say a big Thank You to everyone who planned the day so successfully, with a particular Thank-You to the children for all the effort they went to for the Fancy Dress Competition.

The Vicar had a very pleasant surprise in December 1967 and wrote in the magazine:

> What would you do if someone rang up late one evening and asked if you would like to go on a cruise at Christmas? Perhaps your answer might depend on whether you like the sea or not. This is what happened to the Vicar a few weeks ago. His first reaction was to say it was not possible because he would have to be in his Church at Christmas seeing he has no Curate. Later, however, when some of his friends heard about the offer to be the Anglican Chaplain on the Franconia's Christmas Cruise they at once offered to be responsible for all the Christmas Services.
>
> How could he say 'No' to such an opportunity? The Bishop was consulted and he gave his full approval, so for the first time in his 30 years in the Ministry he will be away at Christmas, and he trusts his parishioners will not begrudge him and Mrs Smith this surprise opportunity.
>
> Details of Christmas Services and of those who have kindly offered to stand in will be posted on the Notice Board in the Porch.

The week from 18 to 25 January is recognised by all Christian Churches as a week of Prayer for the Unity of the Churches. On the Sunday of this week in 1968 we joined with neighbouring Churches for a combined Evening Service at Highfield. The preacher was the Revd Father Alexander Jones, who had spent many years studying manuscripts and translations of the Bible and was the Editor of the New Jerusalem Bible. This occasion was the first time we had welcomed to our pulpit a Priest of the Roman Catholic Church and he came with the approval of our Bishop. A large congregation from all the local Churches, and some from further afield filled the Church on this special occasion.

In May 1968 Major Victor Blundell resigned as a School Governor, thus severing one more of the last direct links with the Blundell family. Mrs Jean Wainwright was unanimously appointed governor in his place by the PCC on 27 May 1968.

At the 1968 Rose Queen Ceremony, Jennifer Moss was the star attraction. She was a local actress who played the part of Lucille Hewitt in Granada Television's Coronation Street. Jennifer was also the grand-daughter of Uncle Billy (Fairhurst) as he was affectionately known, who kept the sweet shop in the little row of shops, now demolished, which stood in Billinge Road opposite Pemberton Station.

Vicar Becomes Honorary Canon

The Revd Smith had been for many years involved in the work of the Church outside the Parish, as a member of Convocation and Church Assembly, as Chairman of the Diocesan Board of Dilapidations, as a member of the CE Pensions Board, and because of this work he was honoured in 1968 with an Honorary Canonry of Liverpool Cathedral. His Citation of Admission to the Canonry reads:

STUART YARWORTH BY DIVINE PERMISSION LORD BISHOP OF LIVER-POOL TO OUR WELL BELOVED IN CHRIST THE REVEREND ROBERT JAMES SMITH CLERK L. TH. VICAR OF THE VICARAGE AND PARISH CHURCH OF SAINT MATTHEW HIGHFIELD IN OUR DIOCESE OF LIVER-POOL GREETING WE DO HEREBY CONFER UPON YOU SO LONG AS YOU CONTINUE TO RESIDE WITHIN OUR SAID DIOCESE AN HONORARY CANONRY FOUNDED IN OUR CATHEDRAL CHURCH OF CHRIST IN LIV-ERPOOL NOW VOID BY THE RESIGNATION OF THE REVEREND JOHN WILLIAM HARTSHORNE CLERK M. A. AND BELONGING TO OUR DONA-TION OR COLLATION IN RIGHT OF OUR BISHOPRIC AND WE DO DULY AND CANONICALLY ADMIT YOU TO THE SAID HONORARY CANONRY AND INVEST YOU WITH ALL AND SINGULAR THE RIGHTS MEMBERS AND APPURTENANCES THEREUNTO BELONGING (YOU HAVING FIRST IN OUR PRESENCE TAKEN SUCH OATHS AND MADE AND SUBSCRIBED SUCH DECLARATIONS AS ARE BY LAW IN SUCH CASES REQUIRED). AND WE DO BY THESE PRESENTS APPOINT YOU A STALL IN OUR SAID CATHEDRAL CHURCH SAVING ALWAYS TO OURSELF AND OUR SUC-CESSORS OUR EPISCOPAL RIGHTS AND THE DIGNITY AND HONOUR OF OUR SAID CATHEDRAL CHURCH.

IN TESTIMONY WHEREOF WE HAVE SET OUR HAND AND CAUSED OUR EPISCOPAL SEAL TO BE AFFIXED THIS SIXTH DAY OF JUNE IN THE YEAR OF OUR LORD ONE THOUSAND NINE HUNDRED AND SIX-TYEIGHT AND IN THE THIRD YEAR OF OUR CONSECRATION.

(Signed) Stuart Liverpool.

George Perrin, the Vicar's Warden, who was an Inspector with the Inland Revenue, was moved to a job in Southampton in 1968. Preparations were made for the family to move to live in the area and George very sadly and at great loss to the Parish, resigned his positions as Parish Hall Treasurer and Vicar's Warden. Mr D. Horne became Hall Treasurer in his place.

There were more resignations at the same time, from the Infant School, when Miss L. Waddington, Headmistress, retired after 13 years. At a small ceremony on Wednesday 28 August, gifts were made to Miss Waddington on behalf of children, staff from all departments and from the School Managers, all in appreciation of her service to the many children who had passed through her hands.

Mrs Perrin, also from the Infant School, left us at the end of August. Mrs Perrin's resignation was due to the fact that she was leaving Highfield with her husband. On the last day of her service to the School a presentation was made to Mrs Perrin in appreciation of her work at the school.

Following Miss Waddington's retirement, the Infants and Junior Schools were combined in one unit with Mr Elliott as the Head Teacher.

After experiments with various forms of services over the past two or three years, the PCC decided in January 1969, that all Holy Communion Services should be 1662 version, and that the first and third Sundays should be Choral Communion at 10. 30am and Matins on the second, fourth and fifth Sundays, with effect from the first Sunday in February.

The Beginning of the New System of Synodical Government for the Church of England was felt in the Parish at the Annual Parochial Meeting in March 1969, when Mr E. G. Elliott and Mr G. A. Cooke were elected to serve on the first Deanery Synod. At the same meeting, Mr G. Taberner was appointed Vicar's Warden in place of Mr G. Perrin and Mr D. Horne was appointed People's Warden.

The Younger Generation was the name given to a newly formed Group of Young Folk. The Group met each Tuesday in the Parish Hall from 7.30 p.m. onwards for young people aged about 12 years upwards. Mr G. Crabtree and Mr A. Lowe were in charge with a rota of ladies who looked after the drinks.

It was in 1969 that the PCC resolved unanimously to remove the front two pews on either side of the central aisle in the nave, for a trial period, in order to give more room. This provided space for a stage during school productions in Church and for ease of movement at Confirmations, and for activities at Family Services.

Decimal Currency Introduced

The full changeover to Decimal Currency was not to take place until 1971, but the 50p and 10p pieces had been introduced by the end of 1969. The effect on Church collections was pointed out in the following article in the November 1969 magazine:

'It's only sixpence.' The issue of the new coins, particularly the new 50p piece, seems to be causing a bit of commotion and people are getting confused between the new 50p piece and the 10p piece which has been in circulation for some time now. We would not really mind if people did get mixed up and put a 50p piece into the collection instead of a 10p piece, but what we are afraid of is that when the old half-crown goes out of circulation next January, many who have been accustomed to putting the 2/6d piece in the collection will settle for the 10p piece and this will mean a loss of 6d each time. It is only 6d. but this could make a big difference to our annual collection. One of the Missionary Societies has calculated that the substitution of a 10p piece for the old half crown could mean a loss of several thousand pounds to them. None of us needs reminding of the way prices have shot up in recent years and the Church has to meet these rising costs just as much as everyone else. Instead of the possibility of losing 6d. we would ask everyone to re-assess their giving to the Church and see that we do not lose anything by the coinage changes. Many have not increased their giving and perhaps have forgotten that even 2/6d. today does not go as far as it did when they first started to make this coin their 'collection piece'. Perhaps some of us could make it a 50p piece in future. It's only 6d. but we can't afford to lose it. Don't let us down, please.'

An article entitled 'Long and Faithful Service' in the December 1969 magazine gave an account of two stalwarts of the Church:

We offer our grateful thanks and congratulations to Mr David Ashcroft who celebrated 50 years' service in the choir in October. At evensong on the anniversary members of the choir, on behalf of the Church, presented him with a Parker Pen.

Mr Matthew Gunn has found it necessary to retire from his work as a Sunday School teacher after 49 years' service, and the Sunday School teachers are to make a presentation to him at the Sunday School Service on December 21st. We very much appreciate the loyal service given by these gentlemen, and we have reason to believe that there are others with long service and still active, and hope that their work may be an example to our younger generation to offer their services that the work of Christ's Kingdom might be further extended in our Parish.

The Secondary Modern Boys' School was to close at the end of the Summer Term, 1970. Some of the staff were transferred to other Schools, Mr R. Gaskell, Deputy Head, who had been at our Boys' School since it first opened in 1932, retired at the end of term, as did Mrs Rhodes, also of the Senior Staff. Mrs M. Simm of the Junior Staff also retired from teaching. Mrs Simm had been involved in the Rose Queen Ceremony for many years.

At the PCC meeting on 15 May 1970 it was announced that the Local Education Authority were willing to sell the Secondary Modern Boys' School to the School Governors. The cost, after an 80 per cent grant from the Ministry of Education, would be £3,000, on which the Governors could get a 40 per cent grant from the Liverpool Diocese. They would also have to find additional money to fund the adaptations necessary. The PCC agreed unanimously to support the Governors financially in the purchase of the schools. The Infants would eventually move into this building from the old Infant building which would put the whole of the Primary School on one site.

In May 1970 Mr G. Aldington, who for many years had kept the Post Office at the end of Enfield Street, retired. He was thanked for his long service in the choir and as auditor, and he and Mrs Aldington were wished a long and happy future on leaving the district.

In June 1970, it was decided to have the cover for the Parish Magazine printed. This meant an increase in cost to the Church. The photograph on the new cover was taken by John Cooke, one of the young choristers, during a morning service.

At the end of July 1970, Mr James Anderson of Parbold and formerly of Winstanley made and presented to the Church a Prayer Desk, in memory of his parents. Twenty-four years previously he had made the Credence Table for the Memorial Chapel. Mr Anderson, then 88 years of age, started at Highfield Schools when he was 5 years old, and attended the old 'Iron' Church. His mother attended Miss Greener's Sunday School over a century before, when it was held in the building which later became the colliery offices. When Colonel Blundell built the old 'Iron' Church in 1867 she became

Family groups in the choir in 1970. These nineteen members came from just eight families.

a worshipping member there and went to both the Day and Sunday Schools. Mr Anderson's gift reveals some fine hand carving by an old craftsman, who remembered with gratitude his links with days gone by.

The new Holy Communion Series II service was tried during January 1971 before a vote to decide which version to use. Referendum Papers were left in the pews until the end of March, but in April the PCC agreed unanimously to continue with the 1662 service, experimenting with different times for the morning services.

At a meeting of the PCC in January 1971, the Vicar proposed from the Chair that a letter of Congratulations and Best Wishes be sent to our former Vicar, the Revd W. H. Bullough, on his appointment as Canon of Liverpool Cathedral. The proposal was heartily endorsed by all present.

In the past 20 years the cost of living had more than doubled, but the endowment, which provided the Vicar's stipend, plus additional grants from the PCC had not kept pace with inflation. In 1971 the endowment plus the Easter Offering did not reach the Diocesan Minimum stipend, and so the PCC voted to increase the stipend by £250. The Vicar thanked the Council, but asked that no action be taken until after April 1st when he would make another report.

In March 1971, Highfield Cricket Club made application to the PCC to play some Sunday matches on the Recreation Ground. This application was refused, but two years later, another application was accepted, and permission was granted for a limited number of matches.

In 1971 Mr Derek Rimmer made several experiments with microphones and amplifiers in Church to see if it was worth investing in a system for use during the services.

Later in the year 10 new choirboys joined the choir, thanks to a recruitment campaign by Mr Elliott, Headmaster of the Junior School, who had sent 30 boys from school for audition.

On Sunday 14 May 1972, the Church Choir, along with many other choirs and singers of the Wigan district, took part in the Sunday Half Hour Hymn Singing on BBC Radio 2, which was broadcast from St John's RC Church, Standishgate, Wigan.

In July 1972 the PCC discussed the future of the old Infant School. It was decided to retain the building for parish use to accommodate the Playgroup, Guides and Brownies and the Junior BB, but later in August the new Winstanley Primary School was not completed in time to open, due to a builders' strike. The Local Education Authority asked to use former Infant School and the Parish Hall as temporary accommodation, and the PCC agreed to their request subject to satisfactory agreements being made.

At the PCC on 24 October, the Vicar announced that he would be away from the Parish in order to visit his son and family in Australia from 25 December 1972 to 20 February 1973. At the December meeting of the PCC the the Secretary offered the Best Wishes of the PCC to the Vicar for a safe journey and a happy holiday with his son and family in Australia.

As part of the Parish's contribution to the 'Call to the North', which was a campaign to spread the Gospel throughout the North of England, in December 1972, the PCC decided to make the distribution of 2,000 copies of St Mark's gospel their Lenten Task. The Parish was to be visited by a team of visitors, with approximately 10 homes to each visitor. With the Gospel a letter from the PCC was included giving times of Services, details of a welcome Service for newcomers on July 1st., and information on Parish activities.

Mr Harold Gaskell was appointed Hall Treasurer in June 1973, in place of Mr D. Horne who had resigned.

In October 1973 Mrs Eden retired from Sunday School teaching after 63 years. She had also been Magazine Secretary in the 1930s, and for many years had been in charge of the Life Boys. The PCC accorded a vote of thanks to Mrs Eden, wishing her a long, healthy and happy retirement. A presentation was made to Mrs Eden at the Children's Harvest Service later that month.

At the same meeting of the PCC on 8th October, the Council unanimously accorded their very best wishes to Mr E. G. Elliott for a long, healthy and happy retirement from the post of Head Teacher of Highfield Primary School. Mr Elliott had been Head Teacher of the Junior School from 1948 to 1973, and during this time had held many offices in the Parish, including that of Vicar's Warden from 1949 to 1953. Mr W. Spencer of St George's CE Junior School, Wigan, was later appointed Head Teacher in his place.

The Vicar also announced at that meeting a further change to the Parish Boundaries. Because a distant part of the Parish was being developed for housing and the occupants found themselves naturally attending St Paul's Church which is nearby, it was unanimously agreed to transfer that part of the Parish to the Parish of St Paul Goose Green.

The PCC also unanimously agreed to appoint Mrs Sue Gordon as Deputy Organist.

Following the recent experiments with the Holy Communion Series III Service, the Vicar announced in March 1974, that he had not called for a referendum, because he had found very few people in favour of the Series III Holy Communion service. The PCC approved the Vicar's action in returning to the 1662 Service.

Obituaries, 1960–1974

In mid-1960 the Church lost two faithful, long-serving members. An appreciation of Mrs Janie Miller was written in the July Parish Magazine:

> We were deeply grieved to hear of the sad death of Mrs J. Miller of Sledbrook Street. Mrs Miller was a very devoted and loyal member of our Church and those who knew her intimately will assuredly miss her kind and pleasant personality.
>
> Her work for the Church over a long period of years was unquestionably fruitful. As a Sunday School teacher of considerable merit and for many years leader of the Young People's Union Mrs Miller will long be remembered by those who had the privilege of coming under her influence and training. The writer knew Mrs Miller for some thirty odd years and during that time knew nothing but good of her. Mrs Miller's zeal for the Missionary cause both at Home and Overseas was clearly manifested in her life and work. Not only in our own parish but also throughout the Deanery of Wigan, where she was greatly esteemed by many friends of the Church Missionary Society.
>
> Latterly Mrs Miller became Superintendent of our Girls' Sunday School but regretfully, for health reasons, was compelled to relinquish the work she loved so much. We thank God for her devoted life and work. May she rest in Peace.

The August 1960 Parish Magazine recorded the following appreciation of Mr Robert Winstanley:

> On Saturday the 25th June we laid to rest, in the Church Yard, a very old and faithful servant of our Church, Mr Robert Winstanley. What a wonderful record of service he had. Seventy-eight years as a member of the choir, starting in the 'Old Iron Building' following on in the present Memorial Church which we all love so well. We in the choir will long remember him, always first in the vestry for choir practice on Friday evenings, Matins and Evensong on Sundays, surely a lesson to us all in punctuality and faithful service to his Church.
>
> Our association with 'little Bob' as he was so affectionately known to us, was a happy one, we recall the times when pressure of work made a late choir practice necessary, Bob would then look at his watch, informing the Choir Master he had a train to catch, we knew only too well where that train was, and it wasn't in Pemberton Station. The choir parties we used to have, and the choir trips were never complete without Bob singing for us 'The Old Rustic Bridge'.
>
> We thank God for his service, and for the privilege we have enjoyed in serving our Church with him, and also for the example he has left behind, we would do well to emulate. He has now passed to the higher service, leaving behind many happy memories. (A member of the Choir.)

The death of Mr J. W. Brierley in February 1961, aged 79, was a great shock to the Parish. Mr Brierley had been Headteacher of the Boys' School from October 1913 to December 1945. He was licensed as a Lay Reader in 1932 and served in that office until his death. He was Church Treasurer from 1939 to 1951, and a School Governor from 1950. He had been a member of the Ruri-Decanal Conference and the Diocesan Conference, and was for many years a fine Bass soloist on many Parish occasions. The following Obituary was published in the March 1961 Parish Magazine:

The Late Joseph W. Brierley

It was with very deep regret and a great sense of loss that we learned of the death of Mr Brierley following such a brief illness. Many did not even know he was ill. It is difficult to realise that we shall no longer see his familiar figure passing to and fro with measured tread and invarying regularity to his beloved Church. Mr Brierley's life was a purposeful one; Service being the purpose, devotion and loyalty being his characteristics.

He had so many interests in life that it is difficult to mention any to which he gave more time. Education perhaps might come second to his Church, which was, of course, supreme.

It was a privilege to know Mr Brierley and the longer one knew him the more one admired his unfailing courtesy and amiable personality, his sterling qualities and high principles, a man of courage and a loyal friend and brother.

All this was the outcome of a living faith in God and a staunch practice of that faith. He knew where to turn for strength and guidance and he knew that God never failed him.

For many years Mr Brierley gave himself to Highfield Parish. In School, in Bible Class, in Church. Through these avenues he must have influenced hundreds of children and adults and led them on to a way of life of the highest order, and there must be very many who have cause to thank God for encouragement and influence given to them perhaps years ago by their old Headmaster.

There is much more that could be said for we have made no mention of his many interests outside our parish and his hosts of other friends.

We mourn the loss of a great-hearted gentleman. Highfield will not seem the same without him. We thank God for his life and work, and we would not forget that our loss is but a shadow of that felt by his own family to whom we offer our most sincere thoughts at this time. T. HUGHES.

Another long-serving member of the choir, Mr A. V. Shepherd died on 11 October 1962. The following appreciation was written in the Parish Magazine:

We wish to put on record our appreciation of the long service (over 60 years) in our Choir of Bert Shepherd whose sudden death on October 11th took from us a good and loyal servant. Advancing years had begun to tell on him but even though he could not walk in procession on Harvest Sunday he was in his place in the Choir Stalls at both services. May he rest in peace.'

News was announced in the January 1964 Parish Magazine of the death in October 1963 of Mrs L. M. Gullick. (formerly Miss Mabel Greener, of the Pemberton Colliery Manager's family, and one of the last links with the Colliery.) Mrs Gullick had left Highfield some years before but continued her interest in the Church and regularly contributed to Church Funds.

The July 1964 magazine recorded the death of Mr Herbert Gee, Vicar's Warden:

IN MEMORIAM. It is with very deep regret that we have to record the passing of Mr Herbert Gee—the Vicar's Warden. Bert Gee as he was affectionately known to his many friends served his Church with sincerity of heart and mind and found a great joy in so doing. During the long years he was associated with us he served in a number of offices in the Church and brought to them all a loyalty and keenness so much admired.

His death was a great shock to us all for although a few of us had known that he had been feeling a little unwell over the previous week-end none of us thought that his end was so near. Even before his retirement he did what he could for the Church, but after he had retired, and this only last summer, he looked around for more things to do and took on a number of little but important jobs. We shall miss him very much and his place will be hard to fill.

Mr Gee had a musical ability and a number of us have pleasant memories of the evening only a week before his death when he really enjoyed himself accompanying a couple of teenagers in their 'Pop Music' items. Then there was his Old Age Pensioners group which under his direction recently undertook the folding and stapling of the magazines.

To Mrs Gee we offer our very sincere sympathy and in our sadness we rejoice in that he was a faithful and good servant and one in whom the promises of the Lord have now been fulfilled.

'His servants shall serve Him and they shall see His Face.'

Mr William Atherton, former Verger of the Church, died peacefully at home on the evening of Thursday 11 February 1965, aged 78 years. The following obituary appeared in the *Wigan Observer*:

The Revd Herbert Bullough, Rector of Halsall, returned to his old parish of St Matthew Highfield, on Monday morning, to pay tribute to his great friend, Mr William Atherton, and to assist the present Vicar, Revd Robert J. Smith, to conduct his funeral service.

Verger at St Matthew's for 51 years until he retired three years ago, Mr Atherton died at his home, 394, Billinge Road, Highfield, on Thursday last week. He was 78. In April 1959, Mr Bullough presented Mr Atherton, who had then completed 49 years as Verger with a cheque for £50. In his half-century as verger, sexton and gravedigger, Mr Atherton had served five Vicars of Highfield—Revds John Wood, John Woods, Parker Johnson, W. H. Bullough and R. J. Smith.

Born in Pemberton, Mr Atherton moved to Highfield in 1892 when he was five years old. He was confirmed at St Matthew's, married there on Easter Monday 1916, and had served the Church in many capacities. He was secretary of the Men's Bible Class more than 50 years ago, and a treasured family possession still is a presentation Bible given to him by members in 1911. He was a member of the Parochial Church Council, a member of the Church Bowling Club, and Secretary of the old Highfield Dramatic Society for many years. he also assisted dramatic societies at Upholland Parish Church and St John's Pemberton. Well-known and respected, Mr Atherton was both Diocesan and Deanery Chairman of the Guilds of Vergers. He had been a local agent for Middleton and Wood (Wigan) from their earliest days.

Mr Atherton was a sawyer at the old Blundell's Pemberton Colliery for 40 years until its closure. Then, until his retirement 13 years ago, he was employed as a sawyer by Squire Bankes at Winstanley Hall. He leaves a wife and two daughters.

A service at St Matthew's preceded interment in the Churchyard. Representatives of most parish organisations were in a large congregation. Among those present included Captain and Mrs Bankes of Winstanley Hall; Mr Frank Richardson, Headmaster of Goose Green; Mr W. A. Cowan, Verger at Wigan Parish Church, representing the Verger's Guild; and Messrs George Wood, Norman Tonks JP, and Leslie Stone representing Middleton and Wood.

The sad news of the sudden death of Mr George Perrin on 5 June, aged 50, so soon after the family moved to the south, reached the Parish early in June 1969. The following appreciation appeared in the July magazine:

> It was with a profound shock that the news reached us of the sudden death of Mr George Perrin at his home near Southampton. It was but a few short weeks ago that we said goodbye to Mr and Mrs Perrin as they left to make a new home at Cadnam and we hardly got used to their having left us. We sent them away with our good wishes and committed them to the care of their new Vicar. And then came this great shock and very sad news.
>
> What made it worse for most of us was that being so far away we could not do anything to help Mrs Perrin. Many people wrote to her and we remembered her in our prayers and for this Mrs Perrin asks me to express her most sincere appreciation and thanks. I was able to go to Cadnam on behalf of our parish and many friends to take part in the funeral service in the little village Church which had become their new spiritual home, and then on Sunday morning, June 22nd, his cremated remains were placed in the Garden of Rest in our Churchyard after a Memorial Service attended by many parishioners, friends and business acquaintances.
>
> And so we paid our respects and expressed our sincere appreciation of a man who did what he was able to do in the service of Christ and His Church. We thank God for his example and the encouragement he gave to us all.

In the January 1970 Parish Magazine, the death of Mr Ernest Stretton, aged 64 years, a former Chorister and PCC Secretary was reported:

> Last month we had occasion to express our appreciation to two of our Church workers for their long and loyal service to the Church, and we commented on the fact that we knew of others of still longer service. Little did we think that Ernest Stretton who joined the Church choir some 57 years ago would so suddenly pass away. Ernest served the Church in a variety of ways and was for a number of years the Secretary of the Church Council. Whatever he put his hand to was done with meticulous care and attention, and he left no stone unturned to make sure that his work gave the best service he could provide. His attention to the details was first class and if he took on a task one could leave it with him knowing that it would be well done. The Church is the worse off for his passing from us and we give thanks to God for his love of the Church and for his service to Highfield. To his loved ones we offer our sincere sympathy in their loss and trust that they will take courage in the knowledge that those 'who serve God shall see His face.' May he rest in peace."

Miss Hannah Fairley died on 31 December 1971, aged seventy-four years. Miss Fairley had worked as Sunday School Secretary with Mr Richardson many years ago. She had been responsible for the hymns and readings at the Women's Fellowship, and had been connected with the Dramatic Society from the days of the Old Iron Church. She was a member of the PCC for many years. Mrs Arthur Stockley, Mrs Herbert Gee and Mrs

Bessie Hampson were her sisters. They were all grandchildren of William Fairley, FGS, an internationally recognised Mining Engineer who came from Staffordshire, the author of several books on Mining who sent his son Ernest to be articled to Mr Shortrede of Bankes' Winstanley Collieries.

Mr Thomas Hughes, who had been involved in the life of the parish all his life, died on 5 February 1974, aged 91 years. He was born on 13 January 1883, in Little Lane, and attended the Little Lane Mission, which was held in the Reading Room which had been built by Colonel Blundell for his employees. The building is still standing today, now used as a garage.

As a young man he worked as a clerk at Pemberton Colliery until 1914 when he left to join the forces. He went to Chester Barracks but was found to be Grade CIII in health. When he came home his job at the colliery had been taken, and he obtained a post as Clerk/Book-keeper at a Shipping Office in Liverpool, a post which he held until he retired in 1948.

He became a Sunday School Teacher at the Little Lane Mission, and played the harmonium there for the singing. He led the Little Lane Sunday School Procession with their banner when they joined the parish procession at the end of Little Lane on early Walking Days. In 1913 he presented the Little Lane Accounts to the Annual Vestry Meeting at the Parish Church.

On 27 August 1921 he married Selina Parkes, also from Little Lane, and also a Sunday School Teacher at the Mission, and they came to live in Highfield View. The Members of Little Lane Mission always came to Highfield for Communion, and so in 1915, when the Mission closed, most of the members came to Highfield, rather than to the new Church at Goose Green.

Mr Hughes was involved with the work of the Church Missionary Society for most of his life, becoming Treasurer after the death of the Revd J. Woods. In his younger days at Highfield he was involved with the Church Football Team. He was Superintendent of the Boys' Sunday School when Mr W. Richardson was in charge of the Girls' Sunday School and Miss L. Holland was in charge of the Infants. He was Treasurer of the Day School Fund in the 1940s and 1950s, and was a Churchwarden from 1948 until 1963. He was a member of the Liverpool Diocesan Conference in the 1950s and 1960s, and a School Governor from 1953 until his death.

Mr Hughes was a gentleman of the Old School and well-respected. He was a source of information on the early day of the parish and responsible for many of the magazine articles on the Parish History. He was a truly Christian Gentleman who loved and served his Church well.

At the March 1974 Meeting of the PCC Mr E. G. Elliott was appointed a School Governor in place of Mr Hughes.

The Vicar's Illness and Retirement

The Vicar was seriously ill at the end of March 1974. He was absent from duty until the end of July 1974. The Revd Charles Walker, who later became Vicar of St Michael's Wigan, took most of the services during the Vicar's illness, with help from the Readers.

At the Annual Parochial Meeting in April 1974, in the absence of the Vicar, Mr G. A. Cooke took the chair and opened the meeting with prayers; including a prayer for the recovery of the Vicar. Mr W. O. Millard did not stand for re-election to the PCC and accordingly resigned as Honorary Secretary. After the business of the meeting, the Chairman thanked everyone for attending the meeting. The Vicar was sent Best Wishes for a speedy recovery, and sincere thanks were given to all who had helped to make it a very successful year in every respect. At the following meeting of the PCC Mr Neil Gregory was appointed PCC secretary.

At the August 1974 meeting of the PCC, it was announced that the Old Infant School was to be leased to the Wigan Metropolitan Borough Council for use as a Nursery School for Winstanley Primary School. The Local Education Authority were then doing the necessary alterations, and an agreement as to the terms of the lease was to be drawn up. At the same meeting the Vicar, Canon Smith, stated that he would be retiring on the 31st October 1974. A discussion followed on the procedure to appoint a new Vicar. Mr G. A. Cooke, the Deputy Chairman, proposed a long, healthy and happy retirement to the Vicar, thanking him for his work and help in the Church, and expressing the appreciation and gratitude of all concerned.

The following Farewell address was made by Mr G. A. Cooke to Canon Smith after Evensong on his last Sunday, Education Sunday, 27 October 1974.

> Tonight we are met to say farewell and thank-you to our Vicar, Canon Smith. St Matthew's Church, Highfield, has indeed been blessed with its incumbents, in that they have all stayed for a long time. There must be something attractive about this Parish ! But tonight is different, in that Canon Smith is retiring, and not moving on to another Parish.

Mr Cooke spoke of the early career of the Canon Smith and then went on:

> There have been many changes in Highfield since Canon Smith came. Fifteen years ago there were no houses in the fields to the south of the Church. The population of the Parish must have doubled at least in those years with all those new houses. The number of children in our schools has increased tremendously. The Education System has been reorganised, and instead of three schools as we had fifteen years ago we now have one school.
>
> We have seen a great decline in moral standards over the past fifteen years with the Church struggling in many parts of the country with greatly diminishing congregations. Here at Highfield, thanks in no small way to the ministry of Canon Smith—we have carried on and maintained our standards. We can still fill our Church—as we did this afternoon for our children's service, and we can still pay our way without having to beg

for money or to resort to Fund-raising efforts. All this is due in no small measure to the way Canon Smith has guided the PCC and its finances during this time.

As well as all the time and effort Canon Smith has put into administering the Parish, we know that he never forgot to visit the sick. The little hospital in Billinge Road, I know, was dear to his heart, and lately he has delighted in visiting and giving Holy Communion to the residents of the Geriatric Wards at Billinge Hospital.

In addition to all these duties, Canon Smith has been active in the Church in the Diocese and at National level. He has been for many years Chairman of the Diocesan Board of Dilapidations (now the Parsonages Committee). He has served on the Diocesan Board of Finance and the Diocesan Pastoral Reorganisation Committee. He was a Proctor in the Convocation of York from 1958 to 1971 and he was a member of Church Assembly—the Parliament of the Church of England. In 1968 his efforts were rewarded by the Bishop with a Canonry of Liverpool Cathedral.

We know how hard Canon Smith has worked for the Church he loves and serves so well and all this took its toll just before Easter when to the great shock of the Parish he was taken ill and suddenly taken from us. Oh how we missed him, and what a joy it was to have him back again. Canon Smith had intimated to the PCC before he was taken ill that he was thinking of retiring—I don't think that any of us believed him, but we now know that he made the right decision.

Unfortunately we are not only losing a Parish Priest—we shall be losing a verger, a sexton, groundsman, printer, joiner, electrician, heating engineer—you name it—he's done it! We shall indeed need a superman to replace him. I could go on for a long time singing his praises, but I must come to the business of the evening. On behalf of the PCC and the Congregation of St Matthew's, I have been asked to make this presentation to you and to Mrs Smith, as a thank-you for all your work and help and guidance over the past almost fifteen years. With this presentation go our sincere wishes for many years of happy retirement.

Two and a half years ago the PCC voted you a rise in your expenses. You refused to take the whole sum that they agreed to give you then. The Congregation have contributed £175 as their testimonial to you, and to this the Standing Committee have decided to add all the money that you refused in 1962 plus their own donation—We know that you cannot refuse it now—and we know that it will help in your new Highfield—where we hope that you will spend many happy years with good memories of St Matthew, Highfield and its people.

Canon Smith and his wife retired to the Village of Crank, near St Helens, to a house called 'Highfield'. For many years he continued to help where needed in other parishes in the Diocese. He enjoyed nine years of retirement and died in June 1983 and his funeral was held at St Matthew's on 5 July 1983, when the Right Revd David Sheppard, Lord Bishop of Liverpool, conducted the service.

Revd
William Bynon

Fifth Vicar

1975–1982

WILLIAM BYNON was born on 4 March 1943 in Edge Hill, Liverpool, the third of four sons born to William and Violet Bynon. The whole family were regular attenders at St Cyprian with Christ Church, Edge Hill, where William was a member of the Sunday School, Choir, Life Boys, and Boys Brigade, later becoming a Sunday School teacher and eventually Superintendent. He was educated at Old Swan Technical College and later at West Derby Technical College. He knew from an early age that he wanted to enter the ministry. He had been influenced by his Boys' Brigade Officers, by a Christian family life and by the Revd Canon Ernest Nickson then Vicar of St Cyprian's, but resisted the call when his father became ill and financial problems hit the family, and on 5 August 1959 began work in Martin's Bank.

His call to the ministry persisted and in 1962 he was accepted as a candidate for the ministry and attended the Bernard Gilpin Society at Durham for one year before beginning his training at St Aidan's Theological College, Birkenhead, from 1963 to 1966. On 18 December 1965 he married Joan Margaret Thompson, his childhood sweetheart from St Cyprian's. He was ordained Deacon on 24 September 1966 and began his first curacy at Huyton St Michael's with the Revd J. H. Richardson who was then Vicar. He was ordained Priest on 25 September 1967. Two days later, on 27 September, a daughter, Karen Elizabeth was born to Revd and Mrs Bynon. In 1969 he became Curate of Maghull. Here his Vicar left the day after his appointment, and he was in charge of St Peter's until 1972 when he became a Team Vicar of Maghull. A son, Mark William, was born on 15 May 1971. Revd Bynon served at Maghull until he came to Highfield in 1975.

The PCC of St Mattthew's Highfield met on 13 January 1975 to discuss the qualities required in a new Vicar. It was agreed that he should, if possible, have the following qualifications:

A married, family man, aged 35–45; Parochial, Middle Church, and a Good Preacher; Happy to have Church School; A fondness for children; Prepared for hard work; Strong personality for leadership in all things.

On 21 January the PCC met Canon Bullough & Captain Bankes, two of the Patrons of the Parish. Canon Bullough agreed on the list prepared and hoped that all these could be found in one man. A detailed account of the Parish was presented to the Patrons.

At a PCC meeting on 18 February, Revd W. Bynon was introduced to the Council by Canon Bullough and immediately arrangements were put in hand for the new Vicar to move to Highfield.

The Institution and Induction of the Revd W. Bynon as Vicar of Highfield took place on 14 March 1975 at 8 p.m. The Institution was conducted by the Bishop of Warrington, Right Revd John Monier Bickersteth, who preached on Matthew chapter 13 verse 16. The Induction was conducted by the Archdeacon of Warrington, Venerable John Lawton, assisted by the Revd R. N. Arbery, Rural Dean.

Four days later, on the 18th, the Vicar attended his first Annual Parish Meeting at Highfield. In his remarks to the meeting:

The Vicar asked for the re-election of Churchwardens and PCC this year to cope with the problems of the next 12 months. He thanked those who had carried on the work of the parish during the interregnum, those who had cleaned the Church so well, and he spoke of his hopes for the future of the parish and plans for the Church Heating, Lighting and the Graveyard. He hoped to build up the Congregation and said that the Vicarage door was 'Never closed, Never a Barrier.'

At the PCC meeting on 15 April 1975, the subjects of church lighting and cleaning the church by sandblasting were considered. These two schemes were undertaken and completed before the end of 1975. The Church Lighting was installed by Corletts, who had installed the first electric lighting in the Church in 1923. The money was raised by many parish efforts during the year. The cleaning of the Church by sandblasting was financed by a grant provided by the Local Authority.

The Vicar announced that 'a Mrs A. Moss' had contacted him with regard to forming a pram club. The PCC offered Wednesday afternoons in the Parish Hall.

On 2 December 1975, at a PCC meeting, the pattern of Sunday Morning Worship was discussed. It was agreed to try the following: first, third, and fourth Sundays, Family Communion. Second Sunday Family and Parade Service. Fifth Sunday Matins.

The Atherton Window

A Special Meeting of the PCC was called for 7 December when the family of the late Mr William Atherton, who for 53 years was Verger of this Church, offered to present to the Church a stained glass window, designed by Mr Harold Harvey of York, to be dedicated in his memory. This Sunday would be the nearest to his anniversary. The PCC viewed the drawings of the Window and were greatly impressed by the Artist's work. The PCC wholeheartedly accepted the gift. The Secretary was asked to write to Miss M Atherton to thank the family for their most generous gesture.

The Dedication of the window, by the Revd Canon W. H. Bullough, took place at a celebration of the Holy Communion on 15 February 1976. The design of the window contains two main elements—Psalm 84 and Mr Atherton's work as a sawyer at Pemberton Colliery, roughly separated in the composition with the line in the psalm 'For the Lord God is a sun and a shield' depicted in the head. Symbolically, the source of light behind the figure of the man in the doorway—understanding—is the same as 'The God, the sun and the shield.' The elements in the composition, i.e. screen, doors and church, depict different periods of architecture signifying the passage of time—it is in no sense meant to depict St Matthew's Highfield.

The Funeral of Mrs Maud Atherton, aged 87, the widow of Mr T. Atherton, brother of the above William Atherton, took place on February 26th 1976. Mrs Atherton had been involved with many organisations in the church since the early days. She had been a member of the early Dramatic Society in the days of the Iron Church, a member of the PCC, very involved with the Women's Meeting and a founder member of the Women's Fellowship.

The January 1976 Parish Magazine had a new cover photograph of the Church taken by Mr Cyril Worthington. It was printed on fine art paper so that parishioners could keep and frame it.

The recently revived Men's Fellowship held their first meeting in December 1975 and the following account appeared in the January magazine:

Twenty-six men attended our first meeting last month, and our next meeting is in the hall on Friday 9th January 1976, at 7.30 pm. We hope to have a Fish and Chip Supper, and other 'liquid refreshment', so gentlemen put the date in your diaries and come along.

The February 1976 Magazine gave details of the planned House Groups for Lent:

Lent is a time to think seriously about our lives and our faith. This Lent I would like to see a number of House Groups in the Parish. Those who are prepared to offer their house for a weekly meeting should let me know. If we can organise this successfully, then we should find the experience very worthwhile. Further details will be given when we know how many groups can be formed.

Mr 'Jimmie' Muldoon retired from his position as school caretaker and the following appreciation appeared in the March Parish Magazine:

On Tuesday, 2nd March 1976, Mr Muldoon attained his senior citizen's birthday, and retired from his post as School caretaker on the day preceding. He has completed almost 17 years in that post, and during that time he has given faithful and loyal service. For only a fraction of that time I have worked with him in School, but in that short time I have found him to be a very willing and helpful caretaker. We are all certain to miss him—teachers and pupils alike, and we can only place on record our deep gratitude to him for all he has done for us. Some measure of our appreciation was shown in a tangible way on Friday 20th February, when the whole school, pupils, teaching and non-teaching staff, and the School Managers, assembled to present Mr Muldoon with a transistor radio and cheque, the total value of both exceeding £70.

With these gifts go our best wishes to 'Jimmy' for a long and happy retirement. The School Managers join with us all at school in congratulating you, Jimmy, and wishing you and your wife God's Blessing for the future.

Wm. Spencer, Headmaster. W. Bynon, Vicar.

The cost of heating the large Vicarage had become a problem with the increasing cost of fuel. At a meeting of the PCC on 3 March 1976, a new central heating system was recommended including new radiators and pipes plus a separate system for upstairs, so that all rooms could be heated separately.

The Annual Parish Meeting was held after Community Hymn Singing at Evensong on Sunday 4 April 1976. The Vicar's report included the following:

> The Vicar thanked all those who had helped during his first twelve months in the Parish. The Parish was rapidly changing. Approx. 15,000 to 16,000 now reside in the area. The Vicar had visited 1762 people during the year. In the Church we now had new lighting, and the building had been cleaned showing the beautiful Woolton stone to its best advantage. Other improvements had been made and a new Window had been made and dedicated in memory of Mr Wm. Atherton. The Congregation had grown as the following figures show: Communicants have increased in the past year from 4000 to 7385. There were 15,669 worshippers, 102 Baptisms, 11 Weddings, 54 Funerals, 30 Cremations. There would be 83 Confirmation candidates in May. We must try to increase our giving to combat inflation, and look towards a future build-up of the Congregation and our growing responsibilities.

The June 1976 Parish Magazine announced that Mr R. Green had been appointed School Caretaker, and Mrs S. L. Highton had been appointed to the School Staff.

Miss B. Matthewson retired from the Sunday School on 19 September 1976. The following appreciation appeared in the September Magazine:

> After forty years of faithful service in our Sunday School, Miss Matthewson is to retire as leader of the Infants' department. On behalf of the Church, PCC, and generations of children, may we all thank Miss Matthewson for all she has done in this important part of the Church's work.

Miss Irene Twigg took over as leader of the Infants' Sunday School.

Landscaping of Graveyard

The untidy condition of the graveyard had been a matter of concern for many years since the parish had not been able to finance a full-time sexton. At the August and September meetings of the PCC the matter had been discussed in detail and the following report appeared in the October 1976 Parish Magazine:

> The PCC at its last two meetings has been considering the problem of the graveyard.

The dreadful condition of the graveyard before it was landscaped in 1976 and 1977.

Over the last two years a group of men have been struggling, with very little success, to keep the weeds under control. This has proved to be a losing battle, and in spite of a dry summer and lots of weedkiller, the graveyard is still a disgrace to the parish.

The ever-increasing cost of man-power means that the possibility of employing someone to look after the graveyard is completely out of the question—the state of the graveyard is quite beyond one man's capabilities.

The Council has taken all these things into consideration and have decided to landscape the whole of the graveyard and turn it into a lawn cemetery.

All this will cost a considerable sum of money (the estimated cost is £2,500), but we feel it has to be done, and hope that you will give all your support in removing this eyesore from our parish. We know that you will all be thrilled with the end result when it will be a pleasure to visit the resting place of your loved ones.

Further details will be given in next month's magazine.

The Standing Committee of the Church Council.

An appeal was launched which met with a very generous response. The poor weather of the following winter held up progress for a time but eventually the job was completed and the graveyard was left in the hands of teams of volunteers who regularly week by week mowed the grass and trimmed round the headstones.

The confirmation candidates this year gave sufficient money as their gift to the Church to purchase a beautiful silver paten costing £83. The paten or plate was dedicated on Advent Sunday, 28 November 1976, at the Family Communion when it was used for the first time.

A Walking Day picture taken in 1978, showing the shops at the corner of Billinge Road and Enfield Street and the Booking and Ticket Office at Pemberton Station, all now demolished.

This year the Women's Fellowship presented the Church with 100 kneelers costing £172.80 as their gift to the Church. The new kneelers were dedicated at their Anniversary Service on Sunday 7 November 1976 at 6.30 p.m.

The 1977 Annual Parochial Meeting was held on 27 March. At this meeting Mr Graham Taberner resigned from his position as Churchwarden and Mr Roy Thomas was appointed in his place. The following appreciation appeared in the April 1977 Magazine:

> For almost fifteen years Mr G. Taberner has been the Vicar's Warden, and has served faithfully, fulfilling the duties of Churchwarden. Mr Taberner now feels the time has come for him to resign from this office. May I, on behalf of the Church and congregation thank Graham for all that he has done. Our thanks must also go to his father, wife and family who have been with Graham, a team working together for the welfare of the Church. Well done, Graham, and many thanks.'
>
> At the Annual General Meeting the Vicar's choice for a successor to Mr Taberner was Mr Roy Thomas. Roy was born and bred in Highfield and has attended Church with his family all his life. Mr Horne and Mr Thomas are two excellent men who can be relied upon to fulfil the duties of this high office in the Church of England.

The Women's Fellowship, to mark their 21st birthday, presented a new Festal Altar Frontal and a wooden case which were consecrated on 8 May 1977.

3 November 1977 was the 21st Anniversary of the formation of the Women's Fellowship, which was celebrated with a Dinner dance, with Canon and Mrs Bullough, Canon and Mrs Smith and Revd Bynon and Mrs Bynon as special guests. After an

excellent meal, a toast in champagne, and music by Mr and Mrs Wayne, a very enjoyable evening was had by all.

At the Annual Parochial Meeting held on 12 March 1978, the Vicar announced that he hoped to have news of a Curate in the near future. The parish would have to look forward to finding £10,000 for a house and £2,000 *per annum* towards the Curate's stipend.

A Curate for the Parish

At a meeting of the PCC on 11 April 1978 the Vicar announced that he had succeeded in obtaining a Curate for the parish. Mr George Thomas, aged 31, married with a daughter aged 5, had accepted his offer of a Curacy.

George Thomas was born on 4 September 1946 in Bootle, Liverpool. His parents were George and Norah Thomas. He attended Bootle Grammar School and then St John's College York from 1965 to 1969, where he trained as a teacher. He taught from 1969 to 1975 at Alsop Comprehensive School and Yew Tree Comprehensive School. He had attended Sunday School at St Matthew's Church Bootle from an early age 'because he was bored at home!' As a teenager he joined the choir at St Matthew's and was involved in Pathfinders and the Boys' Brigade.

He was influenced to join the ministry by the sermons and example of the Vicar of St Matthew's, Bootle, the Revd Dennis Gatenby. In 1969 he married Joan Dickinson whom he had known at St Matthew's all his life, and a daughter Jill was born in 1972 at Walton, Liverpool. In September 1974 he was accepted as a candidate for the ministry and the family moved to Durham for three years while George completed his training at St John's College, where in 1978 he was awarded a Diploma in Theology. Mr Thomas was ordained Deacon in Liverpool cathedral on July 2nd in the morning, and was received at Highfield at the evening service. A party from the parish attended the ordination service. The PCC agreed to buy No. 32, Melrose Drive as a home for the Curate for £9,750.

The August 1978 Parish Magazine included the following letter form the new Curate, the Revd G. Thomas:

32, Melrose Drive,
Winstanley.
Dear Friends,

A word never very far from my mind these days is 'privilege'. It is a privilege to be among you, to meet you, and get to know you. It is a privilege to be your Curate and share with you in God's work here. It is a privilege to lead worship, to preach the word of God; to be with people in their time of need, to listen to them, to speak God's words of comfort and strength to them.

It is a privilege to be part of St Matthew's, Highfield, to work with your Vicar and learn from him. It is a privilege to visit you in your homes, talk with you on the road and to pray for you.

Joan, Jill and I thank you from the bottom of our hearts for the very warm welcome you have given us—not only in the hall on my first Sunday, but also whenever we have met you, and especially as you have gone out of Church. Your smiles and handshakes are so friendly, —thank you so much.

Our sincere thanks to the Vicar, Churchwardens and PCC for all they have done for us. We are delighted with our house and all the many kindnesses and good wishes we have received. I am grateful for all the help I have been freely given.

Please pray for Joan, Jill and Myself; for the Vicar and me, as we seek together to be servants of God; and for yourselves and us, that we may all together be formed into the Joyful Body of Christ in this Parish.

Love and Best Wishes, G. Thomas (Curate).

The Curate, supported and encouraged by the Vicar was soon involved in the work of the parish, particularly in the field of Youth work as the following letter in the October 1978 Parish Magazine shows:

Dear Friends,

Will St Matthew's be as flourishing in 1998 as it is today? The Church of the future lies with the young people of the present. The responsibility for enabling these young people to grow in the Church lies with the adults of the Church. The Body of Christ here in St Matthew's includes young and old alike—we are all one in Christ.

It is with such thoughts in mind that we begin our two new Youth Groups. The younger group (aged 10–14) meets in the Church School each Wednesday from 6.30–7.45 p.m. The older group (15 upwards) meets at our house each Sunday at 8 p.m. Members of both groups ought to be Confirmed regular attenders at Church. Our aim is to enjoy ourselves through various activities and to learn more of what it means to be a Christian. Enquiries about membership may be made on the appropriate evening or to the Clergy or to any of the Leaders.

What an exciting privilege to be engaged in such work! And the whole Church is involved. These young people will feel part of the family of the Church, if you ask regularly how they are getting on, encourage them in their activities and especially, pray for them by name.

These two groups are new limbs of the Body of Christ and therefore they will need to be solidly joined to all the other parts if they are to grow into the Church of tomorrow.

Tell out my soul the greatness of the Lord
To children's children and for evermore.

Best Wishes to you all. G. Thomas, Curate.

The 10–14 Club became known as The St Matthew's Under Fifteen Fellowship, SMUFFS. This imaginative name was coined by Andrew Porter.

The original architect's drawings of the Church had been kept in a folder in the Vestry. Mr Martin Hedley, one of the Patrons of Highfield had arranged for some of these drawings to be framed. These 1891 drawings were to be hung in the Vicarage for safety's sake.

During the past months a group of ladies, Miss S. Walker, Miss S. Gaskell, Miss B. Matthewson, Miss I. Twigg and Miss M. Moore had spent a total of over 500 hours sewing and repairing the Church Banners. They used over 25 reels of thread with 100

The Platform Party at the Day School Rose Queen in 1978: Mrs E. Gaskell, Deputy Head;
Revd W. Bynon, vicar; Mrs J. Bynon; Mr W. Spencer, Headmaster; Mrs Smith;
Canon R. J. Smith; Mrs D. Lavin, PTA Secretary.

metres of thread on each. Both banners had practically been re-made. A grateful vote of thanks was accorded to them for their efforts.

At a meeting of the PCC on 6 June 1978, the Treasurer, Mr G. A. Cooke gave details of an envelope scheme for Church collections to replace the old St Matthew's Church Fund, using the existing Church Fund Collectors and the Electoral Roll.

At the PCC meeting on 3 October 1978, Mr G. A. Cooke resigned from his position as Organist and choirmaster, but offered to continue until a replacement could be found. A vote of thanks was passed to Mr Cooke for his services which were originally 'only on a temporary basis' but which lasted for 14 years. Mr Cooke continued as Church Treasurer, and in the November 1978 Parish Magazine wrote the following letter:

> On behalf of the PCC I want to say a very sincere thank-you to all of you who are helping to make the 'Weekly Envelope Scheme' such an encouraging success. Over 570 people now have envelopes and the regular weekly contributions have averaged over £211 over the first seven weeks of the scheme. This is a magnificent response, and the PCC can now look forward with confidence to the future.
>
> We hope that any of you who have not yet got envelopes, and would like to join the Scheme, will ask the Vicar or Churchwardens who will see that you get your envelopes as soon as possible.
>
> A regular weekly offering in this way will help the PCC to plan ahead, to meet its commitments, and to go forward with God's work in this Parish.

Gordon A. Cooke. Hon. Treasurer.

16 December 1978 marked the first of a series of 'Olde Englishe Nightes' organised for the Parish by Mr and Mrs H. L. Stockley, (Bert and Barbara). The Squire on this first occasion was Mr W. Spencer with his wife Edna as his Lady. The evening consisted of a procession of the Squire and his Lady, escorted by the stewards, a superb meal prepared by the ladies of the Catering Committee, speeches and toasts from the High Table with Mr Stockley as Master of Ceremonies, and songs and dancing. The entertainer on this first occasion was Mr M. Monk. The evening proved to be highly successful and became an annual event for the following three years. The Curate and his wife Revd and Mrs George Thomas took the part of Squire and Lady in 1979, the Vicar and his wife Revd and Mrs William Bynon took the parts in 1980, and Mr George Elliott, the former Headmaster of the School and Mrs Elliott took the parts in 1981.

The Men's Fellowship decided to form a Bowling Team and applied for admission to the Wigan and District Churches Amateur Bowling League in 1979. Any interested Church Members were invited to join.

Following discussions in the PCC, it was decided to have a printed Parish Magazine from March 1979, in place of the Duplicated Magazine which had been in existence for many years. In his letter in the February magazine, the Vicar thanked all those who had been involved in typing and duplicating the magazine monthly for many years, also the team of retired gentlemen who assembled and stapled the magazine ready for distribution.

In the April 1979 Parish Magazine an appeal for help with the graveyard was made:

> In a parish like Highfield there are always a large number of jobs requiring to be done to the buildings, grounds and graveyard.
>
> It is so important that everything looks its best because everything that we do is to the Glory of God, and we cannot give him second best.
>
> An appeal was made for people to mow and keep tidy the graveyard, to make a new notice board for the porch, to Spring clean the inside of the Church, and for a group who would run a creche during the 10. 30am service.

At the 1979 Annual Parish Meeting held on 1 April it was announced that Mr Cyril Bell would take over as Organist and Choirmaster on 1 July.

On Friday 11 May 1979, a recording was made in Church, of Community Hymn Singing, to be broadcast on Radio Merseyside on Sunday 20 May, under the title 'United in Song.' The Vicar introduced each hymn with a few informative words. Mrs A. S. Gordon played the organ and Mr G. A. Cooke conducted the choir and congregation in the singing of the hymns.

The Curate, Revd G. Thomas was ordained priest on 1 July 1979, and a coach party of parishioners went to the Cathedral for the service. The Revd Thomas celebrated his first Communion at the Evening Service at Highfield and Mr Cyril Bell commenced his duties as Organist and Choirmaster on the same day. He was welcomed to the parish in the July 1979 Parish Magazine as follows:

> On the 1st July we give a warm welcome to our new Organist and Choirmaster Mr Cyril Bell. Mr Bell has been organist and choirmaster at Haydock Parish Church for the last twelve years, and we know that he will maintain the excellent standard set by Mr Gordon Cooke and Mrs Sue Gordon. Mrs Gordon is to continue as our Deputy Organist

The November 1979 Parish Magazine recorded the sixty years that David Ascroft had served in the Choir:

> Congratulations to David Ascroft who has now served in St Matthew's choir for 60 years. Last month David was presented with a Bible from the PCC and people of the Church with a special token from the Choir and a Certificate of long service from Mr Bell the choirmaster and organist. Well done David, and our thanks to you for your dedication and example.

Miss Sally Walker who had been a Sunday School teacher for 44 years decided to retire and the following tribute appeared in the December 1979 Parish Magazine:

> After 44 years as a Sunday School teacher Miss Sally Walker has decided to retire. Sally must have taught 1000s of children and she will be a great loss to the Sunday School. On behalf of the Sunday School, the Church and the 1000s of children and adults we would like to express our thanks to Sally for her long service in the work of her Lord and Saviour. Thank you, Sally.

The same magazine carried the following news:

> On December 2nd, Advent Sunday, a new Baptismal Candle holder will be dedicated during the Family Communion Service at 10.30 a.m. The original candleholder is no longer large enough to accommodate all the candles needed for each Baptism Service. Mr Roy Barton has generously provided and made the new holder, which will be dedicated in memory of Roy's mother, Mary Ellen Barton, who died earlier this year. Once again we express our thanks to a member of the congregation for a wonderful gift which will be long used and cherished.

At the same service a new Chalice, the gift of the Women's Fellowship was also dedicated

The Diocesan Centenary

At a meeting of the PCC on 10 January 1978 a letter about the Diocesan Centenary Celebrations which were to be held in 1980 was read out by the Vicar. Mr Roy Thomas was appointed to be our representative on the Deanery Centenary Committee. At a later meeting Mr Thomas reported on the Deanery Centenary Committee meeting. The Centenary appeal gave us a target of £1,119 per year for seven years towards a Diocesan Target of £1,000,000.

The first Service to Celebrate the Centenary of the Diocese of Liverpool was held in the Cathedral in November 1979. The January 1980 Parish Magazine records the event:

> On Wednesday 14th November 1979, a congregation of 2,500 people met in Liverpool Cathedral for a service of Thanksgiving and Dedication. It was a wonderful service and perhaps it is best summed up by printing the brief explanatory note in the Order of Service which we used:

1980 marks the century in the history of the Diocese of Liverpool. This service is therefore in preparation for the celebrations of that year. Thanking God, as the Psalmist says, is good in itself, but it is also a challenge to all Christians to greater commitment in his service. So in the course of the worship representatives from the deaneries and parishes will present their 'declarations of intent' to the Bishops of the Diocese, as tokens of the service they promise to offer to meet the challenge of this great occasion. In response to the same challenge an Order of Christian Witness will be inaugurated during the service, when representatives from the parishes, who will speak on their behalf, will be admitted to that Order as pioneers of Christian witness. All who are present are asked to share in the promise that is made.

The Vicar was asked by the Bishop to be the Director of this new Order whose object is to meet for mutual support and fellowship, study, action and prayer. There are now representatives from more than one hundred parishes in the 'Order', and it is hoped that all the parishes will be represented eventually.

The Wigan Deanery Centenary Walk was held on Whitsunday, 25 May 1980. Parishioners were transported in five double-decker buses to Wigan. The procession round the centre of the town in which 29 parishes took part, consisted of three sections, each headed by a Bishop, which joined together and processed via New Market Street, Mesnes Street, Standishgate, Market Place, Market Street and Parson's Walk and assembled on the Mesnes School Cricket Field for a service of worship which was all part of a great act of witness to show Wigan that the Church is still alive, and a power for good in an evil world. The Centenary was also celebrated by a great gathering at Haydock Park Racecourse for a Diocesan Family Festival Day in a unique demonstration of faith, solidarity, family unity and goodwill. The Wigan Deanery also held a Centenary Carnival at Haigh. Highfield entered a float representing the mining industry in our parish.

At the New Year's Eve Dance, presentations of flowers and gifts were made to the ladies who had catered and cleaned for many years and who had sadly decided to retire. Mr Harold Gaskell paid tribute to the long and devoted service of Mrs Ashcroft and Mrs Muldoon, with their worthy assistants Mrs Williams and Mrs Prior. The February 1980 Parish Magazine records:

> Many thousands upon thousands of Highfield people and their guests have been spoilt over the years by the magnificent buffets these ladies have presented and by the immaculate condition in which they have kept the hall for use. They have served us with love and devotion beyond the bounds of duty.

The Anderson Window

Mr Donald Anderson had made it known that he would love to purchase for the Church a stained glass window in Memory of his parents. The theme of the window was to be of the mining industry in this area. A brass plaque was to be placed underneath the window with all the names of the mines in the area. The layout of the above was to be by Mr Simm and Mr Harold Harvey. A draft was to be given to the PCC for approval.

The Anderson Window, 1980, with the Vicar and Mr Donald Anderson,
who gave the window in memory of his parents.

The Dedication of the new window took place at the Celebration of Holy Communion on 2 March 1980 at 10.30 am. The Revd Canon W. H. Bullough dedicated the window and preached. The April Parish Magazine gave details of the window and also of Mr James Anderson:

The scenes in the window depict activities in the coal industry in which Mr James Anderson was involved.

In the top left of the window there is the 'Old Iron Church' built in 1865 by Colonel Blundell. In the top right of the window is the King Pit Headframe. Mr Anderson was responsible for all the shaft apparatus including winding ropes and guide ropes.

Between the two is the King and Queen Pit Engine House built in 1870. Mr Anderson was responsible for all building work and his last big job was the building of Summersales Colliery and the bricking of the shaft.

In the centre of the window is a 'Box Wagon' used for transporting coal to Liverpool docks. Mr Anderson was in charge of the wagon building and repair shops. At the age of 19 he could build a complete wagon in a week and the piece rate for the job was £3 4s. od.

In the bottom left of the window can be seen men inspecting the Engine Pit. Mr Anderson was responsible for all the shafts and rode down on top of the cage each Friday to inspect them.

In the bottom right of the window is seen the Engine Pit pumping rod of the great 84 inch beam engine. This was built by James Lindsey and Co. at the Haigh Foundry in 1820. It was modified in 1873 and scrapped in 1932. When it was built in 1820 it was believed to be one of the largest beam engines ever built.

Mr James Anderson, 1882–1971

Mr Anderson was born 98 years ago in a cottage near the wood where May Mill is now standing, just 300 yards from the Church. His mother—maiden name of Winstanley—was born in the same cottage. She attended the Iron Church when it was first built and went to the Day and Sunday Schools. Her family kept the 'Hare and Hounds' and the farm attached to it in 1810.

Mr Anderson attended the Iron Church and the Day and Sunday Schools when Mr Duddle was the Headmaster and Miss Rawlinson was the Headmistress. At the age of 14 he was bound apprentice to Jonathan Blundell and Son in the joinery and carpenters shop at the Colliery. he was put in charge of these shops at the age of 27. When Colonel H. B. H. Blundell died in 1906 it was Mr Anderson who put the flag at half mast on the Church.

The Colliery at that time paid for all preparations for Church activities such as bazaars, school trials and sports etc. and Mr Anderson was involved in all these activities. The schools belonged to the Blundells and it was part of Mr Anderson's job to keep them in repair.

In 1970 Mr Anderson (aged 88) made and presented to the Church a Prayer Desk in memory of his parents, and twenty four years before that made the Credence Table for the Memorial Chapel. Some of the other activities performed by Mr Anderson are recorded in the lovely new stained glass window.

Mr and Mrs Anderson lived all their married life in Highfield until they moved to Parbold in 1954. We here at Highfield remember with deep gratitude the wonderful work performed by Mr James Anderson and his family for so many years.

The Holy Communion Service on 31 August 1980 marked the Commissioning of the Parish Youth Mission 'Hot Gospel.' The Mission lasted for one week and was held in the Parish Hall. On the first night 180 young people attended. There were Christian

Rock Bands during the evening sessions and the Greenbelt film was shown. The Revd Tony Adamson was the missioner and the response was described as 'Terrific!' The Mission ended at Evensong on the 7th September, when the Curate, Revd G. Thomas was the preacher.

Miss Margaret Anderton, a member of the Choir, a former member of the PCC, and a youth leader decided to leave the parish for a rather special reason as was told in the November 1980 Parish Magazine:

> We are delighted to hear that Miss Margaret Anderton is to relinquish her teaching post and go into full time Christian Service. Margaret is going to the Mayflower Family Centre in London as House-keeper/Pastoral Worker in January.
>
> Well done Margaret for responding to the Lord's call. We shall miss you here at Highfield but look forward to hearing about your new work for the Lord.

At the December 1980 meeting of the PCC it was announced that £1,374 had been raised at the Christmas Fair. Thanks were expressed to Harold and Eileen Gaskell and Joan and Derek Rimmer for organising the Social occasions throughout the year. The ladies catering teams were also thanked for their efforts. In the January and February 1981 Parish Magazines an appeal was made for volunteers to help the catering teams and also the bar teams.

A Parish Weekend was held at Thornleigh, Grange-over-Sands from February 27th to March 1st 1981. The speaker was the Bishop of Warrington. Food, fun and fellowship were enjoyed in great abundance by everyone. The Bishop's theme was 'The Resurrection Community, the people of promise and hope, with a belief in new life and new starts.'

Details of the Annual Parish Meeting held on April 5th 1981 were recorded in the May magazine:

> Mr D. Horne retired from his position as Churchwarden. He was thanked for his work over many years, also for his work as Parish Clerk, keeping registers, attending Baptisms, Weddings and Funerals. He was appointed to the Honorary Position of Churchwarden Emeritus. Mr Harold Gaskell was appointed Churchwarden in his place. Mr Peter Broadhurst was appointed Deputy Warden in place of Mr Gaskell.

Mr Harry Brighouse moved from the parish to live in Up Holland in 1981. This meant that it was impossible for him to attend to all the duties expected of a Boys' Brigade Captain and so Harry decided to resign as Captain of our 14th. Wigan Company. Harry was a boy in the Company when it was founded in 1944. he became an Officer and served for 34 years, 21 of which were as Captain of the Company. Harry was thanked for his loyalty and work for our Company. The new captain is Mr W Harrison.

Dry Rot found in School

It was at a meeting on 2 June 1981 that the PCC were first informed of a problem which was to take up much of their time for the next two years. The first evidence of dry rot in the school was discovered which eventually led to the demolition of the old building and the subsequent building of the new Junior School.

*The Junior School, built for girls and infants in 1894 by Colonel H. B-H-Blundell,
demolished because of dry rot in the summer of 1982.*

Following the investigations into the extent of the dry rot in the Junior School, the
following article appeared in the September 1981 Parish Magazine:

> The Church School. At the time of writing we have just been informed of a serious
> problem at our school. Extensive dry-rot has been found in all the classrooms and hall
> of the Junior School. We have been forced to evacuate the school so that repairs can
> begin immediately. The children are being taken each day by bus to the Richard Evans
> School in Ashton. This school is almost empty and due to close next year because of the
> falling numbers of children attending. The total cost of the repairs to the school are
> expected to be approximately £50,000 and the repairs are not likely to be finished before
> next Easter. Special events are now being planned in order to raise money towards the
> cost of the repairs. Our thanks to Mr Spencer and his staff for giving up part of their
> holidays to pack and then move all the desks, chairs and materials to Ashton. I am sure
> that this serious problem to our Parish will be overcome just as every other problem has
> been overcome in the past. Best Wishes. W. Bynon.

The cost of the repairs to the school plus the extent of the dry rot forced the PCC and
the School Governors to consider whether or not they should replace the old building
with a new one. At a meeting of the PCC on 1 September 1981, with the School
Governors and Mr W. Spencer, Headmaster present, a wide ranging discussion of the
problem, including a discussion whether or not the PCC should consider allowing the
school to become Controlled status rather than Aided status as existed, and looking, as
far as possible at the costs involved, the PCC decided to build a new Junior School, and
immediately opened a School Building Fund. At a meeting of the PCC held on

2 November 1981, Canon Yendall, the Diocesan Director of Education and Mr Robin Whalley, the Architect were present, together with the School Governors and Mr W. Spencer, Headmaster. The meeting was told that the approximate cost of the school would be £343,204 of which the Parish would have to find approximately £45,000. The PCC decided to go ahead with the project.

In June 1981 Mrs Audrey Moss and Mrs Pat Gore were recommended to start training to become Readers. In the August magazine Audrey and Pat told how they were called to this service.

Women's Fellowship 25 Years Old

The November 1981 Parish Magazine carried the following article celebrating the 25th Birthday of St Matthew's Women's Fellowship:

Women's Fellowship. 25 years—Quarter of a Century.

25 years ago on 1st November 1956, the Women's Fellowship came into being. Canon W. H. Bullough was then the Vicar of this parish. It was his idea to close the two small groups of Women's Classes and form a Fellowship for young and old. A letter was put out in the parish and on Thursday night, November 1st 1956, 175 women met in the new Parish Hall. Every name and address was taken.

The parish was small in those days and 175 women was a surprise even for Canon Bullough. This was something he never expected and he never for one moment thought that in 25 years time the Fellowship would have well over 100 members and would have done such good work for Church and Charity.

During those 25 years the Women's Fellowship has carpeted the Church throughout, bought vases, stands, flowers, Hassocks, Hymn Books, large door mats, a Church Boiler, a Vicarage carpet, Invalid Chair and given donations including curtains for the Parish Hall, contributed towards Church Lighting and Church Schools, two silver chalices and a beautiful frontal, made and worked by Miss Graham of Wigan and Mrs Anderson of Blackburn and also a lovely oak chest to house the frontal.

Charity does not begin at home, it begins by helping as much as one can all who are in need, so we have given to World Refugee Fund, Training Guide Dogs for the Blind, cancer research, Multiple Sclerosis, Hope School, Red Cross, Samaritans, CARE, Spastic Society, NSPCC, TV's to Billinge and Pemberton Hospitals, Heated cots and infant respirator, Casa Materna Home, Italy, Moral Welfare Association, Graveyard Fund, Tear Fund, Wigan Hospice, Sue Ryder Homes, St Margaret's Home and the Relief of Pakistan. All in all almost £7,000 has been made and divided between Church and Charity.

Once or twice the Fellowship has been likened to a social club, but let me assure you it is not so. It belongs to St Matthew's Church and its roots were buried 25 years ago deep in the teachings of Christ. What is it then that has kept this Fellowship together for so many years? Certainly not by write-ups in the papers, we work and enjoy ourselves not by boasting about our activities but knowing that somewhere, someone helps and guides us.

Now we have in this year of 1981, £1,000 to dispose of, and the committee have decided to give £200 to Wigan Hospice and £800 to the Parish Hall to help to modernise the kitchen. The Hall which was built by men of this parish, is badly in need of repair. Next year, God willing, we intend to work for our new Junior School.

With the exception of holidays, the Fellowship meets every Thursday evening, mostly in the Hall. On second Thursdays of each month an Evening Hour Service is held at which a collection is taken for flowers for sick members. On the 1st and 3rd Thursdays we have social events. The last Thursday in each month a Holy Communion Service is held in Church, at which new members are admitted and presented with a badge which was designed in 1960. Each member should wear her badge with pride and thank God she belongs to St Matthew's Women's Fellowship. Joan Bradley.

The Anniversary was celebrated at Evensong on 1 November 1981, All Saints Day, when the preacher was Revd W. H. Bullough.

The January 1982 Parish Magazine announced the publication of 'Founded on Coal' by Ray and Derek Winstanley, an excellent history of Highfield and Winstanley including two chapters on the Church and the School.

Formation of St Matthew's Fellowship

A very important meeting of the PCC was held on 2 March 1982. For some time, plans had been discussed to form a Fellowship which would provide social facilities for the Parish in the Parish Hall and extension. The PCC agreed to the Constitution of St Matthew's Fellowship which would be held in the Parish Hall, including a licensed bar. Thanks were expressed by the PCC to Mr Fred Holcroft for all his work on this constitution. It was decided that one of the first tasks of the Fellowship would be to refurbish the kitchen in the Hall to improve the facilities for the catering groups.

Outline plans for the new school were shown to the meeting which met with approval.

Vicar to Leave Highfield

The biggest surprise of the evening was the announcement by the Vicar that he was to leave Highfield, and his last Sunday would be the first Sunday in August.

At the Annual Parish Meeting on 28 March 1982 Mr Roy Thomas was re-elected Warden to help ease the change of the interregnum. The Vicar announced his resignation, and said how sad he was to leave Highfield.

At the PCC meeting on 4 May 1982, Mr N. Gregory resigned from his position as Secretary after ten years in that position. He was thanked for his valuable work by the Vicar. Mrs M. M. Cooke was appointed Secretary to the PCC in his place. Details of how the new Vicar would be chosen and appointed were explained to the meeting by Mr G. A. Cooke.

At a meeting of the PCC Finance Committee on 18 May 1982, Revd G. Thomas was appointed Chairman of the School Appeal which was to discuss arrangements for the finances of the new school building which dealt with an appeal letter, appeal via the local press and a buy-a-brick scheme, along with all the other Parish money-raising efforts.

The July 1982 Parish Magazine contained the Revd W. Bynon's Farewell letter:

My Dear Friends,

'Goodbyes' always involve an element of sadness. In our case especially so, as we have been so happy here at Highfield. It has been a great joy to see the Church grow, the buildings renovated and improved, and the Church grounds properly maintained. Above all, Highfield is the place where we have seen the Lord at work, drawing people to himself, and transforming many lives.

It is with praise and thanksgiving to God for all that he has done in the seven and a half years, yet also with sadness at leaving so many with whom we have become deeply involved that we say 'Au Revoir' for now, but we hope to see you again in the future. It is through the love of Jesus Christ as our Saviour and Living Lord that we will most assuredly meet in the life to come, even, if not again in this life.

Our new address is: All Saints Vicarage, 1, Park Avenue, Hesketh Park, SOUTHPORT.

Joan and I hope that you will call and see us when you come to Southport, we would be delighted to see you. Above all, we would ask you to find a small place for us in your prayers. We face a marvellous and yet daunting task in Southport. To make a new start in a Parish which is one hundred and five years old is a great challenge. The fire in 1977 destroyed everything so it is with new buildings that God has called us to begin the task of rebuilding the congregation and organisations for the future. In our own strength nothing is possible, but with our Lord, all things are possible. So please pray that God will empower and lead us in His wonderful service.

We will certainly miss you all and this grand parish of Highfield and there will be forever in our hearts a deep sense of love for you and your beautiful Church.

May God bless you all, Bill and Joan Bynon, Karen and Mark.

In the August 1982 Parish Magazine, the Churchwardens expressed their appreciation of the work of the Revd W. Bynon:

His ministry has been much appreciated. We thank him for the innovations he gave to us, the new graveyard, the Over Sixties, the Men's Fellowship, etc. and for the spiritual blessings many people, especially the sick and sad, have received from him.

The Curate, Revd G. Thomas, also expressed his appreciation of the Vicar:

Bill Bynon has been a good boss to work for. I'm grateful to him for his help and guidance; for enabling me to work out and discover what ministry is about and for allowing some of our more daring escapades to take place.

I am also thankful to him for our Christian fellowship over the last four years, for our prayer together and for our discussions on ministry and church life.

Joan, Jill and I wish him and Joan, Karen and Mark God's richest blessings upon them as they leave us and continue in God's wonderful ministry in Southport.'

Mr Fred Foster, an old boy of Highfield School, wrote the following article which was also included in the August 1982 Parish Magazine:

Memories of Highfield School, 1935–42

When I heard the news that the old school had to come down, I felt that a piece of my life was going with it. I thought back to the days that I had spent there. We started school in those days in the care of Miss McAvoy, a very kind lady who was in charge of the nursery and at the grand age of 4½, I entered her class. We used to have a sleep in the afternoon on the small beds, complete with green blankets and pillowcases. At the end of each term, we all took our bedding home to wash, carrying it in the pillowcase, pretending to be coalmen! Misdemeanours were punished by a slight tap on the hand, after which you turned to your classmate and said, that didn't hurt! Not so with Miss Holland the Headmistress. If you ran foul of her, a few stinging slaps on the legs made you regret your mistakes.

Miss Broomhall, in the next class was, to me, a rather large, forbidding lady, who wore her hair in a long roll around her head. Her ample figure was clothed in white blouse and long grey skirt. We all used pencils to write with, and if for any reason you broke the point off the pencil and had to go out to her for a re-sharpen, she always rapped your knuckles with it first. There was a reason for this, because most points were broken off by pressing the pencils into holes in the desks.

We all loved going into Arthur Dickinson's shop near the station, where he had a soda fountain and sold penny drinks. Sometimes Miss Broomhall would select one of us to go down to the shop and bring an apple back for her.

Near to Arthur's shop was the one run by 'Uncle Billy' Fairhurst. He must have been made uncle to generations of Highfield children. I can see his shop now, with wine gums, cherry lips and sherbet dabs, not forgetting those fabulous 'lucky bags'.

The next class was run by Miss Starkey, but for some reason, I skipped this class and finished the infants' school in the one run by Miss Simm. About this time the 2d. Saturday matinee at the 'Carlton' was showing Flash Gordon as the serial. I recall that we used to fasten our gaberdine macs like capes around the neck and pretend to be our hero. Many's the time that we reached home, soaking wet, as we sailed matchsticks down the gutters and watched them disappear down the nearest grid.

I started the Junior School in Miss M. Barton's class, or Bottom Miss Barton as she was known, to distinguish her from Miss E. Barton otherwise known as Top Miss Barton. This meant that I had again 'skipped' a class, Miss Gulley was teacher in the first class of the Juniors. Some time around this period we had a new teacher in school, Mrs Savage, who, I believe was a missionary's wife. She was a real character. She brought crab apples to school for us to use as subjects for art, after which we could take them home. They always looked more appetising than they tasted! The first time Mrs Savage was on playground duty in the boy's playground there was an uproar. Usually, when the lads saw the teacher put the whistle to her lips they would make a dash for the toilets which used to be on the far wall of the playground, so as to prolong playtime. This day Mrs Savage followed them in, something that had never been done before. The result was that several boys had minor accidents. They never tried it again with her!

I also recall some of the games we used to play, games like Skilly, All across, throw-on-t'can, call-a-ball. Jack Bilsborough from Enfield Street was king at all across. No-one ever stopped him. He used to come across last with his fist swinging and no-one was foolish enough to get in the way! In those days, whether it was real or imagined, there seemed to be a division at Pony Dick, a case of 'us' and 'them'. We thought that only 'posh' people lived up the hill, and sometimes it appeared to us that the teachers crawled to them a bit. Once, when the teacher was out, the whole class had been misbehaving and when she came back, she caned the lot of us. We all lined up and took it, until it was the turn of a girl from the 'posh' area. The cane fell like a feather, there was a groan from the rest of the class and the teacher's face was scarlet!

Another incident that sticks in my mind was when one boy had been warned for persistent lateness. Finally Miss Johnson decided to cane him after morning assembly. He was brought up to the front and she went to the cupboard for the cane. He made a dive behind the piano which was at an angle to the wall. When she tried to reach him he kicked out with his clogs. It became pure farce, everyone was tittering and her face was getting redder and redder. When she finally grabbed him, she didn't half lay on!!

A lot of us went to school in clogs in those day and after the dances on Saturday nights, the hall floor was like glass and we used it as a skating rink. Clogs were great in the winter, also for making ice slicks in the school yard, that is, until Harry Stretton came out with hot ashes and spoiled them. The sandstone flags by the old Co-op shop were great for making sparks fly; my father threatened me many times when I came home with the clog irons off. There was a spell when we only went to school half time because the air raid shelters hadn't been built. This was thought to be great, we used to spend the extra time in the woods in Winstanley, jumping the brook or 'walking the pipe'.

We had big open fires in the classrooms in those days and these were used many times to dry out children's wet clothes or to warm the bottles of milk for our break. The bottles with the cardboard tops were supposed to press down in the middle, but usually went into the milk and splashed you if you were unaware of it.

It was a great life really. We were pretty poor in worldly goods but we were happy. There were forty in a class and I don't remember anyone at that time who couldn't read or write. Some were slow learners but when we read around the class everyone could read. The teachers were dedicated to their work and would help any child who needed it.

It's a pity to see the old school go, with all its memories. Let's hope that the new building will still carry on the traditions and ideals that made Highfield School to me and many more, the best school of all. Fred Foster.

On 5 August at the Women's Fellowship Meeting a cut glass decanter and six wine glasses were presented to Revd and Mrs Bynon. Revd Bynon thanked the Women's Fellowship, but said that he was very disappointed that the decanter was empty. He said that he and his family did not want to move but he felt it was God's will that he should go to help build up his new church in Southport.

A cheque was presented to Revd and Mrs Bynon on behalf of the PCC and congregation at the evening service on 8 August 1982.

The September 1982 Parish Magazine recorded the following letter of thanks:

All Saints Vicarage, 1, Park Avenue, Hesketh Park, Southport.
12th August 1982

Dear friends in Highfield,

At the moment we are surrounded by boxes which when opened will present us with our home once again. It was very sad for us to leave Highfield on Tuesday, and our thoughts and prayers are still very much with you. Joan and I would like to thank you all for your kindness and many gifts and especially for the cheque presented to us last Sunday evening.

Thanking you all once again, Best wishes, Bill and Joan Bynon, Karen and Mark.

The October Magazine recorded details of Revd Bynon's Induction Service at All Saints' Southport on Wednesday 1 September 1982.

The Revd Bynon was Vicar of All Saints Southport from 1982 to 1988 and Chaplain to Hesketh Park Hospital from 1986 to 1988. He was also Priest in Charge of All Souls Southport from 1986 to 1988. In 1988 he became Vicar of St Peter's Newton in Makerfield. His wife Joan became a Reader in 1988.

Revd George Thomas was left in charge of the parish for the next five months.

In the November Magazine it was announced that Revd George Thomas would shortly be leaving the parish to take up an appointment as Vicar of St James, Chorley, and his last Sunday at Highfield would be 2 January 1983.

Obituaries, 1975–1982

Mrs Lucy Chadwick, who had been in charge of the catering in the parish hall for many years, died and was buried on 20 December 1975. Her Obituary appeared in the January magazine as follows:

> It was with sadness that we learned of the death of Mrs Chadwick. After a prolonged illness Mrs Chadwick spent the last month with her daughter in Surrey, and died there on the 15th December. The large congregation at her funeral on Saturday 20th December showed the love and respect that so many people had for this wonderful lady who has served her Church so faithfully for so many years. Her catering in our hall was the talk of Wigan, and she will be sadly missed by us all. We offer our sympathy and prayers to the family at this time.'

The funeral of Mr Thomas Ashcroft took place on 25 June 1976. Mr Ashcroft had been a sidesman at Church for many years, and was one of the bricklayers who put most of the bricks into the building of the new Parish Hall.

On 23 September 1977 the funeral of Mr William Nicholson took place. Mr Nicholson had been a member of the Choir for many years, a member of the PCC, and Covenant Secretary in the early days of the scheme.

The death of the Right Revd Clifford Arthur Martin, Fourth Bishop of Liverpool, 1944–65, was announced in the October 1977 Parish Magazine:

> It was with great sadness that we learned of the death of Bishop Martin. Those of us who remember Bishop Clifford Martin knew him as a Bishop, a father-in-God, a man of outstanding pastoral gifts with a concern for mission and evangelism. He had a quality of communication—the 'common touch'—which was so evident in his meeting with people, in his teaching and preaching, in his shrewd practical judgement, and in a delightful sense of humour.
>
> We thank God very deeply for Bishop Martin's life and ministry.

The funeral of Miss Lilian Holland, who from 1915 to 1954 was Headmistress of Highfield Infants' School, took place on 27 June 1979.

The Funeral of Mrs E. M. Eden took place on 3 August 1979. Her obituary appeared in the September Parish Magazine:

We pay tribute to Mrs Eden who has been a well loved and respected lady in this parish and community. For twenty-two years she was leader of the Life Boys, sixty-three years a Sunday School teacher, a member of the PCC and Women's Fellowship, (before the Fellowship, the Women's Bible Class and the Women's Meeting). Mrs Eden played the piano and was a member of the Parish Dramatic Society and also of the Wigan Operatic Society. Mrs Eden will be missed and we thank God for her life of devotion and service.

A new altar frontal for the season of Trinity was dedicated on 1 June 1980, in memory of Mrs Eden. The frontal was made by Miss B. Matthewson and Miss M. Moore.

The Funeral of Mr W. H. Morton took place on 17 December 1979. A tribute to Mr Morton appeared in the February 1980 Parish Magazine:

> The death of Mr Morton is a very sad loss to St Matthew's Church and school. For many years he was the treasurer of the School Managers and always had the welfare of our school and its children at heart. Mr Morton served this church faithfully and will be sadly missed by the congregation. We offer our sympathy and prayers to Mrs Morton and her family at this time.

Mr Tom Lea died on 8 February 1980, aged 79, and was buried on the 11th. His obituary appeared in the March Magazine as follows:

> The death of Mr T Lea is a very sad loss to St Matthew's Church. Mr Lea was a sidesman for sixtythree years, and rang the Church bell for twelve years (in the belfry). Every Sunday morning he opened the Church at 7 a.m. and prepared the 8 a.m. Holy Communion, and for many years served on the PCC. Mr Lea served this Church faithfully and will be sadly missed by the congregation. We offer our sympathy and prayers to his family at this time.

The August 1980 Parish Magazine recorded a tribute to Ben Jones who had been for some years the gravedigger and for many years a sidesman. He had also been a keen member of the bowling team. In his later years Ben moved into Brown Court where he spread his friendship and his faith.

The funeral took place on 8 December 1981, of Mr George Henry Taylor, aged 70 years. George had been the foreman in charge of building the Parish Hall. He had for many years been a sidesman and a member of the PCC, but will always be remembered for his invaluable work on the Parish Hall.

On 13 October 1982 the Revd George Thomas had the sad task of conducting the funeral of Ernest K. Stockley, aged 49 years. Like the rest of the members of the Stockley family, Ernest had been a member of the Church all his life, involved in the Sunday School, Choir, Boys' Brigade, Sidesmen and Men's groups and as a member of the PCC. He was to be sadly missed.

A week later, on 20 October, he conducted the funeral of Douglas Horne, aged 75 years, who from 1969 to 1980 was Churchwarden of Highfield. An appreciation in the December Magazine reads:

> The Parish and Community at Highfield were saddened by the loss last month of Mr Douglas Horne. Mr Horne truly stands as one of Highfield's most loyal and faithful servants. He served the Church for many years in various capacities: among them as leader of the Over 60s, school governor, parish clerk and Churchwarden, becoming the

first Churchwarden Emeritus in the history of Highfield Church. He was one of those who kept the Church going through the last interregnum.

Although he held important positions in the Church he was always unassuming, content to do his work to the service of God quietly and conscientiously with the minimum of fuss and bother. Most of us will remember him for the real gentleman that he was, for the gifted artist he was and for his humble yet certain faith in the Living God. The assurance of our continued prayers goes to Mrs Horne and her family.

Mrs Mildred M. Cooke died suddenly on 18 December 1982, aged 53 years. Her funeral took place on the 22nd and again Revd Thomas conducted the service, on this occasion assisted by Canon W. H. Bullough who came to give the farewell address. A tribute to Mrs Cooke was recorded in the February 1983 Parish Magazine:

> The sudden death of Mildred Cooke was a great shock and a great loss to this community. She was a much loved teacher at our school, secretary to the PCC, organiser of the flower rota for church and each week she gave of her time to collate and keep in order the envelopes for our planned giving. Many former parishioners who have moved away received a church magazine sent to them by Mildred. She did countless jobs for this parish and our Rose Queens, Nativities and Christmas Fayres will never be the same without her. We shall miss her, not just for all the work she did but for the kind and helpful person she was. We extend to Gordon and the boys our sincere sympathy and our prayers. E. M. G.

Revd G. Thomas Leaves

A farewell letter from the Curate and his family appeared in the January 1983 Parish Magazine. In it he says:

> Saying 'Goodbye' is never easy especially when you are leaving a place where you have been extremely happy as we have been here in Highfield. We shall never forget the tremendous warmth of your welcome when we first arrived some four and a half years ago; that warmth never lessened as the months (and years) went by, indeed it increased and surrounded us so much that we have felt secure and accepted, as part of this wonderful community. It has been a joy and a privilege to have been a part of St Matthew, Highfield and all it includes.

He continues to express his gratitude and ends:

> Thank you for all you are and for all you have given to us. We pray to God that you will continue to grow into the full stature of Christ Jesus Himself, nothing less will do for any one of us. We have learned a great deal and one thing especially about you all, that: 'There's nowt so good as gradely folk'.

> God Bless, George, Joan and Jill.

A presentation was made to Revd Thomas and Joan in the Parish Hall after evensong on 2nd January when Mrs Thomas was presented with a bracelet and Revd Thomas with a cheque. A letter of thanks from them was recorded in the February Parish Magazine.

Revd George Thomas was inducted as Vicar of St James, Chorley, on Friday 20 January 1983 by the Bishop of Blackburn. He has recently completed ten years as Vicar of St James.

Revd W. H. Harrington

Sixth Vicar

1983–

WILLIAM HARRY HARRINGTON was born on 28 August 1933 in St Michael's Parish, Huyton, the eldest son of Harry Harrington, who worked as a Cupelar Furnaceman at British Insulated Callender's Cables, Prescot, and Hannah Harrington. A younger brother Jim was born in January 1939. In 1936 the family moved to Huyton Quarry and the young Bill, as he was called, attended Huyton St Gabriel's Infant School and Huyton with Roby Church Junior School then on to Prescot Grammar School. He joined the choir at St Gabriel's when he was nine and remained a member until he was ordained and this had its effect on his lifelong love of music and worship and his eventual ordination. He attended Sunday School as a child and the Youth Club as a teenager, becoming a Sunday School teacher at sixteen until he joined the RAF at nineteen. While at St Gabriel's two Curates, the Revd S. Coulter and the Revd A. Woods, who came from St Mark's Newtown, both had a great effect and influence upon him as did Mr R. S. Briggs the Headmaster of Prescot Grammar School.

While at school Bill had been thinking about ordination but when he left school he was unsure about his vocation and worked for two years at Cooper's, Liverpool, then the headquarters of a large grocery chain, training to be a food inspector. From 1952 to 1954 he served his National Service in the RAF as a Drill Instructor. He studied for the Ordained Ministry at King's College, London for three years, influenced by Dr Eric Abbott, the Dean of King's College who had great charisma and a deep spirituality. After King's he spent one year at St Boniface College, Warminster, Wiltshire.

In September 1957 he married Ann at St Gabriel's, Huyton Quarry. Ann is also a Huytonian having attended primary school in Huyton and Wade Deacon Grammar School, after school working for a number of years at Henderson's, Liverpool.

William Harry Harrington was made a Deacon on Trinity Sunday 1958 by the Bishop of Liverpool, Bishop Martin, and served his title at All Saints, Childwall. He was ordained Priest in 1959, again by Bishop Martin.

A son, Mark, was born to Revd and Mrs Harrington in May 1960.

The Revd W. H. Harrington and his young family then moved to St Helens, where he was Curate in charge of All Saints Sutton from 1960 to 1964. His first parish was St Michael Ditton where he was Vicar from 1964 to 1976, and from 1976 to 1983 he was Vicar of St Barnabas Mossley Hill, Liverpool.

Ann later studied at St Katherine's College, Childwall and was awarded a B.Ed Hons. Since 1970 she has taught at a Primary School in Widnes. Their son Mark attended the Church Primary School in Ditton, Liverpool College and Lancaster University where he obtained a BA Hons. in Religious studies.

At a PCC meeting on 4 May 1983 the appointment of a new Vicar was first discussed. Canon Bullough attended the PCC meeting on August 17th to discuss the appointment with the PCC and an outline of the parish at present was presented to Canon Bullough. It was indicated that the parish needed a very experienced man—possibly a second or even third Incumbency, with expertise in spiritual and lay ministry. At the meeting of the PCC on 2 November 1983, Canon Bullough introduced the PCC anonymously to 'Bill' saying that he had the full approval of Capt. Bankes and Mr Martyn Hedley—the other Patrons, and he was pleased to tell the PCC that 'Bill' had been offered the Benefice, and had accepted, providing that the PCC really wanted him to come. The PCC later agreed unanimously that 'Bill' should be the next incumbent. The news was announced publicly on the following Sunday.

The Institution and Induction of the Revd W. H. Harrington as Vicar of St Matthew's took place on Tuesday 15 March 1983 at 8 p.m. The Bishop of Warrington and the Archdeacon of Warrington officiated.

The Vicar wrote in the April Parish Magazine:

My Dear Friends,

As I write my first letter from Highfield Vicarage may I on behalf of Ann, Mark and myself, offer you our warmest wishes and greetings. At present I am still the Vicar of St Barnabas, Mossley Hill, but from the 15th March (now recent history, I trust) I shall be your Vicar.

I am most grateful to the Patrons of St Matthew's for the confidence they have shown in me by their offer of this living. With God's help I shall do all I can to justify their trust.

No one is more conscious than I of the excellent work done in this parish by previous Clergy. You have been indeed fortunate to have had a succession of 'good clerics'. And how well blessed Highfield is in having two such dedicated and able Readers, namely Gordon Cooke and Bert Stockley. Nor must one forget those two characters who I feel I can call friends already, —our two wardens, Roy Thomas and Harold Gaskell.

It seems to me that whatever success has been achieved at Highfield has been due to co-operation and team work.

As a new chapter begins in the Highfield story, let us pray that we might face the future with confidence and faith. With God's help we can go on from strength to strength.

I charge you all at the beginning of my ministry at St Matthew's to do all in your power to advance God's kingdom in this district.

What of the future? Only God knows the answer completely! We do know that our 'new school' will soon be ready, maybe our already large population might grow. There is a great yet exciting challenge facing us all. More people to reach, more to integrate into our church life. Looking back one can see quite clearly how God's Hand has guided this parish. Rest assured, His Hand will guide in the future if we commit ourselves to him completely.

May we work together, worship together and play together, as a complete and happy family for many years to come, and may as a result God's kingdom be enriched and His name glorified.

Your friend and Vicar, BILL HARRINGTON.

Foundation Stone of New School

The Revd W. H. Harrington attended his first official function at Highfield nearly two months before his Induction when he was invited to the Laying of the Foundation Stone of the new school. The event was reported in the March 1983 Parish Magazine:

Report on Foundation Stone of new school
School Report: We're on our way!

There was much activity around Highfield on the afternoon of January 28th. On this date we proudly laid the Foundation Stone of our new school. The actual ceremony was preceded by a short service in Church attended by the Mayor and Mayoress of Wigan, officials from the Education Committee, the Architect, the Builder, Governors, the Parochial Church Council, School Staff, representatives of the schoolchildren and many other guests. The service was conducted by the Revd G. Thomas and other clergy attending included not less than three former Vicars of this Parish. Following the Service a procession to the School site took place where at the bidding of the Revd W. Bynon, Mr E. G. Elliott well and truly laid the Foundation Stone. The headteacher gave full expression of thanks and the procession then moved to the Parochial Hall for refreshments. The Stone made of black polished marble was kindly donated by Mr Brian Halliwell.

Change of Headteachers

At the end of the Spring Term 1983, Mr William Spencer retired from his position as headmaster of the school. The Vicar wrote this tribute in the May 1983 Parish Magazine:

My Dear Friends,

Once more it is time for CHANGE. Last year your old Vicar left, in January your Curate left, in March your new Vicar arrived—phew!—Now our Headmaster is retiring and a new Headmistress will take his place. This gives me my opportunity to say a sincere and

Clergy and Readers at the Laying of the Foundation Stone of the new school:
Mr G. A. Cooke; Revd G. Thomas, Vicar of St James, Chorley; Revd W. H. Harrington,
Vicar designate, St Matthew, Highfield; Revd W. Bynon, Vicar of All Saints, Southport;
Mr W. Spencer, Headmaster; Canon R. J. Smith, retired; Canon Neil Arbery, Rural Dean;
Canon W. H. Bullough, Rector of Halsall; Mr H. L. Stockley;
Canon Owen Yandell, Director of Education, Liverpool Diocese.

heartfelt thank you to Mr Bill Spencer as he retires from his post as Headmaster of Highfield School.

Every now and then a 'real character' emerges within a community, enriching its life and moulding it together. Everyone who knows Bill Spencer will agree with me, he is a truly unique character; Highfield School in particular and St Matthew's Highfield in general will always be grateful to Bill. he has devoted himself to the children and staff of our school—there can not be a happier school in Christendom. Bill as a committed Christian, has shown children, teachers, and parents alike, what it means to live out a Christian life that attracts others to our Lord. His love of God, Church and his fellow beings is apparent in all he does, says and is; and what a sense of humour, he could leave most comedians trailing miles behind.

Only those closely connected with the School will know how much Bill Spencer has done, particularly in these last months of working on split sites, Ashton and Highfield. I'm positive that children who have been under his care during these last ten years will always have cause to thank him. On behalf of us all at Highfield and of course former clergy, thank you Bill. We wish you and Edna a long and happy retirement and we look forward to seeing you both many many times. So it isn't so much farewell, just thanks and God Bless from us all.

Your friend and Vicar, BILL HARRINGTON.

Mr E. G. Elliott lays the foundation stone of the new school,
watched by the Mayor and Mayoress and visiting clergy.

Mrs Eileen Gaskell was appointed by the School Governors to succeed Mr Spencer as Head Teacher. The announcement was made in the same Parish Magazine:

> As most people know, Mrs Eileen Gaskell, at this moment of writing—Deputy Head—will commence her duties as headteacher of Highfield C. E. School on May 1st. Her appointment has the unanimous approval of the School Governors and the full backing of the Education Authority.
>
> Mrs Gaskell is part and parcel of Highfield Parish, Church and School. She has served as a teacher and as Deputy Head for many years and has been an integral part of a successful team.
>
> Mrs Gaskell is a committed Christian and an able and dedicated teacher. She knows the school and the children from a-z and I'm sure that Highfield School will continue to prosper under her leadership.
>
> As she begins her duties we assure her and the school of our prayers and best wishes.
> BILL HARRINGTON.

Mr Graham Jarvis who had taught at Highfield from 1978 to 1981 was appointed Deputy Head in Mrs Gaskell's place.

The Baxter Bit in Winstanley, one of the pits visited by A. J. Munby in March 1865 had been closed for several years and the site and colliery tip had become derelict. The May 1983 Parish Magazine contained the following article by Mr A. Winstanley describing how the site had been transformed into a park for the area:

After a year of reclamation, an old derelict spoil tip has been transformed into a pleasant environment.

Situated in Winstanley and originally called 'Baxter Pit Tip', a successful Joint Reclamation Project, undertaken by Todds under the direction of the GMC, has successfully redeveloped the whole area. Headgear from the one hundred year old Baxter Pit has been demolished and the shaft capped, making the area safe. Pathways have been made and grass planted over a large area. The tip has been renamed 'Baxter Park'.

On clear days, Rivington, the Pennines and the large telescope at Jodrell Bank can be seen. This is one of the few large recreational area in the parish which is open all year with no admission charge. The nearest access points from the road are in Beech walk and Grindlow Walk, both in Winstanley.

Mrs Ethel Hall's retirement from the Brownies was announced in the July 1983 Parish Magazine:

> Mrs Hall is retiring from St Matthew's Brownies in June after 20 years devoted service. Although she is retiring as Brown Owl she is still carrying on as Registration Secretary to the Division, and hopefully will be coming to Brownies as unit helper when needed.
>
> We would like to say a big thank you from all Brownies past and present and hope she enjoys her semi-retirement.

The Annual Walking Day Procession had continued from the early days of the Church. It was often a new experience for a new Vicar who had come from outside the district and had never witnessed such an event before. The 1983 Walk was described in the July Parish Magazine:

> It was a glorious day when we set out on our 'Walk of Witness around the parish led by our new Vicar. The procession, banners flowing and bands playing, made its way down Billinge Road, along Tunstall Lane, up the hill of Ormskirk Road, down Enfield Street and back to the cricket field, where a short service of dedication took place.
>
> It was nice to see so many people, both young and old alike lining our route looking for friends and relatives amongst the procession. The cameras also had a busy day capturing moments to be remembered in years to come.
>
> On the cricket field our Vicar said he felt like a politician when climbing the rostrum, but he was reassured his seat was safe. The Vicar thanked the bands, banner carriers and all those who had taken part, and told everybody how much he had enjoyed his first 'Wigan Walk of Witness.'

Sadly some of the old, familiar houses and shops in the parish have been demolished to make way for modern buildings, sometimes for the better, sometimes for the worse. Such an occasion reminded Fred Foster about some of the old characters of Enfield Street in another of his articles:

The Barber's Shop

> Going along Enfield Street the other day, I noticed that some more of the houses had been demolished. The houses that adjoined Weley Street. In this row of houses used to be a veritable institution. George Tennant's barber shop. George died some time ago and

the shop has been closed for a number of years, but I remember it well. How many are there who remember going in for a trim?

When we were boys, we graduated upwards in stages. First of all, you stood on the chair, then as you grew up, you in turn knelt, stood behind, and finally sat upon it. This being the final accolade!

The shop itself was in the front parlour of the house. Sometimes, as you were sitting there, suitably draped in a print smock, a lady would appear at the door and call George through to the back for a cup of tea, leaving you surrounded by waiting men, and hair clippings all over the floor, to contemplate until his return.

The seating arrangements consisted of two long benches, padded with horse hair which pricked the back of your legs when wearing short pants. There were two chairs, and when busy, George would alternate between the two, sometimes haircutting in one, and shaving in the other. He had a fine selection of cut-throat razors which were arranged on his work-top, from which he hung two straps. It was fascinating to watch him sharpen the razors on these. he always kept two razors along with comb and scissors, in his overall pocket for immediate use. I often wondered who cut George's hair?

The usual style for us boys was straight up at the back and sides with the clippers and a straight fringe at the front. George would always put out his tongue when he straightened your fringe, and tell you to close your eyes while he blew the trimmings away. Then it was two blobs of cream from the dispenser on the mantle piece and you looked really smart.

He had two big mirrors in the shop, on opposing walls. As you looked into one of them you could see your reflection gradually disappearing into infinity. Jack Bilsborough used to be the lather boy for George on Saturday mornings, when most of the old men used to come for a shave. It was fascinating for us to watch George wielding the razor. He always held the tip of the nose as he shaved the upper lip, wiping the lather on pieces of newspaper cut for the purpose. As a child, I often wondered what George did with all the hair clippings that he swept up!!

Another wonder to us was the art of 'singeing'. This was supposed to stop you from feeling cold after a trim. George would light a taper from the gas geyser and fan it rapidly over the person's head, leaving a smell of burnt hair in the shop.

There was an old chair near the fireplace which was usually occupied by old Tommy Marsh, who would sit there, cap on and wearing his clogs. He was so thin that his legs appeared to be twined together when he crossed them, he never seemed to have his hair cut, just sat there chatting to all and sundry in a very broad 'Lommara Green' accent. The main topic in the shop was Rugby (Wigan of course) and other items of local gossip. They were happy times to look back on, and it's sad really to see memories of one's childhood being torn down, but that's progress, I suppose.

New School Handed Over

It was just over two years since dry rot had been discovered in the old school. Since the demolition of that school the Junior children had been 'bussed' daily to Ashton to the former Evans Primary School. Finally the day arrived for the new school to be handed over for use. The excitement was evident in the following article written by Mrs Gaskell, Headmistress, for the September 1983 Parish Magazine:

On August 22nd if all goes according to plan the New School should be handed over to the Parish. During that week the children will move back from Ashton so that by the end of the week our children will all be under one roof again. This is a day we have all been looking forward to for two years.

The school as you can see is a lovely building from the outside and I can assure you it is just as nice inside. We have over the past two years raised a great deal of money as a school and as a parish but we are still 'thousands' short, so the money raising must still go on. Any donation or effort will be most gratefully received. During the next few months I will arrange evenings when parents and parishioners will be able to come into school and look around and see the result of all our efforts.

E. M. GASKELL.

At a meeting of the PCC on 12 September 1983 Mr G. A. Cooke and Mr H. L. Stockley were elected to serve as Governors of the school. Mrs A. S. Gordon was later appointed a Parent-Governor.

Boys' Brigade Centenary

The Boys Brigade celebrated its Centenary in 1983 and the Vicar invited the parents, old boys and present members of the Brigade to attend a Centenary Service in Church.

The Boys Brigade was started in 1883 by William Alexander Smith, because he had great difficulty in controlling his Sunday School class at the Woodside Mission Hall in Glasgow, yet as an officer in the 1st Lanarkshire Rifles he could control 100 men with a few firm words of command.

A friend suggested that he use some of his volunteer methods in Sunday School and so the idea of the Boys' Brigade was born.

In celebration of the first ever parade of the BB, held on 4 October 1883, every member of the Brigade throughout the world stood on parade in uniform at 8 p.m. on 4 October 1983.

There was a special Centenary Service in Church, on 4 October, starting at 8 p.m. Following the service, at which a message from Her Majesty the Queen was read, a presentation of a Commemorative New Testament was provided for each boy by The Bible Society.

It was in June 1981 that Mrs Pat Gore and Mrs Audrey Moss were recommended for training as Readers. After completing their training successfully Pat and Audrey were admitted to the Office of Reader and Licensed at a service in Liverpool Cathedral on 24 March 1984. They were presented with their blue scarves by the PCC and 'read themselves in' on Sunday 25 March in Church. The Vicar, writing in the March Magazine said:

We look forward to their admission to the Office of Reader and assure them of our prayers and love, and we trust God will bless them in their calling to this important Ministry.

Opening of New School

The Official Opening of the New School was performed by the Bishop of Liverpool on Thursday 17 May 1984 at 2 p.m. Ron Hayhurst, the Editor, describes the event in the July Parish Magazine:

> It was our day, and according to Bishop David Sheppard, it was a GOOD DAY. The occasion was the official opening by the Bishop of Liverpool of our newly rebuilt Junior School. The children? Well, they made the day from start to finish. The event took place on May 17th commencing with a church service attended by the Mayor and Mayoress of Wigan, the Chairman of the Education Committee, representatives of the builders and architects with other distinguished guests. From our own 'Highfield family', we had the School Governors, teaching staff, Parochial Church Council, children, parents and parishioners. Together with our Vicar, we were pleased to see the Diocesan Director of Education, Canon O. Yandell, Canon W. H. Bullough, Revd W. Bynon, Revd G. Thomas, Revd Father Dumbill and the Revd J. Bingham, the last two being the local Roman Catholic Priest and the Methodist Minister.
>
> The proceedings began with a full Church lustily singing 'Stand up, Stand up for Jesus'. Following Prayers and a Reading, the children acted out the drama of dry rot being found during the summer of 1981 and the decision to demolish and rebuild. The action was conveyed to clergy and congregation in graphic detail, as were the various ways in which funds were being obtained, i.e. Smartie tubes of coins, jumble sales, discos etc. The Bishop then gave his address, but what could a Bishop say after that? The children had said it all! The final hymn, 'Lord, all the world belongs to you' was then sung and, following the blessing, the guests proceeded into the new school
>
> School Captain Johannah Whitter made a presentation to Bishop David after he had unveiled a commemorative Plaque, and Councillor J. Riley JP proposed a vote of thanks. You cannot keep children down for long, and here again they were hard at it, presenting excerpts from their recent well loved production of 'Oliver'. Once again, we were able to appreciate the Artful Dodger, Fagin, Oliver himself and others. How much our guests really appreciated their efforts was made plain by the outstanding applause. The school was then on view to the guests and finally refreshments were made available. Our distinguished visitors remarked that they had not previously witnessed such a child oriented opening! Why not? It is their school and by taking part they are unlikely ever to forget this wonderful day. That is how it should be. Yes, Bishop David—it was a GOOD DAY, and thank you for sharing it with us! EDITOR.

Curate Appointed

It was announced at the PCC meeting on 12 March 1984 that in September the parish should once again have a curate. A married 40-year-old ex-teacher had expressed interest. This would be his first curacy. The Vicar announced in the July Parish

Revd Graham Keegan, Curate, being welcomed by the Vicar in September 1984.

Magazine that Mr Graham Keegan was to be made Deacon at Liverpool Cathedral on Sunday 30 September and would become our new Curate. Mr Keegan (as he was then) wrote in the same magazine:

> It was one dark Saturday evening in Winter, when the name of St Matthew's Highfield first entered our lives. Now six months later, here we are looking forward greatly to our move to live and work amongst the people about whom we have heard so many nice and welcoming things.
>
> May I first of all introduce my family. My wife, Pam, is a teacher in Liverpool. At the present time she works in the morning at Knotty Ash Primary School. Our son Mark is 13 and in the second year at St Margaret's High School and Lindsey, our daughter is 10 and is at our local Primary School. Mark likes playing the drums in—dare I say it—our Scout Band and Lindsey enjoys camping with the Guides.
>
> I left school at 16 and followed the family tradition in the Post Office but at 25 I trained as a teacher and that is where I have spent most of my working life. At the moment I teach at Childwall Primary School. About four years ago, just after a very

The party of parishioners who went to Liverpool Cathedral for the ordination of Revd Keegan.

significant birthday, I was recommended for training for the Ministry and I enrolled on the Northern Ordination Course. This course is designed for men and women who because of family commitments would be unable to undertake residential training. The course lasted for three years and after one or two 'hairy' moments on the way, I am now expecting to be ordained Deacon in the Cathedral on September 30th. And so to that telephone call on a Winter's Saturday night. . .

Many people have been kind to me during the pressures of the last three years but it's Pam, Mark and Lindsey who have given me the most encouragement and support and have shared the tensions and the pleasures of training.

We have recently driven out to Highfield on several occasions and have looked at the lovely sandstone church of St Matthew's and the beautiful new school and the Church Hall and cricket field and we have been thrilled with what we have seen and now we are preparing for our move to the Wigan Deanery. We have one or two domestic details to finalise—selling our house, organising schools for Mark and Lindsey and leaving St James, West Derby where we have all worshipped for many years.

We consider ourselves fortunate to have the opportunity of this new phase in our lives and we are looking forward with growing excitement (and a little apprehension) to our move in August. In the meantime, we would value your thoughts and prayers and we can assure you that St Matthew's Highfield and its people will never be far from our thoughts and always in our prayers.

With love, Pam, Graham, Mark and Lindsey.

Graham Keegan was made Deacon at Liverpool Cathedral on Sunday 30 September 1984 at 10.30 a.m. A party from Highfield went to the Cathedral to take part in the service. Afterwards everyone returned to Highfield where a welcoming lunch was held in the Parish Hall. The Revd Graham Keegan's first service at Highfield was Evensong on that day. In his letter in the October Parish Magazine the Vicar said:

> We welcome Graham and his family into our midst and assure them of our prayers. We feel certain they will be happy here. We trust God will bless Graham's ministry at St Matthew's, and pray that this part of God's Kingdom will provide a sound base for a long happy and fruitful ministry in Christ's Holy, Catholic and Apostolic Church.

Fellowship Lounge Opened

Since the formation of St Matthew's Church Fellowship in 1982 the committee had been considering ways of improving the facilities available to members. At the Annual General Meeting of the Fellowship in 1983 the Vicar took over as President. Over the first year of the Fellowship a good profit had been made. Visits were made to St Wilfred's Standish to see how it might be possible to improve our own premises. Plans were drawn up to extend the annexe to the Parish Hall to provide a Member's Lounge for the fellowship and new toilet accommodation. At a meeting of the PCC on 12 September 1983 approval was given for the committee to go ahead with their plans. Building commenced early in 1984 and was opened for use by the members in October 1984.

The Lounge was designed to accommodate up to 100 people in pleasant surroundings. Through the kind generosity of Mr and Mrs Tom Butler of Butler's Catering, the committee were able to purchase about seven thousand pounds worth of carpeting, chairs and tables for just £100. To mark this kindness the committee decided to call the extension The Butler Lounge and a brass plaque recording this was unveiled in the Lounge at the Patronal Dance on 21 September 1985. Sadly Mr and Mrs Butler both passed away at the end of November 1984 before they could see their gifts in situation.

The Vicar's letter in the November 1984 Parish Magazine recorded the retirement of Mr Cyril Bell:

> Mr Cyril Bell, who has been our organist and choirmaster for the past six years retired on Sunday, October 28th. He has completed 62 years as a church organist, serving in various churches of the Liverpool Diocese. His has been a long and distinguished career. His love of Church music has meant more to him than anything else. I'm sure that I speak on behalf of everyone at St Matthew's, as I record our warmest thanks and appreciation for his devoted work as organist in this parish. Vicar.

Mrs A. S. Gordon who had been Deputy Organist with Mr Cooke and Mr Bell took over as organist and choirmistress.

At the meeting of the PCC on 6 November 1984 it was announced that Canon W. H. Bullough had completed 25 years as Rector of Halsall. A letter of congratulations was sent from the PCC.

At the end of April 1985 work began on the open-cast mining of the old Colliery site between Foundry Lane and Little Lane. The work took two years to complete and then the land was reclaimed and landscaped so removing for ever many of the reminders of Blundell's Pemberton Collieries.

The Revd Graham Keegan had served as Curate for a year being busily involved in all the activities of the parish, particularly in the area of work with young people, preaching, teaching, and visiting the old and the sick. On St Michael's Day, September 29th 1985 Graham was ordained Priest in Liverpool Cathedral. The preacher was Bishop Trevor Huddlestone. Again a party from Highfield went to Liverpool to take part in the service, and afterwards returned to the Parish Hall for a celebration lunch. In the evening at 6.30 p.m. there was a Holy Communion Service at which the officiating priest was the Revd Graham Keegan.

The Vicar congratulated Graham on his ordination in the October 1985 Parish Magazine:

> During these last twelve months Graham has become an integral part of St Matthew's and its ministry. Graham has proved himself a devoted, sympathetic, loving and able Curate. As his Vicar I know he is a man of considerable ability with many God given gifts. Along with you all I wish him well for his future ministry here and subsequently in other pastures. Our best wishes also go to Pam, Mark and Lindsey. They have adapted remarkably well to their new lifestyle and are very much a part of our parish family.

In the same (October 1985) Parish Magazine Mrs Gaskell recorded Mr E. G. Elliott's resignation as a governor of Highfield school:

> Mr Elliott resigned as a foundation governor of our school at the end of the summer term. The governors presented him with a golf club at a short ceremony after our last meeting, thus making sure that he will always remember us when he plays his weekly game of golf. Mr Elliott's connection with Highfield spans 37 years; from his appointment as Headmaster in 1948 to his resignation from the governing body this summer. George has served Highfield well and in turn we wish him well for the future. Thank you George for all your care and support during the years. EILEEN M. GASKELL.'

On Sunday 15 December at 6.30 p.m. we celebrated our first Christingle Service in aid of the Church of England Children's Society. A packed Church raised the total of £196.31.

Activities in the Parish Hall

The January 1986 Parish Magazine listed all the weekly events held in the Parish Hall as follows:

Sunday	12 p.m.	Sunday School
	8 p.m.	Modern Sequence Dancing
Monday	2 p.m.	Baby Clinic
	6 p.m.	Tap and Ballet Classes
	7 p.m.	Weightwatchers (Lounge)
Tuesday	2.15 p.m.	Over Sixties
	7 p.m.	Indoor Bowls
Wednesday	1.15 p.m.	Pram Club

	4.30 p.m.	Tap and Ballet Classes
	8 p.m.	Modern Sequence Dancing
Thursday	9.45 a.m.	Morning Coffee (Lounge)
	1.30 p.m.	Ladies' Keep Fit
	8 p.m.	Women's Fellowship
Friday	1 p.m.	Indoor Bowls

On Friday and Saturday evenings the Hall is usually in use for a parish social occasion or let for wedding, birthday and anniversary celebrations.

The April 1986 Parish Magazine announced details of the Parish Weekend to be held later in the year:

THORNLEIGH, Grange over Sands. 31.10.1986—2.11.1986

The Parish weekend at Thornleigh has now been booked and we are looking forward to another occasion when we can spend a few days away together. If the weekend proves as popular as was the last occasion when we went to Thornleigh, then place will be in great demand. So get your booking form from the clergy and reserve your place now. The weekend is intended for all members of the family and there will be opportunities for discussion as well as leisure and of course worship.

The price will be around the £27 mark for adults and proportionately less for children—details are on the booking form. Book now!

In her report to the 1986 Annual General Meeting Mrs S. L. Highton, Secretary reported the following appointments made by the PCC during the year:

Three new patrons have been appointed. The Vicar, Revd W. H. Harrington, Mr G. A. Cooke and Mr H. L. Stockley join Canon W. H. Bullough and Mr Martin Hedley of the Blundell family as patrons of our church. They have together the responsibility of appointing the incumbent. The appointments were made on the recommendations of the PCC.

Following the resignation of Mr E. G. Elliott as a school governor, Mr R. Thomas was elected by the PCC to take his place.

A Charity sub-committe had been formed, headed by Mr Gordon Bennett to organise events for raising money specifically for charity. Such varied events as the V. J. Celebration night, Fancy Dress dance, Bonfire and Carols, and the welcome return visit by the Haydock Male Voice Choir, have been much enjoyed; enabling the PCC to help those less fortunate than ourselves.

A Parish Visitation

The Archdeacon of Warrington made an Official Visit to the Parish in November 1986. The Vicar outlined the programme for the visit in the November Parish Magazine:

The Archdeacon's Visit begins with a service of Holy Communion at 6. 30pm on Sunday, November 16th, followed by a question and answer session with the Archdeacon in the School Hall. This is an open-to-all meeting and offers a rare opportunity to ask questions (and put points of view) to one of the Diocesan hierarchy.

The Archdeacon will spend Monday in the parish with the clergy and will visit our school and a few people at random. In the evening he will dine at a home in the parish. Then at 8 p.m. there will be an extended PCC Meeting in our School Hall. As well as elected members attending we hope that Leaders of organisations will also come along.

The Archdeacon's visit will be designed to help us to 'take stock' of our beloved St Matthew's. To make his visit a success depends upon the co-operation of as many people as possible.

In the same magazine congratulations were offered to Mr Roland Butts who celebrated 65 years as a chorister:

It was in the Autumn of 1921 that young Roland joined the choir of St Matthew, Highfield. The Church choir soon became part and parcel of his life. When he left Highfield for Up Holland, Roland joined the Church choir there. However, the pull of Highfield Church proved very strong and Roland eventually came back to St Matthew's.

It doesn't take a mathematician to realise that Roland has completed 65 years as a Church Chorister. His achievement is all the more remarkable in that he seldom misses choir practice and is usually in the choir stalls twice every Sunday.

At evensong on October 12th Roland (on behalf of all at St Matthew's) was presented with a Royal School of Church Music tie, an RSCM Certificate and a kiss from our Organist and Choirmistress, Mrs Sue Gordon.

Well done Roland, may you and your voice keep going for many many more services.'

Another stalwart, Miss Sally Gaskell, was offered the congratulations of the parish after 48 years as a Sunday School teacher:

Sunday School teaching for 48 years is no mean achievement. Miss Sally Gaskell has decided to retire. We had hoped that she would have made it 50 years, but it is not to be. The parish owes Sally a debt of gratitude and hopefully a presentation will be made on November 16th at 6.30 p.m. Meanwhile, from all of us; thanks Sally for all your love and dedication. Enjoy your well earned rest!

The Ramblers held their first walk in August 1986. Their reports have become a feature of the Parish Magazine since that date. The December issue carried the following report:

A new Venture has been organised going under the name St Matthew's, Highfield, Ramblers. Our first walk was held on the 31st August when we went by coach to Ambleside, had lunch there, then set of on our walks. One to Wansfell (6½ miles) and the other to Lily Tarn (3½ miles). The companionship, laughter and friendship on our first walk was thoroughly enjoyed by everyone with a firm view to repeat it often.

The week of prayer for Christian Unity commenced on Sunday 18 January 1987. There was a united service at St Matthew's on Thursday, 2 January at 8 p.m. The preacher was Father Peter Wilkinson from Up Holland Northern Institute. Despite adverse weather conditions there was a very full attendance at an inspiring service with Christians from different denominations.

At the meeting of the Fellowship Committee on 21 April 1987, Fred Holcroft resigned from the position of Secretary. David Whitter took over as Secretary.

In June 1987 it was announced that Pat Gore and her family were moving to Chorley. The following tribute was paid to Pat in the Parish Magazine:

Pat has made a lasting contribution to St Matthew's. As well as being a Reader, she has written the children's page in the magazine, organised the visiting rota, been a Youth Club leader, brought faithful ministry to the Women's Fellowship and to the Wednesday Study group. She has served on the PCC, the Deanery Synod and latterly on the Diocesan Synod. As well as her official duties she has always been willing to help where needed. Her contribution to this parish has been considerable and we thank her for all that she has done.

G. Keegan.

Mrs Joan Rimmer retired from the school on 31 August 1987. Joan had taught at Highfield for twenty years. Mrs Gaskell paid the following tribute to her in the November 1987 Parish Magazine:

> Mrs Joan Rimmer retired from school on 31st August after 20 years teaching at Highfield. She has always been a most loyal member of staff and has worked hard for the PTA. Joan has trained the children for the Rose Queen since 1969 and always maintained the same high standards in her school and social work for this school. At the end of the Summer Term the children presented Joan with a beautiful dress ring and the staff and the PTA made presentations when she retired. We wish Joan and Derek and long, healthy and happy retirement.

In 1987 proposals were put forward to the Diocese for the reorganisation of the Deaneries. It was proposed that the existing Wigan Deanery should be divided into two new Deaneries, Wigan East and Wigan West. The PCC at a meeting on June 9th expressed the wish to preserve the status quo but were prepared to accept the proposals.

The August 1987 Parish Magazine records the retirement of Mrs Kathy Gregory from school:

> Mrs Gregory who has worked on school meals at Highfield for over 20 years retired on Friday, July 3rd. Mrs Gregory joined our P. T. A. at its very first meeting and she has supported our school most loyally ever since. With Mrs Downham she has been responsible for the refreshments at the Garden Fete since 1969. We are truly grateful for what she has done and wish her a long, healthy and happy retirement. E. M. Gaskell.

Revd G. Keegan Moves to Ince

At a meeting of the PCC on 5 October 1987 it was announced that Revd G. Keegan, Curate, had been offered the living of St Mary's, Ince, and would be leaving Highfield in the near future. The PCC congratulated Graham on his appointment and wished him well.

Graham wrote of his move in the November Parish Magazine:

> I am sure that you will have heard the news that we are soon to be moving to the parish of St Mary's, Ince, where I am to be the new Vicar. At the present time we don't know the exact date for the move but we think it will be late November or early December.

Since the news was announced I have spoken to so many people who have connections with St Mary's.

(Graham goes on to give details of his new parish and ends:)

Since coming to the Wigan area three years ago, we have been very happy living here. Our move to Ince will mean that we are not moving too far and we still hope to keep our contacts with our many friends at St Matthew's.

With all my best wishes, GRAHAM.

The Revd Graham Keegan was inducted as Vicar of St Mary's, Ince, on Friday 11 December 1987 at 8 p.m. His last Sunday at Highfield was November 29th. After evensong on that day a farewell was held in the Parish Lounge. Graham was presented with a cheque and Pam with a Silver bracelet as a farewell gift and reminder of their time at Highfield.

Graham wrote in the December Parish Magazine:

I have no hesitation in saying that these have been the most exciting years of my life. There are many reasons why I say this. I will always treasure my memories of ordination services in the Cathedral and the many and important occasions that have taken place in the parish. But chiefly I will treasure the many opportunities which have come my way of being close to people in the crises of life. In theory, I have been there to help and support, but in fact I have been privileged to share and learn from their experience and their faith.

I have many thank you's to say. First of all to my Vicar. The relationship between a Vicar and his curate has often had problems. But not in this case. I will always be grateful to Bill for allowing me the space to develop my own ministry without feeling under pressure. He has been sensitive to my strengths and my weaknesses, and I am grateful to him, and to Ann for their kindness to me and to my family. I trust that the parish as a whole will accept our sincere thanks for the many happy memories which we all take with us. Wih love from GRAHAM, PAM, MARK and LINDSEY.

In an appreciation of Graham's work in the parish the Vicar wrote in the same Magazine:

It hardly seems three years and two months since Graham and his family came to live amongst us. Since September 1984, Graham, Pam, Mark and Lindsey have become part and parcel of St Matthew's Parish. We thank them all for living amongst us and contributing so much to the life of our church and community.

As Vicar of this parish I am probably in the best position to say how much hard, dedicated and loving work Graham has done. God has undoubtedly used him well and St Matthew's has been enriched by his ministry.

I trust that the experience of his ministry here will stand Graham in good stead as he begins his work at St Mary's.

On behalf of all at St Matthew's, I say thank you to Graham, Pam, Mark and Lindsey. You all have our prayers and best wishes.

BILL HARRINGTON

Mrs Dorothy Downham retired from school at the end of December 1987. Mrs Gaskell writing in the December Magazine said:

This month we shall be saying goodbye to Mrs Dorothy Downham, a long serving dinner lady and a member of our PTA since its beginnings in 1969. Dorothy is usually found in the kitchen at most parish and school events and we are most grateful for all she has done for us. We all wish her a long, healthy and happy retirement. E. M. Gaskell.

Paul Wright to train for Ministry

Writing in the January 1988 Parish Magazine the Vicar announced Paul Wright's acceptance for training for the ordained ministry:

> May I on behalf of everyone at St Matthew's offer the heartiest congratulations to one of the younger members of our Church family. Twenty one year old Mr Paul Wright recently attended a Church Selection Conference for those interested in offering themselves for the ordained ministry.
>
> As a result of the Conference the Advisory Council for the Church's Ministry has recommended Paul for training for the Stipendiary ministry. We are delighted for him and his parents, Bill and Dorothy.
>
> At present Paul is reading History at Preston Polytechnic. When he leaves Preston he will do a two year foundation course at Aston (plus voluntary work) then a three year Theological College Course.
>
> Well done Paul. VICAR.

The Vicar had read the Bishop's letter to launch the Church Urban Fund at the services on Sunday 24 April 1988. The Liverpool Diocese was asked to raise £500,000, but would receive much more back in the years ahead. The Bishop of Liverpool was to attend a gift day at Wigan Parish Church on Tuesday, 14 June to receive money raised to that date. Over the next two years a total of £3,154.93 was raised by the parish for the fund.

At a meeting of the PCC on 7 June the Vicar gave a very sincere thank-you to all those who had made the celebration evening in honour of his 30 years in the ministry so special. Special thanks were given to Bert and Barbara Stockley for all their hard work on 'This is your life.' The evening was something which the Vicar would remember for the rest of his life.

In the August 1988 Parish Magazine it was announced that Mrs Audrey Moss, one of our Readers had been elected to the General Synod of the Church of England. The Vicar wrote:

> I'm sure you will join me in offering our warmest congratulations to Mrs Audrey Moss on her recent election to the General Synod, (the Church of England's Governing body). No sooner had Audrey been elected than she was off to London for the July meeting of General Synod. We are very fortunate to have first hand reports of the work of Synod from time to time in our parish magazine.

Change of Headteachers

Mrs Eileen Gaskell retired from the Headship of Highfield School at the end of 1988. The Vicar wrote the following tribute in the December 1988 Parish Magazine:

Another chapter in the story of St Matthew's Highfield is fast drawing to a close. On December 20th Mrs Eileen Gaskell will retire from her post as Headteacher of Highfield C of E Primary School. She commenced her duties as Head on May 1st 1983. Now five and a half years later comes this opportunity to say a sincere and heartfelt thankyou to Eileen as her retirement draws near.

Eileen started her role as Headteacher under the most daunting and difficult circumstances. Due to the building of the new Junior Department, half of the school was housed at Ashton. Having to lead a Split School was certainly not an ideal start. In spite of the obvious problems the life of our school flourished and no child suffered. In August 1983 the new building was ready and all our teachers and children were back on one site.

The successful negotiating of this transitional period in our school history was very much due to a magnificent team effort by parents, teachers and children. However, it must be said, without the right person at the helm, it could have been a different story.

Eileen has proved to be an exemplary Headteacher. She has led from the front and given unstinting, selfless devotion and service to teachers, children and parents alike. She has helped to mould the school, church and community in general into the one family we proudly call 'Highfield'.

There can be no Headteacher anywhere who has worked harder than Eileen. Visitors to her room would look in amazement at her teaching timetable.

As a teacher, Deputy Head and Head, Eileen has served twenty years in our school No doubt there are many hundreds of children and parents who will always have cause to thank her.

On behalf of everyone at Highfield past and present (including former children, teachers and clergy), thank you Eileen.

We wish you and Harold a long and happy retirement—knowing you both as we do we feel sure it will be an active one as you continue to serve our Church and Parish. As you will be continuing to live amongst us it isn't farewell, just thanks and God Bless from us all.

Your friend and Vicar. BILL HARRINGTON.

In the same magazine the appointment of Mr Graham Jarvis as Headteacher was announced:

The School Governors recently appointed Mr Graham Jarvis, Deputy Headteacher, to the Headship of Highfield C E Primary School. We congratulate Mr Jarvis on his appointment and wish him well for the future. Mr Jarvis began his teaching career as an assistant teacher at Highfield in 1978. In 1981 he moved to St Paul's C E Primary School to a promoted post. In 1983 he returned to Highfield as Deputy Head and in January takes up the position of Headteacher.

St Matthew's Choir, Walking Day, 1989, with Mrs A. S. Gordon, Organist and Choirmistress.

At a meeting of the PCC on 7 August 1989 a decision was made to reclaim the overgrown land round the graveyard. The Liverpool Diocesan Care and Repair Committee were given the contract and work was expected to commence at the end of Summer.

At the same meeting members learned of the proposed new link road from the M57 to the M61. Fears were expressed that this new road which passed over the railway at Pemberton station, very close to Highfield Church and School would cut the parish in two, and the PCC agreed to make an official objection and to ask the Diocese to support our case.

Mr Paul Wright who was training for the ministry preached his first sermon at Highfield Church. The occasion was recorded in the October 1989 Parish Magazine:

> Special, rare or unusual occasions, always remain in the memory of those who have experienced them. They should certainly be recorded for the benefit of those who were absent.
>
> Such an occasion was our Evensong Service on Sunday September 10th. During that service the sermon was preached by our own Paul Wright.
>
> Paul (as many of you know) is training for the sacred ministry of the Church of England. He obtained his degree over a year ago. As part of his training for Holy Orders he has spent the last year working as an assistant chaplain for the world-wide mission to seamen.
>
> In his sermon Paul gave us a history of the mission and an interesting and sometimes moving description of his work amongst seamen. Considering it was Paul's first sermon

at St Matthew's (hence the special occasion) he did extremely well. A first sermon is always a nerve-jangling and demanding effort, especially in front of ones own people.

Didn't he do well! Oh, I did enjoy that! Bill and Dorothy (his proud parents) must be chuffed! These were just three of the comments I heard after the service. Well done Paul and thank you from all in church that memorable evening.

Paul has still a long way to go before ordination so I ask you all to remember him in your prayers.

Your friend and Vicar BILL HARRINGTON.

Mrs Ethel Hall's retirement from the Guides was recorded in the same magazine:

Ethel Hall—a familiar face associated with the Guides, Brownies and Rangers at St Matthew's—retired from services in July this year not by choice, but in the Girl Guide Movement when one 'reaches a certain age' you must come out of uniform. It does not mean that Ethel has finished with Guiding, far from that, last week for instance she was at Brownies testing four young girls for their Cook's badge. However in July the District Guiders held a Surprise Barbecue for Ethel when she was presented with a silver owl to add to her collection of owls and from the Guiders at St Matthew's and from the Ranger Guides she received a basket of dried flowers.

Mrs Hall was also presented with a gift from the PCC at the December Parade Service.

On 25 July 1989 it was announced that the the the Rt. Revd George Carey was to be the new Archbishop of Canterbury. The Vicar welcomed the appointment in the September Magazine and said:

I personally thank God that George Carey heard the call 'Follow me. He seems to be a breath of fresh air. A man who knows what it is like to live with ordinary people—apart from his background he has also been vicar of a parish. He is also a scholar, a true leader, a man who upholds and teaches the traditional apostolic faith.

The Bishop of Liverpool wrote a Pastoral Letter about the Decade of Evangelism which was printed in full in the October Parish Magazine. In it the Bishop asked each parish to do three things:

1. Work out an imaginative programme of sustained prayer.
2. Conduct a Mission assessment programme in your neighbourhood.
3. Let him have, by September 1992 a carefully written statement of our particular plans for the Decade.

The PCC at its meeting on 8 September 1992 detailed these plans as follows:

1. Building a new cricket pavilion and lounge.
2. Replacement of the old Infant School building.
3. To maintain the Community Life of the Parish.
4. To maintain full Church services with music.
5. To continue to support Evangelism prayerfully.

These plans were presented on behalf of the parish by Mr Colin Whittick at a special service at Liverpool Cathedral on 16 September 1992.

At a PCC meeting on 20 February 1989, the question of overhauling the Church organ which was now 30 years old was first discussed. Over the following two years details had been discussed and the contract was finally awarded to David Wells of Liverpool at a cost of £9,300 plus VAT. The organ was completely overhauled and cleaned and a new computerised capture action was added. The work was finally completed at the end of 1990 in time for the Carol service on 23 December 1990.

The Vicar was pleased to write in the January 1991 Parish Magazine of the appointment of an Honorary Curate for the parish. He wrote:

> I am now in the happy position to be able to announce that as from January 1991, the Revd Ernest Traverse will be Honorary Curate at St Matthew's. Ernie is a retired Priest and will continue to live with his wife, Nora, in Billinge. many of you have already met Ernie and Nora—many more, I trust will meet them soon. On behalf of all at St Matthew's we give a very warm welcome to Ernie and to Nora.

Death of Mr E. G. Elliott

Mr E. G. Elliott, former Headmaster of Highfield C. E. Primary School died on 31 January 1991, aged 79 years. Mrs Gaskell wrote the following appreciation in the March 1991 Parish Magazine:

> Mr Elliott arrived in Highfield on September 1st 1948. He had spent the war years as an instructor in the Tank Regiment. My first memories of him were as a good steady batsman in the Highfield 1st XI. George kept up his interest in the club long after his playing days were over. Later as a parent, when Cameron and Jane attended Highfield School, I could appreciate the happy fulfilling atmosphere he created there.
>
> In January 1969 I became his deputy and the friendship we already had was strengthened. The year 1969 saw the birth of our PTA, the Rose Queen and garden fete and the joining of the Infant and Junior Schools under his headship. Harold and I knew George as a friend from 1948. His daughter Ruth joined us in the dramatic society and David was a member of the Cricket Club. Mrs Elliott was secretary to the Women's Fellowship and to the Ladies section of the PTA. George was a member of the PCC and a sidesman.
>
> After his retirement George became a governor of the school and during the interregnum he steered the governors through the planning and building of our new school. The laying of the Foundation Stone is a day I will long remember and I know that George was a delighted guest of honour. It was an honour well deserved.
>
> When I became Head I was pleased to still have George as a governor. he always attended meetings, travelling back from Cheshire to his beloved Highfield in all kinds of weather.
>
> A few years ago Harold and I were privileged to join Mr and Mrs Elliott, their family and friends on the occasion of their Golden Wedding.
>
> I know many people in Highfield will remember George with great affection. He was a gentleman.

At a meeting of the PCC in May 1989 it was reported that there was continuing trouble from young people using the Church Porch as a meeting place. It was felt that the time had come to consider fitting gates to the porch and enquiries were made from local builders. As a result of these enquiries two offers were received and gratefully accepted by the PCC:

The first offer was from the family of the late Mr Paul Gaskell, for many years Treasurer of the Church and member of the PCC, who wished to donate the Church Doors in his memory. The doors are made in oak to match the existing woodwork of the Church. They were dedicated on Sunday 17 March 1991 at the Morning Service during which the Wardens led the Vicar and the family to the main doors of the Church where a short service of dedication took place.

The second offer was from the Birchall family who wished to give the doors in memory of the late Mr John Birchall. Happily the Birchall family agreed to give the new doors for the Parish Hall Lounge.

The April 1991 Parish Magazine records the retirement of Mr Ronnie Green:

> It is with mixed feelings that I write informing you that Mr Ronnie Green retires as School caretaker on Friday 19th April. In all my 33 years association with Church Schools I've never met anyone to equal Ronnie Green. Caretaker is such an apt name for Ronnie. He started his duties in 1976 and has given our school fifteen years dedicated and loyal service. Nothing has been too much trouble for Ronnie. When there have been break-ins, damage caused by vandals, other problems, he has responded immediately, no matter the time of day or night. He has done endless repair jobs far above the call of duty, thereby enabling the smooth running of our school and saving the governors considerable amounts of money. I know I speak for the Staff, the Governors, the PCC and the whole community in thanking Ronnie for his devotion to duty and his loving caretaking at our school. Ronnie will be missed by all. Happily though, I'm sure we will still see him and his wife Margaret at our Church. Margaret retires one week after Ronnie (so he's only got 7 days to get those household chores done.)
>
> We wish them both a long, happy and healthy retirement.

The condition of the Church carpet had been causing concern for some time and at a meeting of the PCC on 20 February 1989 the Women's Fellowship offered to start a Carpet Fund with their annual donation to the Church. An appeal was launched and over the following fifteen months over £7,000 was raised. The carpet was laid in May 1991.

In 1991 Mr G. A. Cooke and Mrs J. Wainwright retired as school governors. Mrs Wainwright had been Treasurer of the Governors for many years. At the October meeting of the PCC Mrs Janice Holding and Mrs Sue Gordon were appointed Foundation Governors and Mrs Jennifer Halliwell as Parent Governor.

At the AGM held on 14 April 1991 Miss M. Moore asked if anything could be done to improve the condition of the Canteen building used by the Youth Organisations of the parish. At a meeting of the PCC on 29 April Mr Gordon Bennett offered to oversee the repairs. A Committee was formed from organisations using the canteen to discuss what needed to be done. The PCC and the Fellowship agreed to fund repairs up to £2,000 initially. The repairs were done during the school summer holidays.

In the October 1991 Parish Magazine the following letter of thanks appeared from the Youth Organisations:

> On behalf of the youth organisations of the parish, we would like to thank the PCC and the Fellowship Committee for their great generosity in paying for the alterations to the Youth Centre (the old school canteen). Over the Summer break, under the watchful eye of Mr Gordon Bennett, the window frames (such as they were) have been removed and bricked up. Also, a new wooden floor has been laid to replace the original that has

suffered from 'sulphate attack' to the sub-floor concrete. The gift from both the PCC and the Fellowship Committee indicates a lot of care for future parishioners' welfare by these improvements. There is still more work required to finish the job and we are sure that our parishioners will give their support to future fund raising efforts by the organisations in order to finish the work.'

Another gift to add to the beauty and interest of the Church was the offer by Miss Margaret Atherton of a Vicar's Board in memory of her mother. This was accepted by the PCC with grateful thanks at a meeting on 8 April 1992. The Vicar's Board is to be dedicated at a service on Sunday 27 June 1993 by Revd Canon W. H. Bullough.

Centenary of Foundation Stone

Ron Hayhurst, the Editor, recorded the celebration of the 100th Anniversary of the laying of the Foundation Stone of the Church, in the June 1992 Parish Magazine:

> On Sunday April 26th 1992 at 10.30 a.m. St Matthew's Church celebrated the 100th anniversary of the laying of the Foundation Stone; and what a celebration it was!
>
> As might be expected, a very large number of parishioners attended this memorable service. The preacher and celebrant was Revd Canon W. H. Bullough AKC who had been the Vicar of the parish from 1944 to 1959 and had therefore, been present at the 50th anniversary of the dedication.
>
> The service began with the processional hymn 'Thy hand O God has guided Thy flock from age to age' and continued with the Holy Communion Service up to and including the Creed. Preceded by the cross and choir, the congregation singing 'Blessed City. Heavenly Salem', they were led out of church to the foundation stone which is situated at the east end of the building. At the site the Vicar said a prayer of thanksgiving for all who had worked and worshipped in the old Iron Church, and especial thanks were given for Colonel Henry Blundell who built this lovely church as a memorial to his wife. The congregation responded with the reciting of the general thanksgiving before returning back into the church where the Holy Communion service continued.
>
> In his address, Canon Bullough gave three key words to mark the occasion: Rejoice, Resolve and Remembrance. There was much to be thankful for in the gift of the church, and the resolve of many who had well maintained the buildings, and especially the remembrance of the greatest gift of all, the Son of God, who gave His life for us.
>
> At the conclusion of the service, the recessional hymn 'The Church's one Foundation' was lustily sung to close a rearkable service. Finally the congregation were invited into the Parish Hall where an assortment of refreshments were provided; and so, on to the next hundred years!

In 1988 the PCC had met with the Archdeacon of Liverpool to discuss the possibility of a new Vicarage. The existing Vicarage needed extensive repairs and was expensive to heat and the PCC had decided to make enquiries about possible schemes of improvement or replacement. Discussions went on over the next three years without any decisions being made. In 1991 the new Diocesan Surveyor came to inspect the building and estimated that repairs would cost £25,000. After discussions with the Parsonages Committee it was decided to put the repairs in hand and in 1992 the improvements involving double glazing, a new damp course, a new roof, new doors at the rear and repairs to the wall between the vicarage and the graveyard were carried out at a cost of £30,000, the PCC agreeing to contribute £2,000 towards the cost.

Extension to Parish Lounge

Due to storm damage to the old pavilion the Cricket club expressed a wish to replace their old building with an extension to the Parish Lounge to provide changing rooms and a lounge/meeting room. This proposal was brought to the PCC in May 1990.

The proposed extension, costing between £20,000 and £30,000 was to be funded by the Cricket Club and the Hall Fellowship. The proposition was carried unanimously by the June 1990 PCC meeting. The extension would be owned by the Parish and the Cricket Club would contribute one third of the cost.

Writing in the April 1991 Parish Magazine, Dave Whitter, Secretary of the Hall Fellowship says:

> For as long as most of us can remember, Cricket has been an integral part of Parish life in Highfield. To a considerable number of people, both men and women, Saturday afternoons in the summer would not be the same without a few lazy hours, basking in the sunshine (hopefully), quaffing a little light refreshment, (solely to keep the dust down, of course), and watching 22 idiots chasing after a little red ball waving a lump of wood! Many of our older male readers have achieved their finest hour dressed in the white flannels of Highfield Cricket Club.
>
> Our playing area is second to none in the area, and the Lounge Bar provides wonderful facilities for after the match social activities. However the club is sadly lacking in one aspect, and that is in the changing facilities. You will know the existing Cricket Pavilion as the rather derelict looking building at the side of the graveyard. Unfortunately this building was rather badly damaged in the storms last year and would cost an inordinate amount to repair. It had proved impossible to obtain insurance cover on the building, so all the costs involved had to be paid by the Cricket Club. Quite frankly the state of the building is such that it is not worth repairing, and so we have decided, with PCC permission to build a new pavilion as an extension to the Parish Hall.

A good deal of voluntary work was put in on the extension during the summer of 1991 and in the August 1991 Parish Magazine, Dave Whitter writes again:

> In the very near future we will all be able to benefit from the facilities offered by the extension to the Lounge at the Parish Hall.
>
> The extension, built primarily as a cricket pavilion, incorporates a lounge, kitchen, 2 changing rooms, showers and toilets. Access will be gained from the existing lounge.
>
> The building has been erected using voluntary labour wherever possible, and a considerable debt of gratitude is owed to the men (and boys), predominantly from the Cricket Club, who have not only contributed considerably in a financial sense, but have given generously of their time and expertise over the past few months. It is hardly fair to single out individuals, but without the assistance of such as Martin, Cameron, Lee, Brian, Ronnie, Tony, Ken, et al. Under the expert guidance of Frank Dodd, and the unflagging enthusiasm of Harold Gaskell, (does that man never stop?); the building

Mr Brian Statham of Lancashire and England opens the Cricket Pavilion in August 1992, with the Vicar and Mr Harold Gaskell.

would have cost us twice as much. Numerous others have also shovelled, carried, mixed, shifted, set up, knocked down and made the occasional 'pigs ear'.

In fact, if you add the bar demolition team of Colin, Bob, Jeff, Roy and the two Johns to the list of unhired labourers, you will get some idea of the commitment involved.

The amount of work involved has been considerable and makes one doubly appreciative of the efforts put in by volunteers when the original Parish hall was built. What a job that must have been!

The 1992 Annual General Meeting of the Parish was held in the H. F. Gaskell Lounge for the first time. The room had been named 'The H. F. Gaskell Lounge' in honour of one who has been described as the Mr Cricket of Highfield, who has done so much for cricket at Highfield over a lifetime. Harold has given so much service to the Club and to the Parish as sidesman, member of the PCC and for many years as Churchwarden. The honour was indeed well deserved.

At the AGM the Vicar said that the new extension was proof of what can be done by a parish which sets its mind to improving facilities.

The new Cricket Pavilion and Lounge was officially opened on Sunday August 30th 1992 by Mr Brian Statham of Lancashire and England. Plans had been made for a Fun Day and cricket match and other attractions, but these had to be curtailed because of rain. It was a memorable day despite the bad weather and £2,000 was raised towards the cost of the extension.

This project completed one of the Parish's aims for the Decade of Evangelism.

Obituaries, 1983–1992

Canon Robert J. Smith died in June 1983. The Vicar wrote the following obituary in the August 1983 Parish Magazine:

Canon Bob Smith
1909–1983

On Thursday, June 30th, Canon Bob Smith died peacefully in Whiston Hospital. His death comes as a great shock to all his colleagues, friends and ex-parishioners. In spite of not being in good health for some months Bob ministered to the Church he loved for as long as he possibly could. Only a few weeks before his death he administered Holy Communion at Billinge Hospital, he 'helped out' during the interregnum at St Matthew's and last officiated at Holy Communion on Thursday, March 10th. He also conducted a funeral at St Matthew's on April 12th.

Before ordination Bob served as a Reader. He decided the world of commerce and business was not for him and studied for the Ordained Ministry at St Aidan's College, Birkenhead. He was made a Deacon in 1937 and served his title at St Catherine's, Tunnel Road, Liverpool. His second curacy was at St Anne's, Aigburth. During the latter part of the war years Bob served as a Chaplain in the Armed Forces. From 1947-52 he was Vicar of St Michael's, Ditton near Widnes. Then Bob moved to St John's, Burscough Bridge. Then as you all know he moved to St Matthew's, Highfield and gave selflessly to the parish and the Church of England in general.

There are many people in Highfield who have good reason to thank God for Bob's ministry. Already I've had many people talking of his preparing them for Confirmation, his officiating at family weddings and funerals etc.

His ministry extended outside the parishes he served. He served in the Diocese, as a member of the General Synod, as Chairman of the Parsonages Committee, and as Clergy Widows' Officer.

To Doris, Diane and Elvin we extend our sympathy and prayers and entrust them and Bob to Our Father's loving care.

'Well done, thou good and faithful servant'.

BILL HARRINGTON.

David Ashcroft, one of the longest serving members of the choir and a keen member of the Cricket Club died in September 1983. The following Testimony was written by Roland Butts, a contemporary.

David Ascroft
1910–1983
A Testimony

David was born on a January day in Enfield Street, and at five years of age began his education at Highfield Infants school (now the entrance hall and administration offices of the new school). At the age of seven he transferred to the 'big boys' school', (now the nursery school). The headmaster was Mr J. W. Brierley, who was also a Lay-Reader and sang many solo parts in Church as he possessed a fine baritone voice. His wife, at that time Miss M. Liptrot, taught class three, is still alive and is interested in the Church.

David joined St Matthew's choir when he was ten, after spending the usual period in the probationers. The choir at that time was under the direction of Mr Arthur Harris, also assistant master at the school. Under Mr Harris the choir reached its zenith, regularly singing Handel's Messiah, Stainer's Crucifixion, and other cantatas, plus an anthem most Sundays, including an eight part anthem entitled 'I saw the Lord'. At this time the boys (all male choir) had the honour to be invited to sing services at Chester Cathedral. During his sixtyfour years David served under seven choirmasters and six vicars.

David left school at fourteen and started work in Blundell's colliery office, and remained there until the nationalisation of the coal industry, when he transferred to the privately owned Windy Arbour Colliery. He served five years in HM Forces during the 1939–45 war, much of that time in the atrocious theatre of conflict in the Far East.

David also served his Lord as a Sunday School teacher, starting as a teenager and continuing until about the age of forty.

Being a sportsman he excelled as a school boy on the Rugby field, and was chosen on occasions to represent the school on the Wigan and Lancashire school boys rugby teams. At the age of sixteen he signed professional forms for Wigan Highfield rugby league club, later to become Liverpool Stanley, now known as Huyton.

David struggled to get to Church as long as possible, but now that struggle is over, the last try has been scored, so tar ra for now, Tashy, from your old pal, BUTTY.

John Berry, one of the builders of the Parish Hall died on 20 May 1987, aged 83. He worked at Samuel Gratrix in Manchester and was instrumental in obtaining many of the materials for the building of the hall at reduced rates. He regularly attended St Matthew's from 1939 to 1963. He was the author of an article on the building of the hall included in chapter seven.

Mrs Beatrice Morton, who was the founder and leader of the Women's Fellowship for many years, and together with Douglas Horne and the Revd W. Bynon, a founder leader of the Over-6os died on 18 August 1987. Joan Bradley, writing in the Women's Fellowship Notes in the October 1987 Parish Magazine says:

> It is with great sorrow I begin this month's writing to tell of the death of our founder leader Mrs B. A. Morton, on 18th August. Many of you like myself will miss her very much. She shared our troubles and our sorrows and helped us over many hurdles. Her keen sense of humour and tales of holidays in Italy brought much laughter to our meetings. Our deepest sympathy goes to Bobby, David and their families. She will always be remembered at Highfield Women's Fellowship with great affection and love.

The Foote Window

Mrs Betty Lovejoy, the daughter of Mr J. H. Foote and the late Mrs E. J. Foote, had contacted the Vicar to say that she wished to donate a stained glass window in memory of her parents. She wanted primroses and the bluebird of happiness on the window. At a meeting of the PCC in February 1990 the Vicar said that it would be necessary to apply for a faculty for the window.

Mr Harry Harvey of York, who had designed the Atherton and the Anderson windows, was asked to prepare a design. Mrs Lovejoy and the PCC approved the design and the PCC wrote to Mrs Lovejoy thanking her for her generous gift.

While the window was being prepared Mr J. H. Foote, Mrs Lovejoy's father, died, and so the window was dedicated to the memory of both her parents.

The Dedication of the window took place on Sunday 29 November 1992 when Mrs Lovejoy's children and grandchildren came from America and other members of the family and friends from England attended. Ron Hayhurst recorded the occasion in the 1993 January Parish Magazine:

> A large congregation was present on Sunday November 29th 1992 to witness the dedication of a new stained glass window in memory of Mrs Eva Johnson Foote who died in January 1990 aged 90 years, and of her husband John Henry Foote who died in January 1991 aged 97 years.
>
> The beautiful window was provided by their daughter Mrs Betty Lovejoy who now lives in the United States of America. It is situated on the West end of the North Aisle and is adjacent to the Anderson and Atherton memorial windows. Both these windows were designed by Mr Harry Harvey of York. The new window was also designed by him and was made and installed by Miss Ann Southeran who was a student of Mr Harvey.
>
> The window incorporates a three part collage arrangement covering family, work and recreation. At the base of the window, a maternal figure knits a sock. The male figure is seen wheeling a barrow to the Parish Hall being one of the several volunteers who built the Hall in the mid-fifties. As he was principal automotive engineer for a local construction firm, a suitable reference to his professional life is incorporated. Both the donor's parents loved gardening and it therefore, appropriate that the window displays garden birds, roses and sweet peas.

A group of the Parish Catering Team in 1993.
Back row: Mrs Kathy Gregory; Mrs Joan Bradley; Mrs Iris Hooke; Mrs Beryl Thomas;
Mrs Mildred Garner; Mrs Jean Hamson; Mrs Audrey Irvine.
Front row: Mrs Dorothy Downham; Mrs Jenny Stockley; Mrs Lilian Pouncey;
Mrs Eileen Gaskell.

In his sermon the Vicar spoke at length of Mr and Mrs Foote who came to live in Pemberton Road during the mid 1930s. They were both immaculately dressed as they walked from Pemberton Road to Church on Sunday mornings; Jack wearing a Homburg hat and kid gloves. They sat in the same place in church and walked home afterwards. Never having a car of their own, Jack rode around in his firm's pick-up truck. He was a sidesman from 1949 onwards and a deputy warden from the late '60s to the early '70s. He was also a member of the PCC from the '50s to the '70s. As a keen gardener, no weed dared grow in his garden, and he tended his beloved lawn until the end of his days. Truly a remarkable man from a notable family. It is fitting that the parents should be commemorated in this manner.

Centenary Celebrations

The forthcoming Centenary of the building of the present Church was first discussed at a meeting of the PCC in March 1990. Over the following three years many meetings and discussions took place, a Centenary Committee was set up, and it was finally decided, at a meeting of the PCC on 11th January 1993, that £5,000 be given to charity, a wall and lychgate were to be built in front of Church, the renewal of the interior lighting of the Church and the floodlighting of the exterior be put in hand. The members of the Centenary Committee are:

Bert and Barbara Stockley,
Roy and Beryl Thomas.
Harold and Eileen Gaskell.
Jeff and Susan McCann.
Dave and Margaret Whitter.

Today and Tomorrow

The Church in Highfield today continues, as it has done through the years, to spread the Gospel to the parish; to serve God through the regular weekly worship in the church, and to serve the parish through the many organisations for young and old which flourish week by week, at the same time being aware of its responsibilities to the world outside the parish by its support of missions and charities and by its contribution to the wider church through its share of the Diocesan finances.

For the future—the plans to celebrate the Centenary are now in hand. The aims of the Parochial Church Council for the Decade of Evangelism have been stated and with God's help will be carried out. The proposed Route 225 road from Orrell via Highfield, Goose Green and Worsley Mesnes to Hindley could physically cut the parish in half and have a devastating effect on the area, and even more on the parish, and must be contested vigorously. Nevertheless the words of Dr Chavasse, Bishop of Liverpool, at the Consecration of the Church in 1910 challenge us to go on: 'In this place you have done much in the past, and now, with the grace of God, you will do more in the future.'

Two Famous Sons of Highfield

Very Revd Alan Richardson

Dean of York 1964–1975

Alan Richardson was born on 17 October 1905 at 375, Billinge Road, Highfield, the son of William and Annie Richardson. His father was Churchwarden at Highfield for many years. His older brother Frank taught at Highfield School before becoming Headmaster of St Paul's School, Goose Green.

Alan attended Highfield School and Wigan Grammar School. He went on to Liverpool University where he graduated with a BA First Class Honours in Philosophy in 1927. He also attended Exeter College, Oxford and Ridley Hall, Cambridge. He was awarded an MA (Liverpool) and MA, DD (Oxford). He began his career when he was ordained Deacon by the Bishop of Liverpool in Advent 1928, becoming Curate at St Saviour's, Liverpool from 1928 to 1930 and Intercollegiate Secretary to the Student Christian Movement at Liverpool 1928 to 1931. He was an Assistant Chaplain at Liverpool Cathedral from 1930 to 1931. He became Chaplain at Ripon Hall, Oxford from 1931 to 1933. During this time he married Phyllis Mary Packhouse. He was Tutor of Jesus College, Oxford in 1934 and then Vicar of Cambo, Northumberland from 1934 to 1938. He was the Study Secretary of the Student Christian Movement from 1938 to 1943, Sixth Canon of Durham Cathedral 1943 to 1945, Sub-Dean 1946 to 1953. He became Professor of Christian Theology at the University of Nottingham 1953 to 1964; an Honorary Canon of Derby Cathedral 1953 to 1964 and finally became Dean of York in 1964.

He was a great writer of Christian books. During his eleven years at York he was responsible for the great restoration of the Minster which took up most of his years at York, but he still continued to write, to lecture in York and in many other parts of the world. He was awarded a KBE in the New Year Honours, 1973.

He died suddenly on 23 February 1975, just two days before he was due to enthrone the new Archbishop of York, the Most Revd Stuart Yarworth Blanch. At his Memorial Service held in the Minster in March 1975, the Archbishop of Canterbury, Dr. Donald Coggan said that God had given Alan Richardson a great work to do and he had done it with distinction and dedication; In his writings he had thrown a solid bridge across the gap between academic thinking and the preaching in parish pulpits, and the other sphere in his life—the resoration of the Minster—was there for all to see. 'If you seek his monument, look around you.'

In the Lady Chapel of York Minster a tablet in the floor records:

In Memory of Alan Richardson, former Dean of York. Remember before God Alan Richardson KBE, DD, Dean of York 1964–1975. The Theologian, Teacher, Pastor who served the whole church and through whose care this Minster stands renewed secure in their hand.

Cyril James Anderton

Chief Constable of Greater Manchester, 1976–1991

Cyril James Anderton was born on 24 May 1932 in Northumberland Street, Goose Green, the son of James and Lucy Anderton. He was baptised at St Matthew's, Highfield. When he was two years old the family moved to Brindley Street, Pemberton, in St Matthew's parish, where the family worshipped at Highfield Church and he went to Highfield School.

In 1938 he joined the choir and attended choir practice twice a week and church four times on Sundays—to Communion, Matins, Sunday School and Evensong. In his biography 'God's Cop' by Michael Prince he says:

I went to church because that's where I wanted to be. I did not have to be ordered there. Even at that age, I felt close to God. Some people hate Sundays. I've always looked forward to them. Church has been a second home to me, my anchor.

In 1943 he won a scholarship from Highfield to Wigan Grammar School. In 1944 he became a founder member of the 14th Wigan Company of the Boys' Brigade at St Matthew's. Later in his life he became a battalion president while he was Deputy Chief Constable of Leicestershire. He became a Sunday School teacher at Highfield and as a teenager he discussed his vocation with the Vicar but decided that Holy Orders were not for him—he wanted to be a policeman and serve God as a layman.

He joined the Military Police in 1950 and married Joan Baron in 1955. He served in various Police Forces for forty-one years during which time he rose quickly through the ranks and served as Assistant Chief Constable of Leicestershire and Rutland from 1968 to 1972 when he became Assistant to H.M. Chief Inspector of Constabulary for England and Wales at the Home Office in London. In 1975 he was appointed Deputy Chief Constable of Leicester and later that year moved back to Manchester as Deputy Chief Constable, and in 1976, aged 44, he became Chief Constable of Greater Manchester.

He was awarded a Knighthood in January 1991 and retired in March 1991. In a tribute, Chief Superintendent Gordon Burton of Wigan Division said:

Sir James has been an outstanding police officer and a man of tremendous charisma who has been well respected by all his subordinates over the years.

Church Officials

Curates-in-charge

Revd S. L. Laidman	1867–1871	Revd T. Evans	1871–1881
Revd J. Wood	1881–1908	Revd J. Woods	1909–1910

Vicars

Revd J. Woods	1910–1936	Revd P. Johnson	1937–1944
Revd W. H. Bullough	1944–1959	Revd R. J. Smith	1960–1974
Revd W. Bynon	1975–1982	Revd W. H. Harrington	1983–

Assistant Curates

Revd A. E. Buer	1911–1915	Revd T. Barton	1940–1941/2
Revd G. Thomas	1978–1983	Revd G. Keegan	1984–1987
Revd E. Traverse	1991– (Honarary Curate.)		

Readers

Mr J. W. Brierley	1932–1960	Mr W. Wilkinson	1941–1943
Mr E. Davies	1948–1953	Mr G. A. Cooke	1953–present
Mr H. L. Stockley	1958–present	Mrs P. Gore	1984–1987
Mrs A. Moss	1984–present		

Churchwardens

Mr W. Richardson	1910–1941	Mr T. Barton	1910–1912
Mr J. L. Little	1912–1914	Mr R. A. Southworth	1914–1923
Mr J. Starkey	1923–1929	Mr I. Massey	1929–1945
Mr T. Hesketh	1941–1948	Mr W. Richardson	1945–1947
Mr I. Massey	1947–1948	Mr T. Hughes	1948–1964
Mr E. G. Elliott	1949–1954	Mr H. Gee	1954–1965
Mr J. G. Taberner	1964–1977	Mr G. Perrin	1965–1969
Mr D. Horne	1969–1981	Mr R. Thomas	1977–present
Mr H. F. Gaskell	1981–present		

Organists

Mr Fannthorpe	1867–1869	Mr R. Dawson	1869–1890
Mr J. W. Duddle	1890–1895	Mr W. Williams	1896–1914
Mr A. Harris	1914–1926	Mr J. Magraw	1926–1951
Mr R. Kay	1951–1954	Miss R. Turton	1955–1956
Mr F. Ashcroft	1957–1961	Mr N. Knowles	1961–1962
Mr G. A. Cooke	1963–1979	Mr C. Bell	1979–1984
Mrs S. A. Gordon	1984–present		

Vergers

Mr J. Berry	1896–1899	Mr W. Stockley	1899–?
Mr W. Atherton	1911–1964	Mr W. Boyd	1964–?

Church Council Secretaries

Mr G. Melling	1920–1924	Mr A. Harris	1924–1925
Mr J. C.Ashurst	1925–1926	Mr J. Starkey	1926–1929
Mr H. Gee	1929–1941	Mrs Clarke	1941–1954
Mr E. Stretton	1954–1964	Mr W. O. Millard	1964–1973
Mr N. Gregory	1973–1982	Mrs M. M. Cooke	1982
Mrs S. L. Highton	1983–present		

Church Council Treasurers

The Churchwardens	1920–1939	Mr J. W.Brierley	1939–1952
Mr P. Gaskell	1952–1956	Mr G.A. Cooke	1956–present

Parochial Church Council, 1993

Ex-Officio Members: Vicar, Revd W. H. Harrington, Readers, Mr G. A. Cooke, Mr H. L. Stockley, Mrs A. Moss, Wardens, Mr R. Thomas and Mr H. F. Gaskell, Deputy Wardens, Mr P. Broadhurst and Mr A. Jenks.

Elected Members: Mrs S. L. Highton, Mrs B. Jenks, Mrs B. Jones, Mrs H. Riley, Miss I. Twigg, Mrs D. Wright, Mr G. Bennett, Mr D. Fisher, Mr W. Garner, Mr R. Hayhurst, Mr F. Holcroft, Mr J. McCann, Mr B. Morters, Mr G. Pennington, Mr D. J. Rimmer, Mr C. Whittick, Mr D. Whitter.

Co-opted Member: Mrs A. Harrington.

Parish Organisations, 1993

Sunday School. 12 noon.	Infants meet in School. Superintendent Mrs J. Hodgson. Juniors meet in Parish Hall. Superintendent Miss M. Moore.
Pram Club.	Wednesday 1.15 p.m. in Parish Hall. Leader Mrs L. Garner.
Rainbows.	Tuesday 4.30 p.m. in Youth Centre. Leader Mrs J. Halliwell.
Rainbows.	Friday 5.15 p.m. in Youth Centre. Leader Mrs E. Dunne.
Brownies.	Monday 6 p.m. in Youth Centre. Leader Mrs E. Holden.
Brownies.	Thursday 5.15 p.m. in Youth Centre. Leader Mrs S. Pollock.
Guides.	Monday 7.30 p.m. in Youth Centre. Leader Miss M. Moore.
Rangers.	Monday 7.30 p.m. in Youth Centre. Leader Mrs S. Pollock.
Anchor Boys.	Wednesday 6 p.m. in Youth Centre. Leader Miss J. Harrison.
Junior B. B.	Tuesday 6.30 p.m. Leaders Mrs M. Brown & Mrs S. Stafford.
Boys' Brigade	Friday 7.30 p.m. in Youth Centre. Leader Mr B. Harrison.
Over-60s' Club	Tuesday 2.15 p.m. in Parish Hall. Leader Mr N. Gregory.
Women's Fellowship.	Thursday 7.45 p.m. Leader Mrs S. L. Highton.
Choir Practice.	Thursday 7 p.m. Choirmistress Mrs A. S. Gordon.
Men's Fellowship.	Last Monday in each month 8.30 p.m. Mr N. Sherrington.
Church Fellowship.	Each evening in Parish Lounge. Secy. Mr D. Whitter.

The School

Headteachers

The Boys' School

Mr Fannthorpe	1867–1869	Mr R. Dawson	1869–1890
Mr J.W. Duddle	1890–1895	Mr W. Williams	1896–1913
Mr J.W. Brierley	1913–1945	Mr E. Davies	1946–1953
Mr A. Coates	1954–1956	Mr G.A. Procter	1956–1964
Mr R.H. Gaskell	1964–1970 when the school was closed and incorporated into the Wigan Deanery High School.		

The Infants' School

Miss J. Sutherland	1873–1874	Miss M.A. Twiss	1874–1877
Miss E. Rose	1877–1880	Miss M. A.Ashurst	1880–1915
Miss L. Holland	1915–1954	Miss L. M. Waddington	1955–1968
		when the Infant School became part of the Primary School under Mr E. G. Elliott	

The Girls' School

Miss M. A. Twiss	1876–1888	Miss E. Rowlinson	1888–1895
Miss A. E. Hitchen	1895–1901	Miss A. Taylor	1901–1910
Miss E. Crebbin	1910–1924	Miss E. Johnson	1925–1933
		when the Girls' School became the Junior Mixed School	

The Junior Mixed School

Miss E. Johnson	1933–1948	Mr E. G. Elliott	1948–1968
		when the Junior Mixed School became the Primary School	

Highfield C. E. Primary School

Mr E. G. Elliott	1968–1973	Mr W. Spencer	1973–1983
Mrs E. M. Gaskell	1983–1988	Mr G. Jarvis	1989–present

School Buildings and their Use

1867	First Iron School Church Opened as all-age school.
1876	Duck Pond Hall Barn converted for use as Boys' School. Infants and Girls remain in Iron School Church building.
1894	New Girls' and Infants' School built

	Iron School Church becomes Parish Hall.
1932	New Boys' Secondary School opened.
	Infants transferred to old Boys' School.
1933	Girls' School becomes Junior Mixed.
1968	Infants School becomes part of Primary School
1970	Secondary Modern Boys' School closed.
	Infants transferred to Secondary School Site.
1983	New School Building for Juniors opened.

1994 as well as being the Centenary of the building of the present Church also marks what would have been the Centenary of the old Junior School which was demolished due to dry rot in 1982.

Bibliography & Sources

Barnton Cricket Club Centenary Brochure. 1980. Geoff. H. Buchan.
Blundell's Collieries, 1776–1966. Donald Anderson.
The Buildings of England. South Lancs. Nikolaus Pevnser.
The Blundell Papers, Lancashire Record Office.
The Carmarthenshire Antiquary, Vol XXIII (1987).
The Carmarthenshire Journal.
Census Returns for Carmarthenshire.
Census Returns for Clitheroe and District.
Census Returns for Liverpool and District.
Census Returns for Wigan and District.
Chester Diocesan Record Office (Archives).
City of London Archives.
Crockford's Clerical Directory 1867 *et seq.*
Founded on Coal. Ray Winstanley and Derek Winstanley.
God's Cop. Michael Prince.
Gore's Directory, Liverpool.
W. Greener's Diary 1852–1858. D. Anderson's papers.
Highfield Parish Archives.
Highfield Parish Church Council Minutes.
Highfield Parish Magazines.
Highfield School Managers Minute Books.
Highfield Service Books.
Highfield St Matthew's Church Fellowship Minutes.
Highfield Vestry Books.
Kelly's Directory. Wigan and District. 1891 *et seq.*
Lancashire and Yorkshire Railway. Vol. 1. John Marshall.
Liverpool Diocesan Bishop's Acts Book.
Liverpool Diocesan Calendars and Directories 1881 *et seq.*
Liverpool Diocesan Finance report 1901.
The Manchester Guardian.
Munby's Diary March 1865, Trinity College Library, Cambridge.
Portrait of a Parish. St John the Divine, Pemberton. Michael A. Mason.
Registers of St John the Divine, Pemberton.
A Service for Rogationtide. Council for Church & Countryside.
The Schoolmaster, Journal of the National Union of Teachers.
Slater's Directory of Lancashire 1890.
The Western Mail.
Who Was Who?
The Wigan Examiner, 1867 *et. seq.*
The Wigan Observer, 1867 *et. seq.*